LA FOLLETTE

AND THE

RISE OF THE PROGRESSIVES

IN WISCONSIN

Robert Marion La Follette

A bronze bust by the American sculptor Jo Davidson
in the possession of the State Historical Society of Wisconsin

LA FOLLETTE
AND THE
Rise of the Progressives
in Wisconsin

ROBERT S. MAXWELL

NEW YORK / RUSSELL & RUSSELL

To Margaret

PREFACE

★ ★ ★ ★ ★ ★ ★ ★ ★ ★ ★ ★ ★ ★ ★ ★ ★

THE INTERPRETATION OF A REFORM MOVEMENT SO COMPLEX AS Wisconsin Progressivism is at best a highly subjective study. Of necessity the topics dealt with in detail have been the result of personal selection, and no effort has been made to cover all the routine activities of the state administration during the progressive era. Instead I have sought to focus attention upon those significant phases of the Wisconsin story which broke new ground or were a departure from traditional patterns. At the same time I have sought to keep in sight the larger aspects of the movement and the interplay of progressive forces throughout the United States.

The personality of Robert M. La Follette cast a long shadow over the events and problems of this era, but this volume is in no sense a biography. Neither is it a general history of Wisconsin. It is a study of the development, the course, and the results of the Progressive Movement in Wisconsin during its initial phase, the years from 1900 to 1915. These were the years when progressivism and reform were on the march throughout the United States; the period conventionally termed the Progressive Era.

In general I have sought to allow the reformers themselves to define what they meant by the term "Progressive." It included the idea of placing more of the machinery and functions of government under the direct control of the electorate and a demand for the removal of corrupt influences from positions of power. Progressivism also envisioned the expansion of government to curb special-interest groups and to promote the economic and social well-being of the individual citizen. Most of its

vii

concrete proposals were embodied in the party's platforms during these years.

I owe a debt of gratitude to a great many people who have aided me in bringing this book to completion. Professor Merle Curti of the University of Wisconsin has contributed much-needed encouragement and has offered many helpful criticisms throughout the entire course of this study. Miss Alice Smith, Miss Ruth Davis, and Miss Josephine Harper of the State Historical Society of Wisconsin have been especially helpful and cooperative in making the resources of the Society available to me. Miss Livia Appel, the Society's book editor, has, by her capable editing, greatly improved the literary style of the manuscript and has saved me from many errors of form and fact. The Committee for the Study of American Civilization at the University of Wisconsin generously provided a grant for additional research and rewriting during the summer of 1951, and the Research Fund of the University of Kentucky made possible a survey of the pertinent manuscripts in the Library of Congress. Both Professors J. Merton England and Carl B. Cone, my colleagues at the University of Kentucky, have read the manuscript and offered many helpful suggestions. Perhaps I am most indebted to my wife, Margaret Dunning Maxwell, who has helped type and retype the manuscript through many versions and has constantly been my most generous critic and unfailing source of encouragement.

All these people have contributed to whatever merits the book may have. The opinions, interpretations, errors, and omissions, however, are entirely my own.

R. S. M.

Stephen F. Austin State College
Nacogdoches, Texas
Spring, 1956

CONTENTS

★ ★ ★ ★ ★ ★ ★ ★ ★ ★ ★ ★ ★ ★ ★ ★ ★

ILLUSTRATIONS

★ ★ ★ ★ ★ ★ ★ ★ ★ ★ ★ ★ ★ ★ ★ ★ ★

LA FOLLETTE

AND THE

RISE OF THE PROGRESSIVES
IN WISCONSIN

1 THE SOIL OF PROGRESSIVISM

★ ★ ★ ★ ★ ★ ★ ★ ★ ★ ★ ★ ★ ★ ★ ★ ★

THE PROGRESSIVE MOVEMENT PRESUPPOSED AN ACCEPTANCE OF the doctrine of progress. To the reformers of the first decade of the twentieth century this was axiomatic; they were certain that man, as a rational animal, was capable of making steady progress in solving his problems and improving his way of life. Few doubts about the ultimate triumph of democracy, either political or social, had yet disturbed America's faith in the future. Hence the progressives were optimistic, self-confident, and eager to reform all that appeared to be in need of reforming.

Progressivism was a volatile and many-sided movement. During the years before the first World War it boiled and fermented in the United States, fundamentally altering the way of life of the citizens of that generation and profoundly influencing the subsequent course of American history. As with most popular reform drives, it was not confined to a single political party but was broader, deeper, and more fundamental than any one party. Both the major parties contained powerful progressive elements that were at times dominant, and the most dynamic third-party movement in the history of our political system bore the name "Progressive." [1]

The roots of the progressive movement are to be found in the political unrest and economic distress of the midwestern farmers in the decades following the Civil War. The successive crusades of the Grangers, the Farmers' Alliance, and the People's Party gave dramatic emphasis to the contention that the times were out of balance and that heroic measures were

3

required to set them right. Again and again these farmer groups headed their platforms with demands for government action to relieve the stress caused by the constantly "appreciating dollar." They also sought government intervention to control the railroads and other monopolistic corporations, the reorganization of the tax structure in accordance with the distribution of wealth, and the reform of nominating and election procedures to insure that the voice of the people would no longer be ignored. As all these proposals found their way, in one form or another, into law during the progressive era, the heritage of the Populists provided a firm foundation for the progressive movement both in the states and on the national level.[2]

Progressivism did not, however, stem solely from the embattled agrarians. Industrial and laboring elements likewise made important contributions. Indeed, it was not until the urban shift in wealth and population became pronounced that this popular reform program met with real success. By 1900 almost a third of the people of the United States were living in urban places and the value of manufactures, produced largely in these urban areas, was more than twice that of agricultural products, though farming was still traditionally the most important occupation.[3] The appeal of the progressive movement was directed toward these urban elements at least as much as to the agricultural classes. The success of this appeal is all the more significant in the light of the fact that the Populists had been unable to arouse enthusiasm in the ranks of labor and that the efforts of labor to organize and liberate itself had been largely unavailing and abortive.

These agrarian and industrial elements were drawn together and cemented by intellectual leadership into the powerful force that became progressivism. This leadership was recruited neither from the farmers nor the trade unionists. It was essentially educated, urban, and professional in character. It was marked by a spirit of moderation and absence of doctrinaire dogmas and gave to the movement a respectability that made its success possible. The resulting combination drew support from business and professional groups which had previously considered the radical farmer and labor parties anathema.

Progressivism was not merely a political phenomenon and it was by no means confined to the national scene. It manifested itself in economic, social, and educational fields and on all levels of government from the municipality to the federal regime in Washington. The states, intermediate in the governmental hierarchy, provided significant examples of federalism in operation as they virtually transformed themselves into laboratories to test and perfect the several aspects of the progressive program. Among the states that became notable for their progressive reforms were California, Oregon, and Wisconsin.

Wisconsin perhaps offered the most striking example of the reforms and innovations that characterized progressivism. Although neither the first nor the most radical state in its proposals, Wisconsin inaugurated, under the leadership of Robert M. La Follette, Sr. and others, a comprehensive program of political, economic, and social reforms that affected the life of every person in the state. These reforms, in turn, served as models that were copied, in whole or in part, by many other states and by the national government.

Like most of its neighbors at the turn of the century Wisconsin was experiencing political stresses, industrial expansion, and shifts of population. Politically it had known a brief period of Granger ascendancy, but had never been converted to Populism. On the contrary, Wisconsin had remained staunchly conservative throughout the decade of the nineties. The control of the state was generally conceded to be in the hands of the Republican machine as it had been for twenty years. This Republican organization was fairly typical of the state machines that flourished in the United States in the late nineteenth century. The dispensation of the patronage, both state and federal, was controlled by a relatively few men who represented the dominant economic interests of the state. Like political machines elsewhere the whole organization was founded on special privilege, which ranged all the way from a free ton of coal for a member of the party faithful to a street railway franchise or a timber or water-power concession.[4]

A second important element in the economic and political pattern of Wisconsin at the turn of the century was the position of the railroads. The railroad network was dominated by two giant corporations, the Chicago and North Western and the Chicago, Milwaukee and St. Paul, which between them controlled half the trackage in the state and did more than half the railroad business. In political affairs these two companies joined with the powerful lumber barons to insure state administrations friendly to their interests. Beginning with the short-lived Potter Law of 1874 the legislature of Wisconsin had periodically sought, without conspicuous success, to bring these giants under the control of the state. Like a majority of the states, Wisconsin had a railroad commissioner, but he was without power and was frequently controlled by the very interests he was supposed to supervise. Thanks to a whole series of court decisions, both federal and state, the railroads had been able to resist all attempts at regulation and continued to levy rates on the basis of "all the traffic will bear." For more than a quarter of a century after the Civil War most of the prominent men in public life in Wisconsin were identified with either the railroads or the lumber interests, and the presidents of the two great systems were important figures that must be consulted before any major decision concerning state policy was made.[5]

The shifts of population in Wisconsin were fairly typical of those in the United States as a whole. In 1900 the state had a population of slightly more than two million, which represented an increase of some twenty-two per cent since 1890. The urban population, however, had expanded almost thirty-seven per cent, and over one-third of the new growth had taken place in Milwaukee. Two-thirds of the state's residents were either foreign-born or of foreign parentage. Of these, Germans comprised almost half (forty-eight per cent) and Scandinavians, chiefly Norwegians, another sixteen per cent. There was a sprinkling of Irish, Poles, Finns, French, Belgians, Swiss, English, and Dutch, but relatively few southern or eastern Europeans. The German element was prominent throughout the state and it completely dominated Milwaukee, where it comprised two-thirds of the population. A great majority of the Scandinavians, on the other hand, lived on the land, and they predominated in many of the rural counties.[6]

The changing industrial pattern of Wisconsin was reflected in the urban shift. At the turn of the century, lumber and timber products still ranked first among the state's industries, but they had declined both relatively and absolutely since 1890. Wisconsin led the nation in this industry, but the rapid depletion of transportable timber heralded the end of this particular type of exploitation on a large scale. Flour-milling products held second place in 1900, but the necessity of importing into the state much of the wheat to be milled indicated that this industry, too, would decline in relative importance. Foundry and machine-shop industries, in contrast, were expanding rapidly. In the course of a single decade the annual value of their products leaped from eight and one-half million dollars to more than twenty-two millions. About two-thirds of the output was manufactured in Milwaukee, which had become a regional center of the new automobile industry and was turning out engines, motors, and complete cars at a rapidly increasing rate. Of equal importance to the future of Wisconsin was the spectacular growth of the dairy products industry, whose output had more than trebled since 1890. It was now the fourth most important occupation in

the state, and Wisconsin held second place among the cheese-
and butter-producing states of the nation as compared with
fourth in 1890.[7]

Yet agriculture continued to be the occupation of the largest
number of Wisconsin breadwinners at the turn of the century.
The census of 1900 listed two hundred and sixty-four thousand
persons as engaged in farming as opposed to one hundred forty-
two thousand in manufacturing. But the value of all agricultural products, reported at $115,861,963, lagged far behind the
total of $360,818,942 for manufactured products.[8]

The economic pattern of Wisconsin in 1900 was fairly typical
of the United States as a whole. Some two-thirds of the people
lived in rural areas and made their living from agriculture, but
three-fourths of the wealth was produced by manufactures, which
were concentrated in the urban areas. One great city, Milwaukee,
overshadowed all other towns and cities, though it comprised
only thirteen per cent of the state's population. The northern
half of the state was experiencing a decline in lumbering, its
chief source of wealth, and was turning to other activities as the
great forests disappeared, leaving behind the barren "cutover"
regions. The greatest growth of population was taking place
along the shore of Lake Michigan, where Racine, Sheboygan, and
Kenosha, as well as Milwaukee, emerged as industrial centers.
The oldest settled section of the state, the southwest, lagged behind as the communities in central and south-central Wisconsin,
located in a fertile belt of rolling prairie, began to develop a
balanced economy based on both agriculture and manufacturing.

Thus the Wisconsin population from whom came the most
fundamental and thoroughgoing of the state progressive movements did not differ noticeably from its neighbors in the other
north-central states. The program developed in Wisconsin was
distinguished from the reforms of other states chiefly in that it
was more comprehensive and far-reaching rather than more
radical. As elsewhere, progressivism in Wisconsin was neither

left-wing agrarian nor socialistic. It was moderate, pragmatic, and non-doctrinaire in approach, including agricultural, industrial, and intellectual elements in its appeal. As the movement developed and unfolded, powerful and able leaders emerged to give it direction. Progressivism in Wisconsin became an article for export both to other states and to other countries. But in 1900 all this lay in the future.

2 LA FOLLETTE AND THE
ELECTION OF 1900

★ ★ ★ ★ ★ ★ ★ ★ ★ ★ ★ ★ ★ ★ ★ ★ ★

AS THE ELECTION YEAR OF 1900 APPROACHED THERE WAS LITTLE
evidence discernible to the casual observer that a political revolution was impending. The state was staunchly Republican and
apparently devoted to the principles of McKinley, gold, and the
full dinner pail. Four years before, despite the vigorous efforts
of Bryan, the Democrats, and the Populists, McKinley had carried all but three of the state's seventy counties and had rolled up
a plurality of more than a hundred thousand votes.[1]

The state's political leaders were all known as careful, conservative, and safe men. Wisconsin's senior senator, John C. Spooner,
had attracted nationwide attention with his speeches on foreign
policy, the new colonies, and the tariff. Henry C. Payne, soon to
become postmaster general, was chairman of the state central
committee and was a prominent figure at national Republican
conventions. Junior senator Joseph V. Quarles, a capable lawyer,
was regarded as conservative, reserved, and amiable. The recent
governors were of the same pattern. Edward Scofield was to be the
last of the Civil War veterans to become chief executive of the
state. Having acquired wealth in the lumber industry, Scofield
had scant patience with those who sought to curb the dominant
interests of the state or to place restrictions upon their operations.
He was a firm believer in free and unrestricted enterprise and a
bitter opponent of Populism in all its forms.

Yet Scofield's administration had not been unprogressive. He
had been re-elected on a platform calling for a reorganization of
the tax system to compel all corporations to "contribute their

10

just and equal share towards the burden of taxation" and a reform of the caucus and convention system for nominating candidates. These important proposals came to naught, but his terms as governor saw the creation of a temporary state tax commission, the passage of an inheritance tax law, and the organization of a civil service system for the employees of the State Board of Control. Additional taxes were levied on private car and express companies. A corrupt practices act, an anti-pass act, and an anti-lobby law were also passed.[2]

This scattering evidence of reform sentiment seems to have indicated a latent demand for a reorientation of the purpose and function of the state government. In contrast to the surface calm, there was an undercurrent of opinion propitious for a major reform drive.

In the political field especially the time was ripe for a reorganization of the Republican machine. Old ex-Senator Philetus Sawyer had retired from active political life and was soon to pass from the scene. "Boss" Elisha W. Keyes had long since ceased to be a major power in state politics and was now, as Madison postmaster, serving as an informant for the Wisconsin group in Washington and as a lobbyist for the major railroads. Spooner, in spite of his reputation, had proved to be a poor politician and indifferent organizer. Among the insiders it was whispered that Henry C. Payne was losing his grip and that Charles F. Pfister, the heir-apparent, was not equal to the task. Congressmen John J. Esch of La Crosse and Joseph W. Babcock of Necedah were both watching alertly for an opportunity to reorganize the state machine in their own interests.[3] Isaac Stephenson, multimillionaire lumberman from Marinette, was irked over the failure of party leaders to reward his service with a United States senatorship and would welcome a realignment of interests. Among the many who were keenly aware of the opportunities that 1900 offered for political leadership was a Madison attorney, Robert M. La Follette.

By 1900 La Follette, then forty-five, had already had a considerable public career. After serving as district attorney of Dane County he had been a member of Congress for three terms ending in 1890. As a congressman he had taken his duties very seriously and had gained the reputation of being studious, attentive, and industrious. He was so industrious, in fact, that he worked himself periodically to the verge of collapse. La Follette was a member of the Congresses that passed the Interstate Commerce Act and the Sherman Anti-Trust Act. He had been active also in the drafting of the McKinley Tariff Act of 1890.[4]

La Follette's political philosophy had been profoundly influenced by the Granger and agrarian uprisings he had witnessed during his youth. "As a boy on the farm," he later recalled, "I heard and felt this movement of the Grangers swirling about me; and I felt the indignation which it expressed in such a way that I suppose I never fully lost the effect of that early impression." Likewise the shock he received from reading such books as Henry George's *Progress and Poverty* left a permanent effect.[5]

Even stronger and more direct was the impression made upon young La Follette by President John Bascom of the University of Wisconsin. From Bascom he acquired a "proper attitude towards public affairs." Most problems of government became to him largely a matter of right or wrong, and he stressed a moral and ethical view of political questions. He spoke often of the need for honesty, maintaining that "the politician cannot exist without absolute, unyielding, uncompromising honesty." In his economic and social outlook he was greatly influenced by the Jeffersonian tradition. He thought of the sturdy independent farmers and small shopkeepers as the bulwark of our government. Implicit throughout his early speeches and writings were the doctrines of the social contract, the rights and dignity of man, the sovereignty of the people, and the benefits of free competition. To him they were self-evident. His contention that "the real cure for the ills of democracy is more democracy" was characteristic of his approach to the problems of government and reform.[6]

When the Democratic landslide of 1890 suddenly terminated his career as representative, La Follette directed his interests and enthusiasms to state politics and tried, unsuccessfully, to become a leader of the state Republican organization. His violent rejection of Philetus Sawyer's offer to bring him into the inner circle and put him on the payroll gained for him the personal ill will and hatred of Sawyer and his friends.[7] Thereafter he was faced with the choice of making war on the party machine or making peace with it. It is doubtful whether he seriously debated the alternatives. For eight years he carried on an unceasing attack on the party bosses, bitter, personal, violent, and unavailing. His most vigorous campaigns resulted in defeats, and he was denounced as a socialist, an anarchist, and a Populist. In 1894 he backed Nils P. Haugen's unsuccessful candidacy for the governorship. In 1896 and again in 1898 he sought the office himself but both times was beaten in the convention by the superior organization, tactics, and checkbooks of the party regulars. Despite these failures La Follette had won and retained a strong personal following composed largely of farmers, small businessmen, University alumni, and Scandinavian groups. He also had the loyal friendship of such men as former Congressman Nils P. Haugen, ex-Governor William D. Hoard, and Assemblyman Albert R. Hall. But after the campaign of 1898 it was obvious that these personal supporters were not enough. If any future campaign was to be successful he needed powerful new political friends and at least a truce with the old enemies, the support of a fair share of the state press, and above all more ample campaign funds.[8]

The issues put forth by La Follette were timely proposals that appealed to the great mass of the state's voters. He urged a primary election law to replace the convention system, more equitable taxation of the railroads and other public-service corporations, and a general anti-trust and anti-monopoly program. In his own mind he was developing ideas for regulatory commissions free from the defects and limitations that had so weakened the Interstate Commerce Commission. During the years since he had held office both his political philosophy and his organizing skill had matured rapidly. For the moment he had been retired to the sidelines, but he was awaiting a favorable opportunity to re-enter the political arena.

By early February of 1900 several candidates were already in the race for the Republican gubernatorial nomination. Behind the scenes party manipulators conferred on prospects and sought alliances to bolster their own interests. The mayoralty race in Milwaukee would be the preliminary to the statewide contest, and the issues, according to ex-boss Keyes, were to be the same in both elections. In Milwaukee the stalwarts of both parties were seeking to re-elect Mayor David Rose over the opposition of reformer Henry J. Baumgartner. Rose, though a Democrat, seemingly had the backing of Payne, Pfister, and others whom the *Milwaukee Sentinel* referred to as the "street car ring." [9]

In La Crosse newspaper editor Ellis B. Usher kept a wary eye on the local scene in behalf of his patron, Congressman John J. Esch. He was convinced that this was the year for someone to take over the leadership of the party. If a new political regime was about to be born, he would like to be a part of it. He had heard rumors that Joseph W. Babcock was busy and he urged Esch to join forces with the Third District representative in a sort of congressional bloc. [10]

In the meantime the avowed candidates for the governor's chair were active, trying to secure support wherever they could. Ira B. Bradford of Eau Claire County was satisfactory to the party leaders and had the nominal support of Esch and his congressional organization. He was favorably known in his own locality, but was almost unknown in the rest of the state and would add little or no strength to the ticket. John M. Whitehead, state senator from Janesville, was an abler man, but was less available as a candidate than Bradford. He was a capable speaker and lawyer, but he was austere and ultra-conservative and had incurred the opposition of the Germans in Milwaukee because of his prohibitionist tendencies. The other candidates, De Wayne Stebbins of Marinette, Alfred M. "Long" Jones of Waukesha, and General Earl M. Rogers of Viroqua, were men of local reputation only. As it became clearer that Governor Scofield did not intend to seek a third term, the field was obviously still open for a candidate with statewide popular appeal.

Thus far La Follette had given no indication that he was considering another campaign. His very silence caused much speculation in the press and among politicians. When interviewed about the coming election, Philetus Sawyer assured the reporter that he planned to keep out of politics and the governor's race "unless they bring in someone who is an enemy and not a friend, and I don't have to say who it is, young man,—then I'll fight; yes sir, I'll get out and fight." The old lumber baron would still go to any lengths to keep La Follette in retirement. But Sawyer was an aged and very sick man; less than a month later he was dead. His successors proved more amenable to peace and compromise.[11]

Behind the scenes the La Follette forces were far from inactive. Friends and supporters were testing sentiment and writing letters in every county of the state. La Follette had even received powerful support from several former opponents. Emanuel L. Philipp, Milwaukee businessman and rising young political leader, joined forces with him and promoted a much-needed truce with the old Republican machine. Isaac Stephenson, the seventy-one-year-old multi-millionaire lumberman, agreed to back La Follette and opened his checkbook to support the ensuing campaign. According to Stephenson there had been an obvious and growing dissatisfaction with the trend of affairs in Wisconsin during 1898 and 1899. He felt that the railroads and allied interests had come to exert a dominant influence over the legislative activities of both parties. The infusion of new blood and a moderate reform program would be a good thing for the state.[12]

La Follette also received valuable assistance from the leader of the congressional delegation, Joseph W. Babcock. This politically ambitious ex-lumberman had already served four terms in Congress and was seeking a larger field for his talents. He was quite aware of the internal disintegration of the Republican organization and, like Usher and Esch, sought to organize the machine to advance his own interests. Babcock was sure that with his support a La Follette ticket would be both popular and successful. It is probable that he thought he would be able to control the new governor and use the state organization to elevate himself to the senatorship, replace Payne as national committeeman, and succeed Sawyer as the real head of the party in Wisconsin. Events were to prove that he misjudged his candidate completely and vastly overestimated his own abilities, but during the campaign of 1900 Babcock's financial assistance and organizing skill contributed greatly to its success.[13]

The preliminary organization for the campaign went on steadily throughout the early spring. La Follette no doubt considered this the crucial campaign of his career. Another unsuccessful effort would probably eliminate him permanently as a candidate for any major office. The campaign was to be waged on the same principles of popular government that he had championed before, but care had to be taken not to antagonize segments of the party.[14] A survey of the state press indicated that La Follette was a much more popular figure than any of the avowed gubernatorial candidates. His visit to Milwaukee at the time of the convention to select delegates to the national Republican convention aroused much speculation in the press as to his intentions. There, in a closely guarded conference, La Follette and Jerre Murphy met with Babcock, Thomas H. Gill, attorney for the Wisconsin Central Railway, and Philipp, and after a frank discussion of the issues received their definite pledge of support in the coming campaign.[15]

La Follette's decision to become a candidate was made not later than this visit to Milwaukee, but for strategic reasons he delayed making a formal announcement for more than two weeks. In the meantime he reached a close understanding with Nils P. Haugen, who undertook to keep the Scandinavian voters in line. He also prevailed upon the chronically ill Albert R. Hall to defer retirement from the Assembly and campaign for him vigorously in the key Tenth Congressional District.[16] At the same time the tempo of the La Follette boom in the state press increased. The rural press was almost uniformly friendly. The Phillips *Bee*, for example, approved La Follette as the favorite candidate; the Soldiers Grove *Advance* praised him as the real Republican leader in Wisconsin and pledged support to his creed; and the previously hostile *Manitowoc Press* suggested that an olive branch be tendered all factions of the party and indicated that it would not oppose the La Follette campaign.[17]

Finally, on May 16, La Follette announced in a carefully worded statement that he would again seek the Republican nomination for governor. He welcomed the "manifestations of better feeling" which existed and promised to foster it in every way possible. He pledged his support of the principles adopted in the last state party platform and made an obvious bid for Governor Scofield's support by praising the progress the last administration had made toward the fulfillment of the party pledges. In an editorial the next day the *Milwaukee Sentinel* commended La Follette's conciliatory tone and predicted that the campaign would be one of harmony, with no diehard, factional candidates, and would provide a fair chance for everyone, including La Follette. This announcement of his candidacy, which doubtless had been long expected, was received with approval by a large part of the state press. The *Hudson Star-Times* expressed the hope that "bygones would be bygones" and promised that, although committed to Bradford as first choice, it would be friendly to La Follette. The *Fond du Lac Commonwealth* commented that no one doubted his ability and predicted that if elected he would make a good governor.[18]

Babcock, Philipp, and Gill were anxious that their candidate should not appear as a Populist, anti-railroad, anti-corporation man. Through their efforts a personal conference was arranged for La Follette with President Marvin Hughitt of the Chicago and North Western Railway. Hughitt welcomed the candidate in a friendly manner, and La Follette responded with a prepared statement favoring "taxing railroad companies upon the value of their property, just as other taxpayers of Wisconsin are taxed." This promise of equal and fair treatment was quite satisfactory to Hughitt, and the railroad companies maintained a benevolent attitude throughout the campaign.[19]

The La Follette boom quickly put the rival candidates on the defensive. La Follette's campaign seemed to be better organized, more expertly led, more widely publicized, and more adequately financed than those of his opponents, who found themselves struggling to retain control of their own counties and districts.[20] "Long" Jones and others urged the formation of a combination to stop the La Follette drive. But as the weeks went by it became increasingly evident that no such move would be made. Keyes feared that a victory for La Follette would endanger the seat of his friend Spooner and would certainly mean a drive to oust junior senator Quarles. Quarles in turn dourly predicted that a new combine was arising which would be "not only thorough but despotic." [21]

To quiet the rumors that he had designs upon the Senate seats, La Follette issued a statement to the press declaring that if he were nominated and elected he would not be a candidate for the United States Senate and would not use the governor's office to promote the candidacy of anyone. He also extended an olive branch to the holdover state officers by disclaiming any "slate" of

his own and urging that all state officials who had been efficient
should be renominated and re-elected.[22]

Despite these professions of friendliness and cooperation many
observers questioned whether the harmony campaign was more
than a temporary truce. Boss Keyes scoffingly questioned La
Follette's sincerity at the conference with railroad president
Hughitt and was sure that La Follette's whole attitude was a
pose and subterfuge to lull his erstwhile opponents to sleep. The
Sentinel quoted a Washington source as openly dubious about
the so-called "olive branch" that La Follette had extended to the
railroads and corporations. La Follette in turn feared that many
of his avowed supporters had no interest in his program of reform, and he confided to one of his lieutenants that he would
not be shocked at "treachery" on the part of the machine.[23] The
rumors of a deal to deliver the Senate seats and state patronage to
the new coalition continued to circulate. Granville D. Jones,
Wausau business leader and later University regent, felt that
Spooner had been sold out and questioned whether the combination was a La Follette–Babcock or a Babcock–La Follette alliance. The opportunistic nature of the coalition caused much
speculation concerning its leadership and commitments.[24]

As the campaign proceeded, popular support for La Follette
grew in every section of the state and various politicians hastened
to climb on the bandwagon. Even Keyes's son-in-law, John C.
Gaveney, felt that he could not actively oppose La Follette without jeopardizing his own campaign for the state Senate. With
the assistance of Haugen, James O. Davidson, Irvine L. Lenroot,
and others, the La Follette organization made a strong and successful bid for the support of the Scandinavian voters. The *Ashland Daily Press,* which frequently reflected Scandinavian opinion, observed that La Follette's declarations of harmony and his
endorsement of Scofield's administration would strengthen him
in all parts of the state.[25]

In the key metropolitan area of Milwaukee La Follette's supporters set up headquarters and completed their organization down to each ward and precinct. Indeed, it appears that he was the only candidate who had any real organization in the city. Despite the recent election of the conservative Democrat David Rose as mayor, La Follette's supporters were confident of winning a majority of Milwaukee's delegates to the state convention. La Follette made numerous trips to the city for conferences with the directors of the state Republican campaign committee and his own personal workers. That there was relative good feeling and harmony among the several elements of the party was evident on all sides. In response to questions put by a *Sentinel* reporter La Follette smilingly commented that the "contest is a friendly struggle this year." He consistently refused to denounce or disparage any of the other candidates.[26]

Such expressions of cooperation and moderation only served to infuriate Governor Scofield. The two bitter personal campaigns that La Follette had waged against him for the governorship were still fresh in his mind. To him the harmony campaign was a ruse and subterfuge of the radicals and Populists to gain power. He refused to be conciliated. In an open letter to the *Sentinel* he assailed La Follette in direct and personal terms. Branding his avowed hostility to political machines as farcical, Scofield warned that if elected La Follette would build up the most complete and personal machine in the history of the state. He denounced the candidate as a radical and a party bolter, and as a tool and ally of the railroads and other special interests. At least there was no question of Scofield's reaction to La Follette's campaign.[27]

If the governor hoped to incite La Follette to make a bitter and personal reply, he failed completely. La Follette refused to be provoked into abandoning his attitude of a "friendly contest" and he ignored Scofield's letter without comment. The state press reacted immediately and sharply in La Follette's favor. The *Oshkosh Northwestern*, which was friendly to Scofield, regretted

La Follette at the Time of His Election as Governor in 1900

La Follette Campaigning at Cumberland, Wisconsin, in 1897

the attack and agreed that the governor had surrendered "the dignity due the office." The *Appleton Evening Crescent* thought that Scofield had "made the mistake of his life." Other papers joined in denouncing the diatribe, and the *Sentinel* editorialized that the attack would not hurt La Follette but would increase his strength.[28]

The long preparation and thorough organization of La Follette's campaign were now ready to bear fruit. He had personally visited most of the counties of the state, and his lieutenants had covered every township. He had conciliated most of the elements in the party and had expressed a moderate attitude toward the great corporations. He had avoided antagonizing the other candidates and, with the exception of Governor Scofield, the state's major political figures. Thanks to generous financial backing he had been able to keep a corps of paid workers busy mailing letters and pamphlets, calling on potential voters, and later taking people to the polling places.[29] Most important, he alone of the candidates offered a clear, intelligible program of reform, including a direct primary, equality of taxation, and increased control of monopolies. By his fair, moderate, and reasonable attitude he had prevented the chief danger to his candidacy, the formation of an anti–La Follette bloc. The pre-convention "harmony" campaign had produced results. The probable nomination of La Follette was conceded even before the meeting of the first county convention.

The initial contest for delegates indicated the pattern of the campaign. In a short but decisive battle La Follette carried "Long" Jones's home city and county of Waukesha and gained a comfortable majority of those delegates who were pledged to vote for him at the state convention. The same day La Follette carried Scofield's home county of Oconto by a similar majority, thus administering a rebuke to the governor for his intemperate outburst.[30]

The several local candidates obviously had no chance. The

state Republican committee had made no move to organize any combination against La Follette, and by the time the first county convention met it was certain that it would not attempt to do so. On July 1 "Long" Jones, protesting that he was "not a bit sore," withdrew from the race and indicated that he would support La Follette. A few days later both Bradford and Whitehead also retired from the contest. The *La Crosse Republican and Leader,* which had supported Bradford, promptly endorsed La Follette and praised him for his friendly and constructive campaign. La Follette confided to Nils Haugen that the situation was "in the bag," but he did not intend to let up. This time he was determined to leave "as few sore spots" as possible. About the same time Congressman Babcock gleefully wrote James O. Davidson that "we have them whipped to such a finish that Bob won't have any opposition when the convention is called." Then, waxing even more confidential, he assured the state treasurer, "There is one thing, my dear boy, about this campaign: the plans were well laid long before Bob made his announcement." [31]

It was at this juncture that Senator Spooner confounded the political observers by announcing, two years before the expiration of his term, that he did not intend to seek re-election in 1903 but would return to his private law practice. In spite of Spooner's efforts to remain neutral in the state campaign and La Follette's assurances that he had only the highest regard for the senator, rumors of a deal for Spooner's seat had circulated widely. Perhaps Spooner, whom reporter Lincoln Steffens later called a "timid man," preferred to retire gracefully without a fight. Political leaders expressed surprise and regret at this sudden decision and hoped that he would reconsider, but at once they began to lay plans to take advantage of the proposed vacancy. Most prominent among the men suggested to fill the seat were Payne, Babcock, and Esch. All were known to be ambitious. [32]

The rest of the pre-convention contests were easy victories for the La Follette forces. County after county selected La Follette delegates to the state convention. The remaining rival candidates, De Wayne Stebbins and General Rogers, also withdrew, leaving La Follette the only candidate to go before the convention. In reviewing the campaign the editor of the *Sentinel* praised the manner in which La Follette had made the race. Not only had he been moderate and conciliatory, but there was no evidence that he had "surrendered a principle, mortgaged an appointment, or given assurance to any interest or influence unbecoming an honorable man." [33] As the time for the convention approached the press became almost uniformly friendly to La Follette. Only Governor Scofield threatened to renew the bitter personal warfare, and he was dissuaded, with difficulty, by his friends. La Follette gave no sign that he was aware of the governor's hostility.[34]

The convention scene at Milwaukee on August 8 was a fitting climax to the "harmony campaign." La Follette was nominated by acclamation, and the defeated candidates, Bradford, Whitehead, Stebbins, and Rogers, joined in pledging their support to him in the coming general campaign. There was virtually no anti–La Follette sentiment visible in the entire convention. He was not a "factional" candidate. He had become the choice of the whole party.[35]

The party platform was a clear-cut, plain-speaking document, but it reflected the same spirit of moderation and conciliation that had characterized La Follette's pre-convention campaign. It praised the outgoing administration of Governor Scofield as "clean, capable, and business-like." It endorsed the services of Senator Spooner and regretted his decision to retire from public life. The keystone of the document was the plank calling for a "primary election" system, which was to provide the principal issue for La Follette in the coming campaign. Other major planks urged a "justly proportionate" basis for corporation taxation, extension of the anti-pass and anti-lobby laws, continuation of the tax commission, and a general program for the regulation of monopolies.[36]

La Follette was completely exhausted and almost in a state of collapse from his efforts in the preliminary campaign. A vacation was in order if he was to take any important part in the fall contest and election. Again Isaac Stephenson came to his assistance and organized a week's cruise through the Great Lakes on his yacht. There, away from the summer heat of Madison, and with the company of only a few close personal and political friends, La Follette rested, lolled around the deck, and made plans for the coming campaign. He returned from the cruise rested and relaxed, with definite plans for the approaching race. "Fighting Bob" and "Uncle Ike" became, for the time being, close friends and political allies.[37]

In the drive for votes before the general election, the efforts of La Follette and the state ticket were merged with the national campaign. After much preliminary planning the formal Republican campaign was opened with a rally at La Crosse on September 9. There vice-presidential candidate Theodore Roosevelt, flanked on the platform by Senator Quarles and La Follette, was the featured speaker. Ten days later La Follette opened his personal campaign in Milwaukee. The *Sentinel* described him as being "in splendid voice," and his utterances made a deep impression on the audience, which followed him with close attention. In typically La Follette fashion he spoke for three hours, hammering in his points with great force and earnestness. Always a great actor, he was at his best before the Milwaukee audience, which broke into spontaneous outbursts of applause whenever he paused. This keynote speech, which made a strong plea for a thoroughgoing primary law, was reprinted widely throughout the state.[38]

The Democrats had nominated Louis G. Bomrich of Milwaukee for governor and had adopted a typical Bryanite platform, denouncing imperialism, expansion, and monopolies.[39]

As he could count on strong support from his fellow Germans, Bomrich could be expected to make a vigorous race, but even the most optimistic Democrat hardly expected either Bryan or Bomrich to carry the state in November. On the other hand, the enthusiasm of the Republican candidates was contagious. The popular and dynamic Roosevelt made numerous speeches in the state. Senator Spooner campaigned vigorously for both the national and the state ticket, repeatedly praising La Follette and the state platform. The Wisconsin congressmen also took part in the general campaign, supporting the whole ticket. Nils Haugen and "Yim" Davidson did yeoman service in canvassing the Scandinavian neighborhoods and making speeches in Norwegian to secure the vote of that group. Popular pro–La Follette speakers of German descent largely counteracted the natural disposition of many German voters to support Bomrich. No group was overlooked in the comprehensive drive for votes.[40]

But perhaps the greatest single load was carried by La Follette himself. During the campaign he traveled almost sixty-five hundred miles, delivered more than two hundred speeches, and spoke to an estimated two hundred thousand people. His oratorical ability and dramatic presentation of important issues made supporters of many who once had been opposed to him. His speeches were characterized by logical reasoning, humorous asides, and passionate pleadings. Evidently his vigorous and emotional approach appealed greatly to his listeners. It became evident that not only could La Follette carry his own weight but that he was a tower of strength to the whole ticket in Wisconsin.[41]

Throughout the campaign La Follette grew increasingly aware of the importance of the other political races taking place in the state. Especially was he concerned about the personnel of the incoming legislature, which would determine the fate of his program of reform. He had personally persuaded veteran assemblyman Hall not to retire, but he was less successful in clearing the way for some of his other personal friends. He feared that the

elements in the state which secretly opposed him would concentrate on electing a hostile Senate and Assembly. Reports
from the field did nothing to quiet his misgivings; at least one
close supporter complained bitterly that no olive branch had
been extended to him and charged that the Republican organization was backing his opponent. Other elements of the party, apparently, felt under no obligation to support La Follette's personal followers for state and local office.[42]

The Republican campaign for "Mac and Teddy and Bob"
swept to a smashing victory in the November election. McKinley's plurality was even larger than it had been in 1896. La
Follette rolled up a plurality of more than a hundred thousand
votes over his Democratic opponent and carried all except five
counties in the state. The other state officers were re-elected by
comparable margins.[43] Just as it had been a united campaign for
the whole Republican ticket, so was it a victory for the entire
party with little outward evidence of any factional differences
or unusual strains or stresses. The old party leaders had worked
vigorously with the personal supporters of La Follette for the
election of the entire ticket and there had appeared no important
differences within the party over issues and programs. Far from
being a personal victory or a political revolution in Wisconsin
politics, the success of La Follette and the Republican ticket in
November, 1900, was the result of the combined efforts of the
entire party. It was based upon thorough party organization, a
well-filled war chest, exploitation of popular issues, and vigorous,
dynamic leadership. It was a rather typical story of a Wisconsin
Republican triumph. It had been a true "harmony" campaign.[44]

3 BLOCKED BY THE STALWARTS

★ ★ ★ ★ ★ ★ ★ ★ ★ ★ ★ ★ ★ ★ ★ ★ ★

THE ATMOSPHERE OF HARMONY AND GOOD FELLOWSHIP CARRIED
over into the first days of the new administration. In an unevent-
ful but "impressive" ceremony Robert M. La Follette was inaugurated as governor on January 7, 1901. Retiring Governor Scofield, pale but self-possessed, shook hands with his successor and
escorted him to the Assembly chamber but did not tarry to attend
the reception or inaugural ball. Other prominent conservatives,
however, participated in the festivities, which the press called
the "biggest in history." [1]

Though outwardly composed and confident, La Follette was
apprehensive about the composition and temper of the incoming
legislature. He foresaw that in the upper house the vote on the
key administration proposals would be close. Rumors, originating
in Milwaukee, that the stalwarts would attempt to organize the
Senate and control the selection of committees belied their expressions of loyalty and friendliness. The new legislature was
composed largely of political amateurs. Of the assemblymen
sixty-four were attending their first session. Only one, Albert R.
Hall, had had as much as ten years' experience as a lawmaker. In
the Senate nine members were serving second terms, and a large
proportion of the others had had experience in the Assembly. An
overwhelming majority of the members of each house were Republican, and none had actively opposed the incoming administration in the 1900 campaign. [2]

When the legislature convened La Follette presented his reform program directly and forcefully. He abandoned the old
custom of having the governor's message read by a clerk and de-

livered his address in person. He stressed only two major pro-posals, one economic and one political reform. He called for legislation taxing the railroads on an ad valorem basis according to their actual property valuation and a comprehensive primary election law to replace the caucus and convention system. These reforms had constituted the principal planks in the Republican platform of 1900 on which La Follette had been elected, and they were closely identified with his name in the minds of most of the voters. In his campaign speeches he had laid great stress on the need for direct nominations and had repeatedly referred to the direct primary as the "first plank" in his program of reform.[3]

Wisconsin's primary election legislation dated back to the Keogh Law of 1891, which applied the primary principle to local elections in Milwaukee County. Succeeding legislatures had made changes in the caucus and convention system to per-mit more direct control by the voters and in 1899 had extended the Milwaukee law, in modified form, to other towns and cities in the state. Discussions of a general primary law had appeared periodically in the press. Such party stalwarts as Elisha W. Keyes had written favorably of the proposed reform, and a model law for a statewide primary had been distributed by the *Sentinel*. In 1897 such a bill had been introduced by Assemblyman Wil-liam T. Lewis of Racine. It failed of passage, but not before it had been debated in the Assembly and widely reported in the press throughout the state.[4]

By 1900 many other states were considering reforms in nomi-nating procedures. In Pennsylvania and California, for example, there had been piecemeal legislation of a local and optional char-acter since the post-war era. In Kentucky and many of the South-ern states optional direct primary laws had been enacted during the decade of the eighties, and the move to apply the direct pri-mary system to large cities and populous counties was a charac-teristic of the decade 1890–1900.[5] The demand was widespread, however, for more comprehensive and far-reaching legislation.

The corrupt manipulation of city and state governments and the prevalence of "bossism" throughout the country had already attracted the attention of those crusading journalists whom Theodore Roosevelt later dubbed "muckrakers." Chief among the remedies that students of government most frequently proposed was the mandatory statewide direct system of primary elections.[6]

About 1896 La Follette himself had turned his attention to the direct primary as a corrective for the abuses of machine politics, and in succeeding years it occupied an increasingly important place in his plans for reform. Early in 1897 he presented his first comprehensive discussion of the topic at the University of Chicago in a speech entitled "The Menace of the Political Machine." He advocated that the state "abolish the entire system of caucuses and conventions and substitute the secret direct primary election in its place as a nominating device." The application of the Australian ballot to the primary election, he argued, would complete the destruction of the "corrupt political machine." To La Follette the system of conventions and caucuses had become synonomous with "bossism" and machine rule. Soon La Follette was a popular speaker on direct primary reform throughout the Middle West. The address he delivered at Ann Arbor, Michigan, the next year was widely reported in the press and served as a model for numerous pamphlets on the subject. By the time of the campaign of 1900 the voters of the state were familiar with the issues of the direct primary. Indeed, it is probable that the Wisconsin electorate was the best educated group in the country on the subject of convention abuses and nominating elections. In every speech La Follette and his lieutenants stressed the need for this reform. The Ann Arbor speech was reprinted as a campaign document and distributed by the thousands. Through the press of the state the public followed closely the arguments for a primary system, and many editors used their columns to explain the proposed changes and their probable effects. If the voters of Wisconsin approved anything in addition to a continuation of Republicanism in 1900, it was the adoption of a general primary election system as advocated by its champion, Robert M. La Follette.[7]

For several weeks before the legislature convened administration leaders had been busy preparing a detailed comprehensive bill providing for direct, secret primary elections for all local, county, and state offices. A number of legislators had collaborated in drafting it and La Follette gave his approval to the measure as drawn. On January 29 identical bills were introduced in the Assembly and the Senate which were at once referred to appropriate committees and started on the way toward passage. The initial reaction from the state press was favorable, and the editor of the *Sentinel* described the Stevens bill as a carefully drawn, "practical" measure which the committee should speedily approve. La Follette took every opportunity to speak in its behalf and in several rousing speeches before farm audiences urged his listeners to bring pressure to bear on their representatives to speed its passage.[8]

The legislature, however, was already showing signs of splitting into rival factions. La Follette's fears that many unsympathetic candidates would be elected to the Senate were more than realized. It soon became evident that most of the older political figures in the state did not intend to look to the governor for leadership or to support the reforms he advocated. The political honeymoon that followed the harmony campaign was one of the shortest on record.

Early in January Edwin D. Coe, a federal pension agent, sent up a trial balloon in the form of a letter to the *Sentinel* denying that the legislature had to pass a primary law. The whole question was a matter of method rather than principle. The caucus, he said, was one representative system. Rapidly the split widened between the supporters of La Follette and the conservative politicians led by Pfister and Philipp. Each group blamed the other for the break in party harmony and represented itself as the Republican Party, its opponents as a faction. Coe now took the position that the convention had only "recommended" the primary election reform. A convention, he contended, had no power to demand action by the legislature. The administration forces, on the other hand, regarded the primary election plank as a party pledge which was binding on all Republicans, since all had supported it during the campaign. La Follette insisted on the passage of a general primary bill, not an experimental piece-meal measure such as the conservatives would substitute.[9]

The conservative leaders charged that the governor had rejected the counsel and cooperation of the older leaders of the party and had formed a clique of his personal followers to carry out his program. Philipp, who had supported the La Follette ticket, charged that "long before any attempt was made to organize a faction in opposition to the Governor, there was a faction organized and disciplined to carry out his program." He bitterly complained of the "atmosphere of mystery" that enveloped the executive chamber and the whole capitol. Everywhere, he said, there was evasion, suspicion, and secrecy. The old legislative leaders were ignored on questions of policy and they resented it. Elisha Keyes protested that it was almost impossible for anyone except La Follette's henchmen to see the governor on any subject. Jerre Murphy (the governor's private secretary) would act as sentinel and size up the visitor before he would be permitted to enter. The conservative politicians also strongly resented the attitude taken by the close friends of the administration. Philipp charged that they acted as if "they were the anointed ones and in possession of the ark of the covenant." Anyone who presumed to express an opinion that had not been previously approved by the governor or Jerre Murphy became "corruptionists, corporation corruptionists or corrupt hirelings."[10]

As the break developed into an open feud, La Follette tended to doubt the good faith of many who had supported him. He suspected that their real purpose was not to promote reform but to prevent any effective change in the "old corrupt system." He saw the lobbyists descend upon the state capitol in increasing numbers. The railroads, threatened with the taxation bills, and the bosses, threatened with the direct primary, joined forces. To La Follette the breach became a struggle to the death between the people and the machine, and the whole fight centered upon him personally.[11]

A most significant indication of the approaching breakup of the Republican forces was the purchase of the *Milwaukee Sentinel* early in February by Charles Pfister. By a wide margin the *Sentinel* was the leading morning journal in Wisconsin. It had long been a power in Republican politics and exerted a strong influence throughout the state. In the campaign of 1900 it had done much to promote harmony and peace within the party. Though somewhat reserved, it had given friendly support to La Follette and the convention platform. The change in ownership foreshadowed a shift in policy which did not take long to become apparent.[12]

The defection of the state's leading journal was dramatized by the visit of the *Sentinel's* new editor, Lanning Warren, to the governor. La Follette, by his own account, refused to consider Warren's demand that he call off primary and railroad legislation in return for support on other issues. According to La Follette, Warren announced as he stalked out of the office, "If that is your answer, the *Sentinel* will begin skinning you tomorrow." Philipp described the incident as a peaceful effort to reach a compromise on the primary question that would prevent a split in the party. Keyes reported to Senator Spooner, with much satisfaction, the sale of the *Sentinel* and gleefully predicted that it would be "our paper." [13]

The "skinning" began at once. As public attention was centered on the primary election bill, the measure drew the full fire of the *Sentinel* both in editorials and under the guise of news reporting. The bill was denounced as a populistic and socialistic device that would lead to anarchy. A loyal Republican state, it claimed, could not pass so radical a bill. La Follette was denounced as a dictator, a demagogue, and a wild-eyed radical. By the end of February, 1901, the Republican Party was hopelessly split.[14]

The Stevens primary election bill slowly worked its way through the obstacles in the Assembly. After extensive public hearings before the Joint Committee on Privileges and Elections, it was favorably reported and eventually, on March 22, was approved by the Assembly without substantial change and sent to the Senate. It was only by exerting all his energy and influence that La Follette had been able to keep his forces organized to down the opposition in the lower chamber. The vote at each step was dangerously close. Isaac Stephenson made a trip to Madison to bolster support for the bill among assemblymen from northeastern Wisconsin, and Congressman Henry A. Cooper was urged to take a hand to keep southeastern legislators in line. La Follette was forced to order Secretary of State Froehlich to prevent anti-administration activity among his employees. But in spite of the victory in the Assembly the administration grew increasingly pessimistic of the bill's chances. Both friends and foes of the measure freely predicted that it would be mutilated or defeated in the Senate.[15]

The *Sentinel* kept up a constant drumfire of criticism of the Stevens bill. A survey by the *Milwaukee Journal* in late February showed that a majority of the state's newspapers were opposed to the primary election bill. *Die Germania,* influential German-language paper in Milwaukee, "commanded a halt" on the Stevens bill, and the Scandinavian *Amerika* was highly critical of the proposed reform. Pressure was put on other editors to oppose the bill, and a majority of the papers in the state soon became hostile to the administration. La Follette and his friends were painfully aware of this sudden shift in the attitude of the press.

The conflict in the Senate was short and decisive. In the first test of strength the anti-administration forces, the stalwarts, found themselves in complete command. On April 12 a new measure, drawn by Henry Hagemeister of Milwaukee, was substituted for the Stevens bill. This measure, which was quickly approved, retained only the same number to relate it to the bill passed by the Assembly.[16]

The Hagemeister bill, which limited the application of the primary principle to county and village elections, was now returned to the Assembly for approval. Here it was amended to include cities and some state offices and a referendum clause. When the Senate refused to reconsider this modification, the Assembly eventually yielded and approved the Senate version by the narrow margin of forty-eight to forty-six. The measure that went to the governor for his approval or veto had little in common with the bill that the administration had introduced three months before. In fact, its author, E. Ray Stevens, had voted against it at its final passage.[17]

If there were any doubts concerning La Follette's reaction to the Hagemeister bill he quickly dispelled them. With a blistering veto message, in which he denounced the proposal as a subterfuge and a negation of the party pledge, he returned the measure to the legislature. He berated the members who had approved the substitute as tools of the corporations and agents of the "machine." [18]

The stalwart majority in the Senate promptly voted a resolution censuring the governor for "abusing the Senate." The *Sentinel* applauded the resolution and denounced La Follette. It charged that the primary plan was a scheme to control the United States senatorship and that the governor had rejected the Hagemeister bill because it could not be used to that end. It was La Follette, said the *Sentinel,* who was imperiling the unity of the party. He was a dictator who was determined to rule or ruin—a boss who would accept no modification of his proposal. The Hagemeister bill, it continued, was a moderate compromise plan that would allow the people to witness a practical test of the primary election system. La Follette, charged the *Sentinel,* did not intend that any primary bill should become law. The proposal would serve better as an issue for his next campaign.[19]

La Follette later described the fight over the direct primary as another chapter in the long struggle between the bosses and the machine and the people for the control of the government. In his *Autobiography* he cited numerous legislators who had been bribed or threatened into opposing the primary bill. It was better, he declared, to accept nothing than to approve so poor a substitute as the Hagemeister bill. The principle was more important than a "half-loaf." [20]

In the meantime the efforts of the administration to revise the railroad tax structure fared no better than the primary election bill. For years the railroads had practically made their own assessments and determined their own tax rates under a license-fee system based on their gross earnings per mile. They had long been among the largest industrial interests of the state and they refused to submit tamely to either a heavier tax burden or to regulation. The Wisconsin railroad commissioner had been docile and the companies had successfully resisted all attempts to strengthen the office or replace it with a strong type of commission.[21]

But the railroad interests were not unopposed. From the time of his first entrance into Wisconsin politics in 1890 Albert R. Hall had been recognized as the leader of the anti-railroad forces in the legislature. Before coming to Wisconsin he had served in the Minnesota Assembly and had gained a reputation as a Granger, a Populist, and a "railroad baiter." With regularity he proposed that the major railway systems be investigated and that a railroad commission be established with power to fix rates. Just as regularly these proposals were lost in committee. Thanks to the publicity given Governor Scofield's "frank-riding" cow, Hall and his associates had been able to arouse public opinion in favor of an anti-pass and anti-frank law which was passed by the 1899 legislature. That session also created a temporary tax commission to study and make recommendations on taxation with special attention to the proportion of taxes borne by the railroads. This commission's report was later to bear fruit.[22]

At the time of the "harmony campaign" of 1900 the railroads still retained their dominant position in state politics. The presidents of the two leading roads, Albert J. Earling of the St. Paul System, and Marvin Hughitt of the Chicago and North Western, were persons to be conciliated, and La Follette's interview with Hughitt had been largely for the purpose of assuring the old man that the candidate was not a radical on the question.[23] Yet the party platform had stressed the importance of the impending report of the tax commission and the necessity for "each individual and every corporation . . . to bear a proportionate share of the burden of taxation." Such a plank foreshadowed a major change in the state's railroad tax policy.[24]

By the time La Follette took office as governor in 1901 his program for the reform of railroad taxation was well developed. He had been interested in the whole railroad problem since childhood and had become a serious student of railroad taxation and regulation while a member of Congress. But for practical purposes he chose to concentrate his attention on a revision of the tax system and to soft-pedal regulation until after the other reforms had been effected. With this in mind he had prevailed on Hall to refrain from presenting a railroad-regulation plank at the Republican convention and had confined himself to a discussion of the need for reforming the system of railroad taxation. This procedure was typical of La Follette's campaign technique, namely the restriction of the issues to two or three clear-cut pro-

ALBERT R. HALL

WILLIAM D. HOARD

JAMES O. DAVIDSON

HENRY ALLEN COOPER

Prominent Early Progressive Leaders

JOHN C. SPOONER

JOSEPH W. BABCOCK

CHARLES F. PFISTER

EMANUEL L. PHILIPP

Leading Conservative Opponents of the Progressives

posals. By constant repetition and re-emphasis he would expound his program at length before audiences throughout the state. By election time the voters were thoroughly familiar with most aspects of the issues. This campaign of education La Follette followed successfully in all his later campaigns.[25]

When the legislature met in January, 1901, the temporary tax commission made its report. The commission had found that the railroads were paying only half as much on their properties per dollar of valuation as was the average individual. The commission suggested that either the license-fee tax be increased to yield approximately six hundred thousand dollars more annually or the whole system of railroad taxation be shifted to an ad valorem basis and provision made for a physical valuation of the railroads. This latter recommendation had the full support of La Follette, who regarded it as the more scientific method of taxation. He had advocated the ad valorem plan in his campaign speeches and had recommended it in his message to the legislature.[26]

In response to the Tax Commission's recommendations two bills were introduced in the legislature. One, the so-called Whitehead bill, proposed simply to increase the license tax from four per cent to five and one-half per cent of gross earnings for Class I railroads with proportionate rates for the smaller roads. The other bill was sponsored jointly by Stevens and Hall and had the full backing and support of the administration. It provided for complete and scientific physical evaluation of all of the railroad properties in Wisconsin by the Tax Commission, and taxation thereon at the same rate as the general property tax on farms, homes, and businesses.[27]

Numerous other bills applying to the railroads and kindred corporations were introduced, including Hall's pet plan for a railroad commission with power to fix rates and regulate the roads. Old-time politicians feared that the anti-railroad group would go "hog-wild." Without exception the railway attorneys who came to the capitol as lobbyists opposed all the proposed legislation. So active were some of the "lobby lawyers" that friends of the railroads sought to have a number of them re-called before they goaded the reformers to even more drastic action. Unofficial lobbyist Keyes warned president Earling that anti-railroad bills were piling up in the legislature, all of which, he was confident, could be sidetracked.[28]

The same combination of politicians, railroad henchmen, and conservatives that opposed the direct primary law joined hands to defeat the ad valorem proposal and the other railway bills. Long and exhaustive hearings were conducted at which top railroad officials or their attorneys appeared to oppose the ad valorem system. The *Milwaukee Sentinel,* now the mouthpiece of Pfister and the old guard, daily denounced the proposed legis-lation as Populistic and predicted that if such a scheme was en-acted industry would be driven from the state.[29]

In the meantime La Follette's majority in the Assembly melted away. Although he threw the whole weight of his office behind the Stevens-Hall bill it soon became evident that there was little chance that it would become law. The argument of the conserva-tive politicians that more time was needed to study the proposed changes doubtless influenced many members of the legislature to vote against the measure. Some felt that it would be discrimina-tory to increase the tax burden of the railroads while the state's policy respecting the personal property tax was admittedly chaotic. Other members yielded to more direct pressure.[30]

The ad valorem tax bill was killed in the Assembly by a vote of fifty-one to forty-five. It was obvious that taxation reforms were dead for that session. La Follette, anticipating this outcome, used the occasion of a routine veto of a dog-license bill to deliver a new message on taxation to the legislature that same morning. His famous "Dog Tax Veto" was widely reprinted throughout the state. The poor farmer's dog, said the governor, should not be the subject of burdensome taxation so long as the giant railroad corporations were avoiding the payment of their just share of the costs of government. He reviewed the whole history of the tax program and denounced the lobby for corrupting the representatives of the people.[31]

La Follette's program lay in ruins, the Republicans were hopelessly split, and a large segment of the party had repudiated the governor's leadership. Many leaders of the party, including Babcock and Philipp, who had supported La Follette in the harmony campaign now became his bitterest opponents. In spite of the governor's threat to call a special session to redeem the party's campaign pledges, the legislature soon adjourned without taking further action on the reform program. Though the legislature had extended the life of the Tax Commission and had passed some minor non-controversial legislation, it had spent almost the entire session in abortive wrangling and deadlock. As a result La Follette and his personal supporters, now in control of the state's administrative machinery, drew together to form a tight, hard political organization for the purpose of capturing the entire state government. Far from being a decisive victory for La Follette and his progressive Republicans, the election of 1900 had proved to be simply the first battle. The defeat of the progressive program in the 1901 legislature made certain that a long bitter struggle must be fought before such reforms could be achieved. Both stalwarts and progressives looked forward to the coming campaign in 1902 for vindication and victory.

4 CURBING THE BOSSES AND THE RAILROADS

★ ★ ★ ★ ★ ★ ★ ★ ★ ★ ★ ★ ★ ★ ★ ★ ★

THE CONSERVATIVE REPUBLICANS AND STALWART POLITICIANS were determined that there should be no more harmony agreements with La Follette. The fiery reformer had proved himself, in their eyes, anything but moderate and reasonable. Most of the stalwarts thoroughly regretted that they had supported him in the 1900 election and began, early in 1902, to plan their campaign to oust him from office at the end of his first term.

The opposition to La Follette and his progressives centered around the professional politicians and the remnants of the Payne-Sawyer machine. Sawyer, of course, was dead, and Payne, now postmaster general, personally took little part in state politics. He seemed to be chiefly interested in preventing any embarrassment to the national administration stemming from the intraparty fight in his home state. But Charles Pfister, bolstered by his recently acquired *Milwaukee Sentinel,* took an active lead in organizing the opposition to the "Madison Dictator." Among the other stalwarts, Emanuel L. Philipp, rising young refrigerator-car magnate, was already emerging as the most able of La Follette's opponents. Dark, swarthy, and corpulent, Philipp gave the first impression of being a typical city machine politician. But he displayed surprising mental agility, and he had qualities of rugged honesty and integrity that eventually won the admiration and respect of even the most ardent of the La Follette progressives.[1] Philipp had given much-needed support, both personal and financial, to La Follette in 1900, an action that he regretted a year later. On the side lines old ex-boss Keyes kept a watchful eye on the activities at the state capitol. By means of his wide correspondence he continually passed along plans for stalwart action and exchanged bits of gossip with his friends throughout the state and in Washington. As postmaster of Madison, an appointment he retained until his death in 1910, his office was a regular calling place for visiting stalwarts.[2]

The great majority of Wisconsin politicians who were prominent in the national government were adherents of the stalwart faction and opponents of La Follette and his rising progressive organization. Besides Postmaster General Payne, Horace A. "Hod" Taylor and Henry Casson held prominent positions in Washington. Assistant Secretary of the Treasury Taylor, part owner of the *Wisconsin State Journal* of Madison and a close friend of Keyes's and Spooner's, exerted considerable influence in stalwart circles. Casson, as sergeant at arms in the House of Representatives, was a supporter of Congressman Joseph W. Babcock, and was generally popular with the Wisconsin congressional delegation. Like Babcock, he had supported La Follette in the harmony campaign of 1900 but had rejoined the opposition the next year. Both Payne and Babcock occupied high places in the inner councils of the Republican Party. In 1902 Payne was vice-chairman of the Republican National Committee, and Babcock served for twelve years as chairman of the Republican Congressional Campaign Committee. As could be expected, the La Follette wing of the Republicans in Wisconsin received scant consideration from the national Republican organization.[3]

The delegation representing Wisconsin in Congress in 1900 had been largely the selection of the stalwart state organization. Only First District representative Henry A. Cooper was a thoroughgoing progressive. Cooper was a close personal friend of La Follette's, and he served as spokesman for the Wisconsin progressives in Washington and often conferred with President

Roosevelt in their behalf. John J. Esch of the Seventh District
and William Stafford of the Fifth had progressive leanings, but
neither had played a conspicuous role in the early battles of the
La Follette group. Both later became identified with progressive principles and battled for them on the floor of Congress.[4]
Henry C. "Cully" Adams, who succeeded Herman Dahle in
1902 as Second District representative, was neither a progressive
nor a stalwart. So persistently did he attempt to please both
factions that he was accused of being a fence straddler by both.
Four years later, in spite of the support of the Dairyman's Association, he appeared doomed to defeat at the hands of John
M. Nelson, a strong La Follette supporter and Dane County
attorney, when death suddenly terminated his career in the
summer of 1906.[5]

The full force of the progressive organization was directed,
as might be expected, against Third District Congressman
Joseph W. Babcock. He had vigorously supported La Follette
in 1900, and then just as vigorously fought against his reform
proposals. As a result he became the special object of the progressives' animosity, which forced him to fight constantly for his
political life. But despite personal campaigns by La Follette,
Babcock survived attempted purges in 1902 and 1904 before he
finally fell victim to a "fairminded Democrat" who had the unofficial support of the progressive machine.[6]

But by all odds the most important member of the Wisconsin congressional delegation was Senator John C. Spooner. A
close friend and associate of President McKinley's, Spooner had
twice been offered positions in the McKinley cabinet. He had
gained national prominence by his speeches on the Spanish-
American War, the problems of the Philippines, and American
responsibilities as a world power. The people of Wisconsin were
proud of Spooner and of his national reputation as an orator
and debater. But Spooner, as senator, did not take a personal
part in the conduct of local political affairs. In all the major

campaigns he would characteristically endorse all candidates of the Republican Party and devote most of his attention to national issues. This had been his policy during the 1900 campaign. His announcement in the midst of that campaign that he would not seek re-election in 1902 confused and disconcerted many of the Republican leaders. To the conservatives, he was the best vote-getter in the party. He was, as Lincoln Steffens later called him, the "flower" of the stalwart machine.[7]

This rather miscellaneous group of stalwarts, under the direction of Pfister, organized the Wisconsin Republican League to coordinate their fight against the re-election of La Follette in the coming election of 1902. Because its headquarters occupied the entire eleventh floor of a Milwaukee office building, the organization became known throughout the state as the "Eleventh Story League." The membership included most of the anti–La Follette Republicans in both houses of the legislature and was actively supported by many important conservative businessmen and industrialists. The League chose for its candidate John M. Whitehead, lawyer and state senator from Janesville, who had also been an aspirant in 1900.[8]

La Follette had suffered a physical breakdown in the summer of 1901 and for several weeks was dangerously ill. For months he was forced to exist on a very restricted diet consisting chiefly of milk and crackers. This gave rise to the speculation that he would not be able to campaign again. By the spring of 1902, however, "Fighting Bob" had recovered sufficiently to engage in a spirited speaking tour throughout the state, during which he discussed the primary election bill and the ad valorem tax plan with his usual thoroughness and vigor. He explained to his audiences why these needed reforms had been defeated in the legislature and recited the votes on the two measures. This use of the voting records of the local legislators was the forerunner of the "roll call" which became famous as a La Follette campaign device.[9]

Both the direct primary and the ad valorem tax system made excellent campaign issues. The public had followed the course of both measures to their defeat in the 1901 legislature, and the state press had filled its columns with arguments favoring or opposing the innovations. Even the high school debaters of the state were seriously attacking and defending primary elections in their interschool contests. The Eleventh Story League published articles and pamphlets supporting the license-fee system and denouncing the "complicated and expensive" ad valorem method.[10] To combat the stalwarts the La Follette forces published *The Voters Handbook*, a 144-page paper-bound volume which explained both the direct primary and the railroad taxation questions in great detail. It retold again the story of the failure of the recent legislature, listed all the key roll call votes on each issue, and denounced the bosses and the interests for disregarding the people's mandate. The *Milwaukee Free Press* printed 125,000 of these booklets, enough to supply one to almost every Republican family in Wisconsin.[11]

Despite the most vigorous efforts of the Eleventh Story League, their candidate, the capable but puritanical and undramatic John Whitehead, aroused no more enthusiasm than he had in 1900. In contrast, La Follette drew large crowds wherever he spoke. With great skill he championed the ad valorem and primary election reforms and dramatized these issues as direct personal challenges to his listeners. It was a clear choice, he insisted, between voting for the bosses and voting for the people. Soon, long before convention time, even such dyed-in-the-wool stalwarts as Elisha Keyes and Fred Dennett conceded that their candidate had no chance.[12] As a result the League concentrated on supporting Senator Spooner and securing endorsement of him by the party convention. In the bitter legislative fight over the reform bills Spooner had taken no part but had remained aloof and silent. La Follette, on his part, offered no active opposition to the endorsement of Spooner; he even announced that he did not propose to interfere in the senatorship "unless necessary to protect the success of the platform." Consequently most county conventions endorsed both La Follette and Spooner and selected delegates pledged to support both.[13]

At the state Republican convention the progressives were in complete control and La Follette easily won renomination by an overwhelming majority. The platform repeated the demands for the enactment of tax reform and primary election legislation. It went further and declared that the support of these party pledges was a *sine qua non* of the Republican Party in Wisconsin, and urged the voters to require all candidates to give assurance that they would render such support. Senator Spooner was also endorsed. The convention commended his official career and national contributions, regretted his announced determination to retire from the Senate, and pledged that if he should reconsider this decision and "express his willingness to stand as a candidate in harmony with ... the platform principles" the party would enthusiastically support his re-election.[14] The stalwart press denounced this somewhat equivocal endorsement as a trick to "stab Spooner," but the senator said nothing; La Follette took time to praise his work in the Senate, and the public fully expected the re-election of both. Eventually Spooner agreed to accept the Senate seat and, as re-election came without opposition, he continued his career in Washington with no overt break in his relations with the progressive administration at Madison.[15]

The Democrats nominated for the governorship David Rose, mayor of Milwaukee and conservative machine politician who was chiefly known as an advocate of an "open town" for his fellow Milwaukeeans. As the Democratic platform denounced the primary election reform and opposed "double" taxation, the issue was clear-cut.[16] Against such opposition La Follette lost no time in carrying the battle to every section of the state.

He used an automobile in his campaign for the first time and probably even gained votes among the farmers by the innovation. He concentrated on his two major reform proposals, which he described as part of a great "progressive movement." In some speeches he traced the history of the direct primary movement back to 1868 in Crawford County, Pennsylvania, and cited the successful, though limited, experience that Michigan and Minnesota had had with the primary system. Other speeches bristled with statistics on railroad rates, earnings, and taxes. La Follette was probably the only public speaker in the country who could make a rate table sound exciting. The administration forces, mindful of the consequences of their failure in the 1900 campaign, paid careful attention this time to the election of a friendly legislature.[17]

The opposition press, representing a coalition of Republican stalwarts and conservative Democrats, sought to discredit La Follette by citing rumors of deals, scandals, and underhand methods. One tale was that of the so-called "Kress letters," which hinted at a secret agreement with Payne and the railroads during the 1900 campaign. The whole story was flimsy, and the proofs, when finally presented, were so nebulous that the reaction was in favor of La Follette.[18]

The governor's henchmen, however, unwittingly provided their enemies with far more exciting material for scandal than the cold rehash of the truces of the harmony campaign. In the state convention of 1902 the party had dropped Lorenzo D. Harvey from the ticket as state superintendent of public instruction in favor of C. P. Cary. Harvey, who had served two terms in that office, was eager for a third term, and his friends and associates protested the highhanded methods by which he was replaced. Shortly afterward the story developed that certain book companies interested in the defeat of Harvey had contributed two thousand dollars to the campaign fund and had pledged five thousand more if Harvey was not renominated.

At once the *Sentinel* raised a cry of fraud and demanded that all persons involved in the "schoolbook" scandal be dropped from the ticket.[19]

The progressive lieutenants maintained silence on the whole question for almost two months while the opposition press sought to link La Follette directly with the deal. At length Theodore Kronshage, a Milwaukee progressive, released the details of the transaction. Even his version revealed an unhealthy interest in the state superintendency on the part of the book publishers. According to Kronshage, the contribution of Ginn and Company and other independent textbook companies was not tied in any way to Harvey's defeat. They opposed Harvey because he favored, so they charged, the American Book Company and other firms in the so-called "school book trust." Kronshage had deposited the money in a bank and had then sent a check for the full amount to the campaign treasurer. The entire sum had gone into the general fund for campaign expenses. Eventually La Follette took time during one of his campaign speeches to deny specifically that any deal involving Harvey's defeat had been made with anyone; had any funds been offered with conditions attached, they would have been refused. Personally, he asserted, he was habitually ignorant of the source of contributions.[20] With these explanations and denials the story reluctantly died.

La Follette carried the state over the Democrats in the fall election and was returned to the governor's chair for a second term. It was scarcely an unqualified victory, however. For not only did the progressive Republicans experience the general slump in total votes that is characteristic of off-year elections, but La Follette ran some ten thousand votes behind the rest of the ticket. He also failed to carry ten counties, whereas the other state nominees lost only six or seven.[21] Thus it is apparent that a more bitter fight was made against La Follette personally than against the other progressive candidates. As Rose ran about ten thousand votes ahead of the other Democratic candidates, it appears probable that about that number of stalwarts had "scratched the head of the Republican ticket." The progressive administration was in power for another term, but La Follette and his supporters knew that the decisive and final victory was yet to be won.[22]

The incoming legislature was much more friendly to the administration than its predecessor had been. An overwhelming majority of the Assembly were avowed supporters of La Follette. In the Senate the progressives and stalwarts were so evenly divided that the three Democratic members held the balance of power. As in 1901, the relatively conservative Senate posed the major obstacle to the enactment of the progressives' reform legislation.[23]

La Follette determined to seize the initiative by pressing at once for comprehensive legislation, not only on the primary election and ad valorem tax issues, but also on the broad problem of railroad regulation. In his message to the legislature he stressed the need for immediate and adequate primary legislation. There was great danger, he pointed out, in removing the officeholder from the direct control of the voter. When that was done the candidate felt no responsibility to the elector, since he was not directly accountable to him for his actions. La Follette laid great emphasis upon the importance of principles and ideals in the organization of political parties. The Republican Party in Wisconsin, he said, was not dominated by the personality of a single individual but was built around the deep-seated convictions expressed in its platform. The Republican Party, he contended, was not a La Follette party but an organization devoted to progressive reform which he supported the same as any other member.[24]

In his message to the new legislature La Follette also reviewed the history of the ad valorem tax legislation. He discussed at length the recommendations of the temporary tax commission and the techniques to be used to determine the value of railroad property. His message also included a discussion of railroad rates. By means of a comparative table he demonstrated to the lawmakers that a shipper in Wisconsin paid higher freight rates on his commodities than did a similar shipper in Iowa or Illinois. He urged that the legislature delay no longer in passing an ad valorem tax law and creating a regulatory railroad commission.[25] On the national scene President Theodore Roosevelt was beginning his search for means to put teeth into the activities of the court-curbed Interstate Commerce Commission.[26] Always a master of timing, La Follette sensed that the moment had arrived to press for the whole comprehensive program of tax reform, valuation of railroad properties, and a permanent railroad commission with broad regulatory powers.

In the Assembly, where the La Follette forces were in complete control, administration leaders introduced two comprehensive primary election bills. The committee consolidated these into one, and the resulting measure was rapidly pushed through. In less than a week it was passed and sent on to the Senate.[27]

In the upper house Senator Andrew L. Kreutzer of Wausau became the symbol of the stalwart opposition as he employed delaying tactics and proposed numerous amendments. John C. Gaveney, son-in-law of ex-boss Keyes, secured approval of an amendment providing for a popular referendum on the sections applying to state offices and congressmen.[28]

For more than a month the two houses remained hopelessly deadlocked, neither side being willing to surrender. But, in contrast to the situation in the 1901 legislature, the chief strain was now on the stalwarts in the Senate, who must keep their tightly drawn lines intact if they were to resist the continuous pressure of the administration.

The federal officeholders from Wisconsin, some of whom had

participated actively in the Eleventh Story League's efforts to unseat La Follette, watched the progress of the governor's program with apprehension and alarm. In response to the repeated pleas for help which they received from the local stalwarts the Washington delegation agreed to assume leadership and proposed a compromise solution. With the approval of both senators and most of the representatives, Congressman Babcock came to Madison to take personal command of the stalwarts' campaign. His proposal was to allow the administration's sweeping primary election bill to become law but with a referendum clause that would place the entire plan before the voters in November, 1904.[29]

La Follette and the other administration leaders were at first disposed to have no dealings with the "Babcock Lobby." And as the weeks went by without action, the conservative press freely predicted that no primary legislation would be passed. The primary election idea was declared to be dead. Other stalwarts charged that the "Bobolets" were afraid to submit it to the vote of the people. Eventually it had become apparent that no bill that did not include the referendum clause could be passed. The progressive majority in the Assembly accepted the referendum clause and the governor signed the measure.[30]

In the meantime the struggle for an ad valorem tax system for the railroads was also being pushed to a successful conclusion by the administration forces. The report of the temporary tax commission, when finally submitted to the legislature, made detailed recommendations for the proposed tax reforms. The physical valuation of the railroad properties should be carried out under the supervision of a permanent tax commission. The railroads would continue to pay taxes under the license-fee system for the next three years and the ad valorem computation would be used simply to readjust the total tax upward or downward according to the ad valorem standard. Thus, if the railroads challenged the constitutionality of the new system in the courts, the state would not find a large portion of its revenues impounded. Such a plan required careful and detailed drafting of legislation. Of necessity it would leave much power in the hands of experts.[31]

The Tax Commission's proposals received careful study at the hands of the joint legislative committee. On February 11, 1903, the committee met with the commission and representatives of the railroads to discuss the recommendations. Presidents Marvin Hughitt and Albert J. Earling represented their roads in person, and similar high officials the other lines. Inasmuch as it seemed inevitable that some form of ad valorem legislation would be passed, they sought to assist in drafting the most favorable bill possible. President Hughitt expressed the opinion that ad valorem assessment would lower the taxes for the Chicago and North Western. The present taxes in Wisconsin, he stated, were higher than those in either Illinois or Iowa, both of which had an ad valorem system. W. W. Baldwin, of the Chicago, Burlington and Quincy Railroad, had no objection to the ad valorem system if it were applied as it was to other property in the state. President Earling felt that the railroads were already paying more than their share of the taxes. He would accept the ad valorem system, but he regarded the license-fee plan as much simpler and cheaper to administer. In spite of the optimistic tone adopted by the railroad officials, most of them privately expected to pay higher taxes as a result of the change in system. The tax commissioners had concluded their report with the observation that if Wisconsin had had the ad valorem plan in 1902, the railroads would have paid approximately nine hundred thousand dollars more in taxes.[32]

A bill modeled after the recommendations of the tax commissioners was at once introduced in each house of the legislature. Although the opponents of the bill sought to delay and sidetrack it by requesting additional hearings, the Assembly bill progressed rapidly through the successive readings and on

March 6 was passed by the unanimous vote of 87 to 0. The administration postponed action on the pending primary election bill in order to drive the tax program through the upper house. After a sharp struggle the Senate likewise passed the measure and on May 19, 1903, La Follette signed it, thus enacting into law the first of his major reforms.[33]

The railroad interests had acquiesced in the change in tax policy, but they had no intention of submitting to the rest of the progressives' railroad program. The introduction of an administration-approved bill to set up a railroad commission with sweeping powers over all roads in the state only intensified the conflict that was already raging over comparative freight rates. The data that La Follette had presented in his message to the legislature was challenged as "grossly inaccurate." Both Emanuel Philipp and Burton Hanson, general attorney for the Chicago, Milwaukee and St. Paul, cited figures from their rate books to demonstrate that Wisconsin shippers were well and cheaply served. The whole La Follette program, exclaimed Philipp, was a distinct declaration of war against the railroads. The governor was an evangelist preaching the "doctrine of total depravity of the corporations." [34]

To reinforce his arguments for the need of regulation, La Follette sent a special message, in late April, to the legislature. It was an imposing document of almost two hundred printed pages, including ten pages of tables. It listed all the stations in the state on the two major railroads together with the rates charged for various merchandise and commodities, and in parallel columns comparable towns in Illinois and Iowa with the corresponding rates. The whole document had been checked and approved by Halford Erickson, the state commissioner of labor and statistics. From this table it was apparent that Wisconsin shippers were being consistently overcharged.[35]

This document was at once denounced by the leading stalwarts and railroad attorneys. Emanuel Philipp published a compact little booklet entitled *The Truth about Wisconsin Freight Rates*. In it he elaborated and re-emphasized the arguments which had appeared earlier in the press. He sought to show that in almost every instance La Follette had cited the highest possible rates in Wisconsin to compare with the lowest rates in other states. Burton Hanson alleged that La Follette's message contained more than six hundred errors in a single table.[36]

The opposition threw all its strength into defeating the railroad commission bill. The lobbyists, large shippers, and other stalwarts held a mass meeting to denounce the plan. Congressman Babcock, who had arrived at the capital to organize opposition to the primary election bill, was active against the proposed railroad commission also. Eventually the measure was defeated and the railroad interests breathed easier for the moment. La Follette later admitted that he had not expected the bill to pass at that time but had put it forward simply to occupy the attention of the opposition and to provide a popular issue for the next campaign.[37]

The achievements of the 1903 legislature represented substantial but limited victories for La Follette and the progressives. The primary election law still had to survive a referendum in the general election of 1904 before it could be put into operation. The ad valorem tax legislation, while foreshadowing more equitable payments by the railroads, did nothing to regulate their rates or to prevent gross discrimination which would in effect pass on the added taxes to the public. Yet the eventual enactment of both measures could be foreseen at this time, and the significant contributions of each may be conveniently summarized here.

The Wisconsin primary election law established for the first time a comprehensive statewide system for the popular nomination of all local, county, state, and congressional officers and made provision for complete legal supervision.[38] Within five years more than a dozen other states had enacted new primary election laws or had extended their existing statutes to form a complete system. Among these were Wisconsin's closest neighbors, Illinois, Iowa, Michigan, and Minnesota. The pattern of the Wisconsin law was followed in most of the other states, and its influence was marked in the legislative battles that accompanied each enactment.[39] The nationwide primary movement was not, of course, dependent upon Wisconsin's tutelage. Throughout the country progressive leaders had urged such a reform during the entire period of La Follette's struggles with his recalcitrant legislatures. But it was the role of Wisconsin and "Fighting Bob" La Follette to take the lead in pushing the direct primary idea to its logical conclusion. Wisconsin was the first state to submit to the direct vote of the people all candidates for nomination to political office.

The adoption of the ad valorem tax system provided one solution to the problem of ending the privileged position of the railroads. Assuming that it was desirable to tax the railroads on a general property basis, the state now had an accurate method of determining their holdings. The administration of the ad valorem system was not, of course, inexpensive; by 1904 the annual expenses of the Tax Commission had risen, largely because of the cost of evaluating railroad properties, to more than forty-five thousand dollars.[40] By comparison the old gross receipts tax was simple, easily computed, and largely self-assessed. But as a result of the shift to the ad valorem system the state's revenues from the railroads within its borders increased from $1,900,000 in 1904 to $3,400,000 in 1906.[41] Moreover, the state now knew the exact status of the railroad properties. It was no longer dependent on the companies for assessment. In fulfillment of the 1900 and 1902 campaign pledges, the railroads now paid taxes on the same basis as all other citizens and corporations in the state. Many states copied Wisconsin's ad valorem plan, and later the federal government, at the insistence of La Follette, then a United States senator, undertook a physical valuation of all the railroads in the nation.[42]

The "battle of the rates" continued without respite through the hectic gubernatorial campaign of 1904. Despite two victories at the polls and two violent and bitter legislative sessions, La Follette and his fellow progressives knew that the decisive battle was still to come. The entire reform program, including the gains of the 1903 legislature, would have to be defended against a conservative opposition more united and determined than ever before. For any hope of success La Follette's progressive forces must be as thoroughly organized and as astutely led as their machine opponents.

5 BUILDING THE PROGRESSIVE MACHINE

★ ★ ★ ★ ★ ★ ★ ★ ★ ★ ★ ★ ★ ★ ★ ★ ★

IT IS SOMETHING OF A PARADOX THAT LA FOLLETTE, WHO IDENTI-
fied himself as an opponent of bosses and machines, should himself have organized his progressive followers into a most efficient
political machine and become, as its leader, a highly successful
political boss. He had begun his public career as an anti-
machine candidate and by his own account had won his early
victories in the face of the opposition of the bosses and the
regular Republican organization. His brush with Philetus Sawyer had embittered him against all aspects of party machines
and political manipulation. The denunciation of bosses became
an important part of La Follette's speeches, in which he described in detail the methods they used to control and corrupt
the representatives of the people. The direct primary, he declared, would "break the hold of the corrupt political machine
on American public life." [1]

The coalition that waged the successful harmony campaign in
1900 had, it is true, many of the earmarks of the traditional
political machine. La Follette and his personal friends were
joined by elements of the big city machine of Milwaukee and
various local and personal cliques. None of these were progressive or reform organizations. To all of them La Follette was
merely an available and popular candidate who could promote
their own interests and strengthen the entire ticket. [2]

The subsequent defeat of his reform program in the 1901
legislature convinced La Follette of the futility of further coali-
tions in the interest of harmony. His only hope of carrying

through that program lay in developing a loyal progressive organization capable of defeating the stalwarts at the polls and in the legislature. La Follette and his supporters, therefore, drew together in a close-knit political organization. From this nucleus developed the powerful progressive Republican Party which was to dominate Wisconsin for more than a dozen years. This progressive machine developed slowly during the years from 1901 to 1904. Its victorious campaign of 1902, half-formed though it was, over the stalwarts' Eleventh Story League enabled the progressive leaders to retain control of the state's administrative machinery while they gathered their resources for the final decisive struggle. By 1904 the progressive Republican organization presented a mosaic of many groups and individuals drawn from all economic and social brackets and from all sections of the state.

The central figure in the "Progressive Machine" was La Follette. "Little Bob" possessed that magnetic quality which inspired devotion on the part of his admirers. Few men were neutral in regard to La Follette; one was either a faithful follower or a bitter opponent. "Fighting Bob" was also a dynamic orator. He had the dramatic intuition that enabled him to win and hold the sympathy of his audience. In discussing issues his characteristic method was to reduce every question to its simplest terms and to picture the alternatives as black and white: the choice was between right and wrong. He refused to scatter his oratorical dynamite over a multiplicity of issues, but would concentrate on one or two proposals. These he would present with an evangelistic, crusading zeal that became famous throughout Wisconsin. His speeches were long, but were seldom, if ever, dull. So effectively did he blend logical arguments, statistical evidence, emotional appeals, and occasional humorous asides that people would drive for miles and stay all day to hear "Our Bob" speak.[3]

La Follette was also a vigorous party organizer. In all aspects of politics he was a strict disciplinarian, demanding complete loyalty and fealty on the part of his supporters. In turn he would strongly support the interests of his true friends and willingly drive himself to the very verge of collapse in their behalf. Against opponents he was equally energetic. Many stalwarts charged bitterly that he campaigned against them ruthlessly, in every season, until at last he had "hung their hides on the wall." [4]

In every essential La Follette was a "reform boss." He believed unquestioningly in himself and his cause and, above all, in the ultimate triumph of right and justice. As he learned the tricks of the political trade he became as astute as any of the old-line politicians. This only deepened their hatred of him and his "Bobolettes." [5]

Closely associated with La Follette in his reform efforts were Albert R. Hall and the remnants of the old Populist forces which had fought unsuccessfully for control of the state during the nineties. Hall, mild-mannered and unassuming personally, was nevertheless a determined foe of monopoly and special privilege. His followers, who came largely from the less prosperous rural regions in central and northern Wisconsin, were an embattled, bitter, and pessimistic group. They had been long-time supporters of La Follette and formed one wing of the progressive organization. [6]

Progressivism in Wisconsin also had an intellectual base. La Follette was an active alumnus of the University of Wisconsin and was a classmate and close personal friend of Charles R. Van Hise, president of the University from 1903 to 1918. Many of the University faculty became active participants in the development of the reform program in Wisconsin, including such nationally known scholars as Richard T. Ely, John R. Commons, and Edward A. Ross. The Saturday Lunch Club, which met weekly during legislative sessions, provided an opportunity for the informal exchange of ideas between state administrators and professors. The list of faculty members who served on the various boards and commissions of the state during the progressive era is long and impressive. In 1911, for example, no fewer than forty-six were serving both the University and the state. This use of "experts" in government was a basic part of the political philosophy of both La Follette and Van Hise. In consequence the number of University graduates in state positions steadily increased and the opportunity for college-trained young men to enter useful public service tended to become identified with the progressive cause.[7]

There was strong support for the progressive Republicans in the ranks of labor in all the urban centers of the state. La Follette's initial appeal to these groups was a direct plea to each individual based on reform, democracy, and good citizenship. Especially friendly to La Follette were members of the railroad brotherhoods and other railroad workers who saw in his program the promise of greater security for themselves and a greater sense of responsibility on the part of their employers. In Milwaukee, the chief industrial city of the state, the progressives had to battle not only the stalwarts and the strongly entrenched Democratic machine but also the rising Social-Democrats led by Emil Seidel and Victor Berger. Yet by means of vigorous appeals to workingmen as voters and citizens, La Follette and his successors were able to insure for themselves at least a proportionate share of the labor vote. Eventually labor, both organized and unorganized, benefited enormously as the progressive program was expanded to include employers' liability laws, safety legislation, workmen's compensation, state employment offices, and the Industrial Commission. La Follette's known sympathy for the cause of labor and his untiring efforts to improve working conditions made him a personal favorite among workingmen wherever he went.[8]

Among the various ethnic groups residing in Wisconsin the Norwegians and, to a lesser extent, the Swedes have been especially interested in civic affairs. It was only natural that many Scandinavians should become prominent members of the reform group and play significant roles in the rise of progressivism in Wisconsin. Doubtless the first among these was Nils P. Haugen. A prominent political figure himself, Haugen had great influence with his fellow Norwegians, and that influence he turned into votes for La Follette. Also prominent among the early supporters of La Follette was Norwegian-born James O. Davidson, a perennial officeholder, who counted himself an original La Follette man—having "fought, bled and died for Bob" in two campaigns before 1900. La Follette himself had lived in a Norwegian neighborhood as a boy and spoke the language to some extent. "Our Bob" was a great favorite among them, and he spared no effort to retain their friendship and affection.[9]

The Norwegian press was predominantly friendly to La Follette. The *Skandinaven* of Chicago, which had an almost state-wide circulation and was regarded virtually as a political Bible, was a vigorous champion of the progressive reforms. Madison's chief Norwegian-language paper, *Amerika,* was largely devoted to nonpolitical subjects. Occasionally its editor, Ramus B. Anderson, would let go a blast against some La Follette program, but then he would lapse into silence once more. The stalwarts sought without success to make *Amerika* an anti-administration paper.[10]

Among the younger Scandinavians who campaigned vigorously for La Follette were Herman Ekern, Irvine L. Lenroot, Andrew H. Dahl, and John M. Nelson. All of these were promoted to important state and federal positions as the progressives consolidated their hold on the party. Despite defections, the Norwegians delivered an almost solid bloc of votes for the progressives in each of their campaigns. Even the staunchest stalwarts conceded that they offered "quite a barren soil on which to sow anti-La Follette seed." The careful tending of this potential election crop was one of the important functions of La Follette's new progressive machine. The harvest was seldom disappointing.[11]

In contrast to the Scandinavians the Germans of Wisconsin, the state's largest ethnic group, were largely individualistic in politics. Although staunch supporters of representative government, they were generally conservative and lacked the political solidarity that characterized the Norwegians. Yet both progressives and stalwarts wooed the German vote in each campaign, with varying success. The complete failure of the Eleventh Story League in 1902 was generally attributed in part to the antipathy of the German wards in Milwaukee to its candidate, the austere and puritanical John M. Whitehead.[12]

Milwaukee, the state's metropolis, was largely German in population, and the party workers there appealed specifically to this ethnic group. The old Payne-Spooner-Pfister organization, which had its stronghold in Milwaukee, had sought to organize the wards to deliver the vote as a bloc. The Democratic machine of Mayor David Rose, often in cooperation with the stalwart Republicans, operated in the same manner.[13] In opposition to these entrenched organizations, La Follette formed his own political clubs in the German sections of the city and became increasingly successful in getting out the vote for the progressive cause. The German press, especially the large German-language daily *Die Germania,* persisted in maintaining an independent policy and refused to commit itself or its constituents to either side in the political fight despite the efforts of each group to enlist its support.[14]

Many citizens of German ancestry held important posts in the progressive organization. At least one prominent German name appeared on every progressive state ticket from 1900 to 1914. Among the men of German descent who played a significant part in the progressive reforms were insurance commissioner Zeno M. Host, Republican state secretary Henry Cochems, and normal school regent Theodore Kronshage.[15]

The progressives also received strong support from Wisconsin dairy farmers. Ex-Governor William D. Hoard, president of the Wisconsin Dairyman's Association and editor of the weekly *Hoard's Dairyman,* had been a close friend and advisor of the young La Follette. La Follette's own farm background, his interest in scientific farming, and his vigorous support of the University's College of Agriculture won him many loyal friends among the farmers in every section of the state. The growth of the lucrative dairy industry owed much to the University, and the University came to be closely identified with the progressive machine. The dairy farmers continued to prosper and La Follette was ever solicitous for their welfare. In every campaign he could count on a loyal and powerful following from among the forward-looking farmers of Wisconsin.[16]

And, finally, there was the progressives' angel, Isaac Stephenson. "Uncle Ike," with his vast timber holdings and numerous lucrative business enterprises, could provide the funds necessary to combat the resources of the stalwarts. Stephenson had long been influential in the Republican Party both as an officeholder and as a heavy contributor to the party's war chest. It was no secret that he felt that his generosity and prominence entitled him to climax his career with a term in the United States Senate. He was therefore disillusioned and indignant when in 1899 his supposed friends in the legislature gave the plum to Joseph V. Quarles.[17]

But it was not simply pique that caused Isaac Stephenson to desert the stalwarts and come over to the reform group. He believed that the railroad ring had dominated the state too long in its own selfish interest. An old frontiersman himself, he had sympathy for the underdog and had early admired Bob La Follette's plucky fight against the stalwarts. Far from being the sole cause of Stephenson's disaffection, the election of Quarles to the Senate was simply the final straw which decided him to seek at least a moderate reform in the state government.[18]

According to Stephenson, La Follette had been reluctant to attempt the campaign of 1900, protesting that his poor health and lack of financial support would prohibit a concentrated effort. However, when a plan of campaign was drawn up and Stephenson had advanced a check for initial expenses, Bob's reluctance vanished. The next year Stephenson established the *Milwaukee Free Press,* thus providing the progressives with a much-needed metropolitan daily with which to combat the attacks of the stalwart-owned *Sentinel.* The *Free Press* was probably never a profitable venture, but it crusaded valiantly for the progressives and served as a publisher of their campaign literature. La Follette praised the paper in the highest terms and referred to it as Stephenson's "best monument" and his continuing support of it as an "act of patriotism." [19]

Throughout the early years of the progressive era Stephenson was a heavy contributor to every campaign. His personal influence was not inconsiderable, but it was his financial backing that made his support vital to the success of the progressives. Not only did he help defray the expenses of the statewide campaigns, but he also gave liberally for district and local races. It was largely the Stephenson checkbook that made possible the wide distribution of pamphlets and the thorough canvass of voters that were characteristic of La Follette's campaigns. "Uncle Ike" estimated that he had spent more than a half million dollars to forward the progressive cause. "Without me," he wrote later, "the history of this achievement would have been a blank page." [20]

All political machines are said to run on patronage, and La Follette's organization was no exception. A large number of party workers found their way into profitable jobs in the state administration. Clerks, oil inspectors, and factory inspectors performed dual service during the campaign season. Even the lists of temporary personnel, such as State Fair guards and ticket sellers, were culled to provide the greatest possible number of jobs for progressive workers.[21]

But by far the largest single group of part-time political workers for the progressives were the state game wardens. So notorious became the activities of these so-called conservationists that they became a standing joke in the state press, and writers vied to coin witticisms at their expense. One editor quipped that the game wardens were "strolling around the state . . . hunting for men who will vote for La Follette at the next state convention"; another that "the game wardens are out on the road for La Follette"; and a third that "there should be a closed season" on the class of game the wardens were seeking.[22]

At election time the deputy wardens distributed pamphlets, posters, and sample ballots. In districts where close contests were expected several of them would work as a team, calling on party members, getting out the vote, and even providing vehicles to take voters to the polls.[23] As was to be expected, the stalwarts denounced the zeal of the deputy wardens as evidence of the corruption of the progressive administration. The *Sentinel* charged that there were fifty or sixty of them on the state payroll, all neck-deep in politics.[24]

In truth the expenses of the game wardens during La Follette's three administrations more than trebled. But receipts from fines and licenses also increased rapidly, so that the wardens almost paid their way. According to the report of the state treasurer, the disbursements from the hunting-license fund, which was spent largely for the salaries and expenses of deputy game wardens, rose from $37,000 in 1899–1900 to $85,000 in 1904 and more than $94,000 in 1905. The report of 1904 also listed eighty-two inspectors of illuminating oils by name with salaries and per diem expenses of over $20,000. No expense of this type was listed for 1900. The hunting-license fund receipts grew from about $15,000 in 1899 to more than $87,000 in 1905, in most years lagging behind expenses by some five to ten thousand dollars.

Both the activity and the expenses of the game wardens' department declined after La Follette left the governorship. The civil service law, passed in 1905, curbed much of their political activity. But they continued to provide a solid core of administration supporters during the entire progressive era. Years later, in recalling the controversy over the game wardens waged during La Follette's governorship, former Congressman John M. Nelson smilingly admitted that the progressives had used everybody and every device they could find in the scramble for votes —"just as the stalwarts were doing." [25]

In all their campaigns the progressives also sought the support of "fair-minded" Democrats. The party's nominating machinery, under both the convention and the primary system, was open to all interested persons, and numerous Democrats voted for La Follette and the progressive slate. William Jennings Bryan, titular head of the Democratic Party, was a personal friend of La Follette's and on occasion came to the state to promote his cause. La Follette estimated that the vote of "fair-minded Democrats" in general elections offset the losses caused by bolting stalwarts. [26]

By the end of La Follette's second term as governor these various elements of the progressive machine had been drawn firmly together to form a solid pyramid of political strength. They dominated the state Republican committee as well as the executive department and the legislature. But in the county committees and city wards the progressive forces were still opposed by a considerable number of stalwarts who had held key offices since pre–La Follette days. Both stalwarts and progressives recognized that the election of 1904 would be the crucial and decisive one. With the national presidential election and the local and state races merged into a single campaign La Follette and his supporters would be at a disadvantage, since the stalwarts could expect valuable assistance from the Republican National Committee, of which Henry C. Payne was now chairman. More than that, La Follette's second term as governor would be at an end and he must either support one of his lieutenants, probably a weaker candidate, or run for a third term in the face of tradition.[27]

The maneuvers for the control of the 1904 convention began as soon as the legislative session of 1903 was over. The "shock troops" of the progressive army carefully canvassed every county, visited the voters, and mended political fences with the local party workers. The clerical staff prepared and distributed to the voters throughout the state more than a million and a half pieces of mail. Throughout the summer La Follette himself campaigned on the Chautauqua platform, at county fairs, and at holiday rallies. Progressive leaders groomed candidates in the several districts to unseat stalwart incumbents in the legislature and local offices. Stalwart members of Congress, including erstwhile ally Joseph Babcock, were the objects of an all-out purge effort.[28]

The stalwart leaders began a vigorous search for a candidate whom all could support against La Follette and his machine. All were determined that the Eleventh Story League fiasco of the preceding campaign should not be repeated. Samuel A. Cook of Neenah and Judge Emil Baensch of Milwaukee, both citizens of outstanding ability and favorable reputation, emerged as the most likely stalwart candidates for the governorship. It was agreed that each should make the pre-convention canvass and that the supporters of both would come to the state convention united as anti–La Follette delegates.[29]

La Follette determined to leave no stone unturned to insure victory, for he realized that election of an anti-progressive candidate would jeopardize all the gains made in the previous legislature. The referendum on the direct primary, which was to be submitted to the people in the general election, might be defeated, and his railroad taxation and regulation program might be discarded. With the approval of his friends La Follette became a candidate for a third term and plunged into the contest for delegates with renewed vigor, personally appearing in every county he could.[30]

The *Sentinel* lost no time in denouncing the "third termers." The increased cost of the game wardens' department was paraded as evidence of the political activities of the deputies. The allocation by La Follette of some $458,000 in refunds from the federal government to the general fund instead of to the reduction of the state debt was termed a "looting of trust funds." The textbook scandal was revived. A new charge of corruption, growing out of violations of the anti-pass law by employees of the attorney general's office, further embarrassed the administration. The stalwarts accused La Follette of "gross corruption" and urged the electorate to retire this "dictator" to private life.[31]

The contest for delegates was sharp and bitter, and in many counties disputed elections and two rival delegations resulted. The canvass of both the progressives and the stalwarts was thorough and complete. Even such a veteran machine manipulator as Elisha Keyes was astonished at the resources and competence of the administration forces. In the scramble for delegates no effort was spared, no delegation was conceded, no contest was abandoned by either side. Both progressives and stalwarts used all means and measures at hand to insure the success of their ticket.[32] As the time for the state convention on May 18, 1904, approached, the rival newspapers claimed victory for their respective candidates. Each side denounced the opposition for not yielding gracefully. The *Sentinel* charged that La Follette would attempt to steal the convention. The *Free Press* made a similar charge against the stalwarts.

Never was the La Follette genius for organization better displayed than at the Republican convention of 1904, held in the University gymnasium at Madison. It was obvious that the stalwarts would make a bitter, last-ditch, no-quarter fight to control the organization of the convention. As neither side had an undisputed majority, such control hinged on the decisions made with respect to the disputed delegations. In this matter the progressives had one important advantage. To organize the convention on a temporary basis the state central committee would have to make a preliminary ruling on each case. Since the majority of this committee were progressives, headed by the seventy-two-year-old General George E. Bryant, state superintendent of public property and long-time friend of La Follette's, it was conceded that the temporary organization would favor the governor. The whole progressive machinery was determined that the temporary organization would become the permanent one, and that the stalwarts must be prevented from seizing the convention by any trick, parliamentary stratagem, or use of force. The area reserved for delegates at the gymnasium was carefully fenced off. Special guards were employed to maintain order—former University football players, professional athletes, and other husky characters. A barbed-wire fence was erected outside the building to force the delegates to enter single file. Special delegates' badges were printed and countersigned to insure that none but committee-approved delegates would appear on the floor of the convention.[33] The entire procedure for the crucial first session of the convention was prepared in detail for the convenience of General Bryant, chairman of the state central committee, whose duty it was to call the session to order. The administration left nothing to chance. All nominating and seconding speeches and all motions were assigned to specific delegates; the committee on contests (to be appointed by the chair) was listed; and even a special committee on emergencies was named. The old Civil War veteran

Isaac Stephenson, United States Senator 1907–1915

[Copyright, 1904, by the North American, Philadelphia.]

SENATOR JOHN C. SPOONER.

GOV. ROBERT M. LA FOLLETTE.

He won in the contest before the Republican National committee; his delegation being awarded seats in the convention.

His contesting delegation was defeated. Matter will be carried credentials committee and perhaps to convention floor.

The Tribune was Premature

Cartoon by V. Floyd Campbell in the *Chicago Daily Tribune* of June 18, 1904, reprinted from the *North American* of Philadelphia could keep the convention proceeding according to plan without taking his eyes from his memorandum.[34]

The stalwarts had evidently expected to be voted down and counted out. They had rented Madison's Fuller Opera House for use in the event that they should choose to withdraw and hold their own convention. On the evening before the first session they caucused and agreed upon their strategy, and the next morning, with a corps of strong-armed guards of their own, they marched in a body to the University gymnasium. There, however, only the committee-approved delegates were permitted to enter the convention floor and the others were diverted to the visitors' gallery. With Cook, Keyes, Whitehead, and other leading stalwarts sitting on the platform, the convention was organized with a progressive majority, the stalwart minority report was voted down, and Irvine Lenroot, an avid La Follette partisan, was installed as temporary chairman.[35]

The "bolt" that followed had been fully expected by all factions. The stalwarts retired to the Opera House, where, after listening to rousing speeches by Senators Spooner and Quarles, they nominated Samuel A. Cook for governor and a complete slate for all the state offices. To head their list of delegates to the Republican national convention the stalwarts sought the strongest possible slate and selected Spooner, Quarles, Babcock, and Emil Baensch as delegates at large. After proclaiming itself the true Republican Party in Wisconsin and denouncing La Follette and his machine this rump convention adjourned.[36]

This defection hardly slowed the drive of the "Gymnasium Convention." It nominated La Follette and the other state officers, endorsed the primary election law which was to be the subject of a referendum in November, and approved a reform platform which included a railroad commission. For delegates at large to the national convention the progressives named their most prominent partisans: La Follette, Stephenson, state senator James H. Stout, and William D. Connor. Before adjournment "Fighting Bob" made a crusading speech calling upon the party to complete the return of the state to the people and stand firm on the pledges made in the platform.[37]

In an effort to force the listing of their slate as the regular Republican ticket the stalwarts took their case to the State Supreme Court. The progressives took theirs to the people. From the time of the convention to election day the progressive machine mobilized for furious activity. From the governor down to the youngest deputy game warden the entire organization stumped the state and beat the bushes from the Mississippi to Marinette. In every county La Follette preached primary elections, a railroad commission, and the necessity of completing the job of reform. In many sections he would present the records of the local legislators by means of his now-familiar "roll call." In La Crosse, for example, he recited the voting records of George H. Ray and John C. Gaveney in the past session of the legislature and denounced them for their failure to serve the public interest. These men, he told his listeners, had been elected by the people to vote for them; instead they had voted for the railroads.[38] The progressive campaign was more than a fight for the governorship. The organization supported all the progressive candidates down to the local offices.

Despite the personal letter which Isaac Stephenson addressed to President Roosevelt the stalwart delegates to the national Republican convention were seated as the duly accredited representatives of Wisconsin. This was not unexpected, inasmuch as Postmaster General Henry Payne was acting chairman of the National Committee and Senator Spooner had long held a high position in the councils of the party.[39] Despite this advantage, even the staunchest stalwarts soon conceded that their ticket was unlikely to defeat La Follette; their only hope was to have Cook declared the regular Republican candidate. Keyes gloomily observed that everything depended on the court decision, but even he had little hope. Bob, he conceded, was the biggest campaigner the Western country had ever produced. He was "touring the country in a red devil of an automobile" like a whirlwind, and his lieutenants were working night and day to get out the vote for the progressive ticket.[40]

The progressive cause received valuable and timely assistance from an unexpected quarter. In July of 1904 Lincoln Steffens arrived in Milwaukee to prepare an article on the Wisconsin political picture for *McClure's Magazine*. Steffens was already famous as one of America's most talented political reporters, having exposed graft and political corruption in St. Louis, Philadelphia, and Minneapolis. According to his own account he came to Wisconsin convinced that La Follette was a "charlatan and a crook." He intended to get and prove the specific charges against him. Steffens talked with Philipp, Phil Spooner, Keyes, and Pfister. He also talked with La Follette and other progressives. He even toured the state checking the charges of scandals and corruption being made against La Follette and the progressive organization. When he had gathered his information he departed, leaving both stalwarts and progressives sure that he would support them in his forthcoming article.[41]

When Steffens' article appeared in the October issue of *McClure's Magazine*, a great outcry went up from the stalwarts. In all its essential details it was a vindication of La Follette and his administration. The chief sin of Bob La Follette, the famous muckraker wrote, was that he had taken the Republican Party away from the old gang. Steffens agreed that he had, in truth, become a boss, harder and more efficient than those he had displaced. But he was using his political machine in the public interest, to restore self-government to Wisconsin.[42]

The progressives welcomed the article as a campaign document. It was reported that six thousand copies were distributed in Rock County alone. The stalwart leaders protested against the implications of corrupt practices in the pre–La Follette machine. Keyes, Spooner, and even Stephenson used the press to defend themselves. The editor of the *Sentinel* condemned Steffens as a "yellow-journalist." Steffens actually revealed much less about the activities of the old bosses than he hinted and implied, but the tone of the article was most sympathetic to the progressives, who made the most of its timely appearance. It added hundreds if not thousands of votes to the La Follette total in November.[43]

The stalwarts also suffered a nearly fatal blow when their suit concerning the legality of the Gymnasium Convention reached the Supreme Court. The briefs for the case included scores of affidavits pertaining to the convention, the voluminous testimony of numerous witnesses, and the comprehensive arguments of the respective counsels—a mass of material that threatened to swamp the court under a sea of conflicting claims. Nevertheless the Supreme Court of Wisconsin accepted jurisdiction and hastened to reach a decision before the November election rendered its findings of historical interest only. At last, on October 5, just a month before the election, the high court, with Justice Siebecker abstaining and Chief Justice Cassoday dissenting, handed down a decision in favor of the defendant and dismissed the suit. In effect, the majority of the court decided that the state central committee was exercising its proper powers when it determined which delegations should be seated in the convention, and that Secretary of State Houser was acting within his authority when he declined to certify the contesting stalwart faction as the Republican Party in Wisconsin.[44]

Candidate Cook at once withdrew from the race and the stalwart committee replaced him with ex-Governor Scofield. The party was placed on the ballot as the National Republican Party of Wisconsin, but the organization of the "Opera House" group disintegrated so completely that they privately urged their supporters to vote for the Democratic candidates as the most likely way to defeat La Follette.[45]

The election was a close one. Though the Republican national ticket won a landslide victory in the state with a majority of one hundred and fifty thousand, La Follette polled a plurality of barely fifty thousand. He lost fourteen of the state's seventy-one counties and ran behind the rest of the ticket by forty to fifty thousand votes. Nevertheless it was a great victory. The primary election law was approved by more than sixty per cent of the voters, and supporters of La Follette won complete control of the legislature. The Scofield ticket polled only twelve thousand votes.[46] "Fighting Bob" La Follette had, at long last, broken the back of the stalwart opposition. So completely did the Opera House group disintegrate that they did not reappear as a force in Wisconsin politics for nearly a decade.

The progressive machine in Wisconsin had been built from many diverse elements. Old Populists, idealistic crusaders, University intellectuals, Scandinavian and farming groups, urban workers, professional officeholders, ambitious youngsters, and a disgruntled multimillionaire had combined to rout the old political forces and take over the entire machinery of the state. This union of soil, shop, and seminar was cemented by the magnetic personality and inspiration of "Fighting Bob" La Follette.[47] Under him the organization became a powerful cohesive force that buttressed the idealism and popular appeal of the "Wisconsin Idea" with a well-knit, efficient, and at times ruthless political machine that was capable of controlling and disciplining its members, of producing impressive majorities at the polls, and of enacting its program into law. Despite conflicting ambitions and personalities, this machine continued for a dozen years to promote reform in the public interest. The way was now open for the enactment of the whole body of political, social, and economic reforms which have since become identified with the Wisconsin Idea. La Follette's party of reform and progressivism had become the Republican Party in Wisconsin.

6 COMPLETING THE PATTERN
OF REFORM

★　★　★　★　★　★　★　★　★　★　★　★　★　★　★　★　★

THE DRAMATIC GYMNASIUM CONVENTION OF 1904 PROVED TO BE
the last statewide convention at which candidates for a major
party were chosen in Wisconsin. At the November election of
that year the primary election law was approved in the referendum and since then all party nominees have been selected
directly by the voters. The general reaction to the change was
one of moderate approval, although the innovation failed to
produce the widely predicted improvement in the caliber of the
state's officeholders. In his message to the legislature in 1905
La Follette praised the primary as a bulwark of American
democracy. Anything that came between the voter and the expression of his sovereign will, he contended, was a perversion
of the fundamental principles of representative government.[1]

Privately La Follette regarded the primary as the weapon
with which he could wrest the control of the state permanently
from the hands of the stalwart bosses. His repeated defeats at
state conventions had identified the convention system in his
own mind with machine politics. His later convention victories
did not lessen his enthusiasm for the reform. At one time in the
struggle he is said to have confided to one of his most intimate
friends and supporters, "Give us this law and we can hold this
state forever."[2]

Even before he saw the direct primary in operation La Follette advocated amendment of the law to allow the voter to express his second choice among the candidates. He feared that in
some future primary the progressive vote might be split among

several progressive candidates and a single conservative, the choice of the old stalwart machine, might slip through with a bare plurality. The governor discussed this plan at some length in the message he delivered to the legislature in December, 1905, but it was not until 1911 that a second-choice law was passed. This second-choice system, derided by the conservatives as the "Mary Ann" law, was never popular with the electorate and after a brief time was repealed.[3]

The year 1905 may be considered the climax of the first phase of the progressive drive in Wisconsin. In a long and painstaking session the legislature, now completely dominated by the progressives, enacted a large number of major reforms. In prompt response to La Follette's recommendations the lawmakers enacted a comprehensive Railroad Commission Act, set up a Civil Service system, established a State Capitol Commission, created a State Board of Forestry, and made the Tax Commission a permanent part of the state's governmental machinery.[4] Most of these measures had been included in the party's platform of 1904, and all reflected the progressives' philosophy of government.

The task of drafting a comprehensive and workable railroad commission law was the first tackled by the legislature. The long, bitter controversy over rates which had lasted through two elections had made the legislators extremely rate-conscious. Most of them had individual opinions as to what powers should be included in such a law. In addition La Follette brought to the 1905 legislative session new and conclusive evidence of the urgency of railroad regulation. Before the 1903 legislature had adjourned it had ordered an investigation of the railroad companies' records to determine whether proper returns on the gross earnings license tax had been made. The resulting examination disclosed that favored shippers had been given large rebates which had been omitted from the tax returns.[5] La Follette at once directed that suits be brought to recover the delin-

quent taxes and these cases were, in January, 1905, still pending in court. It was anticipated that the state would collect several hundred thousand dollars from the litigation.[6]

To get a strong, unified, and well-integrated railroad commission law, La Follette and the legislative leaders assigned the actual drafting of the bill to experts. Nils Haugen, member of the Tax Commission and one-time railroad commissioner, drew up the basic draft of the measure, modeling it after the best features of the Texas and Iowa laws. Haugen also solicited advice and help from Senator William H. Hatton, other members of the legislature, and officials of the state's railroads. Burton Hanson, who had fought the regulation program furiously in 1903, gave valuable assistance in drafting some of the technical provisions of the bill. The work of piloting the measure through the legislature without crippling amendments was entrusted to Senator Hatton. As passed it was a sound, moderate, and efficient law.[7]

The Railroad Commission Act provided for the establishment of a commission of three men having special knowledge on railroads, to be appointed for overlapping six-year terms. The commission was given jurisdiction over rates, schedules, construction, maintenance, and service of all the railroads in the state. In addition the law provided that the rulings and orders of the commission were to be considered "reasonable, in force and prima facie lawful"; in other words, the burden of proof that they were unlawful rested with the plaintiff. The law also stipulated that the railroads should not present in an appeal in court any evidence that had not previously been made available to the commission for use in making its ruling. If such evidence was presented, the court was to suspend hearings while the commission reviewed the new information and determined whether it would alter its previous ruling. By such provisions the law created a strong and effective commission, free from most of the weaknesses that had been so glaring in the Interstate Commerce Commission and many of the older state commissions. La Follette sought to appoint as railroad commissioners the best informed experts that were available. After the Senate declined to shift Haugen from the Tax Commission to the new railroad board, the governor named Balthasar H. Meyer, professor of economics at the University of Wisconsin; John Barnes, a leading attorney and Democrat of Rhinelander; and Halford Erickson, commissioner of labor and statistics.[8]

As the first step in determining "reasonable" rates the new railroad commissioners at once began the long, technical, and arduous task of determining the physical value of all the railroad properties in the state. They worked closely with the Tax Commission, which had evaluated those properties in 1904 for tax purposes. The commission also called upon expert engineers to assist in computing the cost of reconstruction. When the study was completed, its figures varied only slightly from those of the railroads concerned.[9]

Two years later the legislature established a mandatory passenger fare of two cents per mile. The same year most of the other public service corporations in the state, whether privately or municipally owned, were placed under the commission's control. The Railroad Commission became a permanent and efficient branch of the government. As a bipartisan, nonpolitical body it continued to function most effectively in spite of changes in administration. Directly connected with regulation of rates was the regulation of railroad services. "Reasonable" and "adequate" service was demanded and secured through the rulings of the commission. La Follette thought that the people of Wisconsin enjoyed, because of the Railroad Commission, the best railroad service of all the states in the country.[10] As the legislature increased the duties of the Railroad Commission it became, through the years, much more than a board to regulate the public carriers of the state and acquired jurisdiction over many kinds of corporation activities.

Besides regulating the rates, practices, services, construction, maintenance, and repair of the railroads in the state, the commission supervised, after 1907, the activities of express and telegraph companies, street railways, and such public utilities as telephone, electric light, water, and power companies. In the same year the legislature added the supervision of stocks and bonds to the duties of the board, and in 1913 a "Blue Sky" law was passed which placed the general regulation of all securities in the hands of the commission.[11]

With the assistance of the commissioners the legislature attacked the problem of the perpetual franchises which previous legislatures had granted the public service corporations. Many of these grants no longer served the public interest; often they actually blocked progress and improvements. The lawmakers at first attempted to solve the problem by giving the utility companies an opportunity to surrender their long-term franchises voluntarily and receive indeterminate grants. But the corporations proved to be reluctant to do so, and in 1911 the legislature revoked the franchises of all corporations and substituted for them indeterminate permits that were to run only so long as the recipients of them functioned in the public interest and provided for municipal purchase if the local government so desired.[12] Thus the Railroad Commission, so called until 1931, was in truth a "Public Service Commission" long before the close of the first progressive era.

The success of the Wisconsin system can be credited to the common sense and thorough knowledge of railroad properties possessed by members of the commission. Even opponents of regulation made no charge of improper influence or methods. The Railroad Commission soon acquired the reputation of being both efficient and ethical. Soon after its organization the president of the Chicago and North Western Railway expressed his confidence in the commissioners' good sense and disposition to be fair. His company would endeavor, he said, to work as nearly in harmony with them as possible. Even the *Sentinel* became a staunch supporter of Balthasar H. Meyer and other commissioners in their determination to keep partisan politics and public clamor out of rate-making.[13]

The drive of La Follette and the progressives to regulate the railroads in Wisconsin paralleled a similar movement throughout the country. Under the leadership of President Theodore Roosevelt Congress enacted the so-called Elkins Act in 1903 forbidding rebates and the Hepburn Act in 1906 specifically giving the Interstate Commerce Commission power to revise rates.[14] Prominent in this fight for federal regulation of railroads was Congressman Henry A. Cooper of Racine, who had been a supporter of La Follette since 1900. With his wide circle of friends, both in his home state and in Washington, Cooper's influence on state and national railroad legislation was considerable. He served as the link between the progressive forces in Washington and Wisconsin. The cordiality and cooperation which existed at this time between the dynamic "T. R." and fiery "Little Bob" was partly attributable to Cooper's mediations.[15]

During his governorship La Follette had a high regard for the strenuous president. In his comprehensive review of railroad regulation he declared that the people had a "brave, able and progressive friend in President Roosevelt. He has declared for them. He cannot be misled. He will not compromise." In another section he quoted at length from Roosevelt's message to Congress on rebates. The two men later became mutually antagonistic and exchanged bitter recriminations, but at this time La Follette accepted Roosevelt's leadership and welcomed his assistance in the battle for regulation.[16]

The battle of the progressives to secure effective legislation regulating the railroads culminated in a "legislative wave" that swept the entire country. Between 1900 and 1907 no fewer than fifteen new or reorganized state commissions were established, bringing the total number of states having regulatory commissions to thirty-nine. Most of these had extensive jurisdiction over all matters of rate regulation and finance. The Wisconsin Railroad Commission differed from most of the others, especially the earlier ones, in that its members were appointed rather than elected. This and the fact that La Follette selected men of known ability tended to give the commission a professional standing which removed it from party politics and to heighten its prestige throughout the state. The Wisconsin solution of the railroad problem is notable not because it was the earliest or the most radical, but rather because it was thoroughgoing, efficient, and successful. Most subsequent state laws on railroad regulation copied the Wisconsin measure or the New York statute of the same year.[17]

The legislature of 1905 was obliged to meet in temporary quarters at the University, the capitol having been almost destroyed in the disastrous fire of February 27, 1904. Besides the appropriations necessary to meet the usual expenses of government and the cost of establishing the important regulatory commissions demanded by La Follette, a large sum was required for the rebuilding of the capitol. No insurance payments were forthcoming, since, only a few months before the fire, Governor La Follette had worked out a system whereby the state would carry its own insurance and had cancelled the policies with the commercial companies. A great howl of criticism rose from the state press and La Follette's opponents denounced his plan for self-insurance as no insurance at all.[18]

To the credit of the legislators, they proceeded to plan and provide for a building that would rank among the most beautiful state capitols in the nation. They reorganized and enlarged the State Capitol Commission which had been appointed in 1903. They approved plans for a completely new and more elaborate structure and made appropriations so that construction could be begun at once. The new capitol was to be built in sections, west, east, south, and north wings being built in turn. The central rotunda was surmounted by a massive dome which could be seen for miles from the surrounding countryside. The proud boast of the later progressives that the entire construction of the new capitol, amounting to almost eight million dollars, was accomplished "without graft" was essentially true. The new capitol became a monument to the vision of the legislature of 1905 and its successors.[19]

The enactment of a thoroughgoing civil service law to be administered by a professional three-man commission was another of the major projects of La Follette's final term as governor. Such a measure was necessary if the other commissions of experts established by the progressives were to be free from constant political pressure. La Follette may also have been influenced, in his determination to put state employees under civil service, by the widespread criticism that was made of the administration's workers, especially the game wardens, during the bitter political campaigns of 1902 and 1904.

La Follette delegated the drafting of the civil service act in large part to John R. Commons, professor of economics at the University. With the help of Charles McCarthy, head of the Legislative Reference Library, Commons drew up a comprehensive measure along the lines desired by the governor. This act, passed by the 1905 legislature, prohibited all state employees from engaging in political activity and gave them tenure based on efficiency. The classified service was divided into exempt, noncompetitive, competitive, and labor divisions. Unskilled laborers were not required to take written examinations but merely to fill out application blanks, and they were employed on the basis of good habits and ability to work. Incumbent employees who desired to continue in service were required to pass a noncompetitive examination. Of the three hundred and eighty employees who took these examinations only seventeen failed to pass, of whom thirteen were game wardens.[20]

La Follette appointed Samuel Sparling of Madison, Thomas J. Cunningham of Chippewa Falls, and Otto Gaffron of Plymouth as members of the newly created Civil Service Commission. The local examining boards throughout the state that were to supervise the competitive examinations served without pay except for expenses. As the system developed the commission assigned an ever-increasing number of positions to the competitive class and encouraged the creation of a permanent corps of personnel.[21] Whereas only eighteen per cent of the state employees of 1900 were still employed in 1904, fifty-eight per cent of the employees under civil service in 1910 were still in the state service in 1914. Most of the turnover, the commission reported, was in the exempt and labor classes; employees of the competitive class were protected by tenure rights and practically all were retained.[22]

Even before the conclusion of his campaign for a third term as governor La Follette had begun to turn his eyes to the national political scene. Washington would provide a larger stage for his talents and offer new worlds to conquer. Much of his original state program had already been enacted into law, and he could be reasonably certain that the incoming legislature would complete the task. To the legislature of 1905 would fall the duty of selecting a successor to stalwart Joseph V. Quarles, whose term as United States senator would expire. Few doubted that La Follette could have the Senate seat almost without contest.[23] When he announced that he would accept the senatorship if it were offered him, the Republican majority in the legislature promptly declared for him; and two days later, on January 25, 1905, a joint session of the two houses overwhelmingly elected "Fighting Bob" to the office, giving him 101 of the 123 votes cast.[24]

La Follette did not at once resign the governorship. Instead he informed the lawmakers that he must first complete the task he had undertaken, and he vigorously prodded them to write into law the numerous and comprehensive proposals he had discussed in his message. After the regular session had ended he discovered that many of the measures passed were defective and that there were several gaps which needed to be filled to complete the desired pattern of legislation. Consquently he called a special session of the 1905 legislature to give further consideration to certain measures and amendments. His appearance at this session was La Follette's swan song as a state official in Wisconsin. In his message accepting the senatorship he impressed upon the legislators that in the preceding four years Wisconsin had built a great reform tradition. This entailed a new responsibility, he added, for the influence of Wisconsin had been felt in every state of the union. "We cannot halt or turn back without bringing disaster to our own state, and discourage all progress along those lines in other states." He urged his colleagues to broaden and deepen the pattern of reform in Wisconsin, and pledged himself to "continue active personal participation" in every contest involving the principles of "representative government." It was obvious that "Fighting Bob" had no intention of relinquishing his position of authority and leadership in the now dominant progressive Republican organization that he had so painfully welded together. Only after the special session had completed its labors did he finally send in his letter of resignation, to take effect on the first Monday in January, 1906.[25] On that day Robert M. La Follette was sworn into office as junior United States senator from Wisconsin, and James O. Davidson became the acting governor for the remainder of the term.[26]

"Yim" Davidson presented a marked contrast to the aggressive and dynamic La Follette. Genial and easygoing by temperament, Norwegian-born Davidson had held a succession of offices in the Republican regime before becoming lieutenant governor in 1903. Though lacking in formal education he had made a creditable record in these positions, having practical common sense and good judgment. He was on friendly terms with the stalwart leaders, but he was a firm supporter of progressive principles and had greatly strenthened the progressive cause by virtue of his influence with his fellow Norwegians. He had been a friend and supporter of La Follette for fifteen years, "willing to make every sacrifice to promote his ambitions, believing in the principles for which he stood." It was only normal that he should look forward to election to the governorship as a fitting climax to his long and honorable career in public office. Consequently he was surprised and shocked to learn that La Follette would not support him for the governorship in 1906 but would actively promote Irvine L. Lenroot, the aggressive young speaker of the Assembly.[27]

Davidson, however, was not disposed to vacate the governor's chair after occupying it for one short year. His fellow Norwegians were strong for him, and many progressives felt that it would be unfair to drop him so unceremoniously. Nils Haugen, always outspoken, told La Follette that it was "due to Davidson to let him be nominated," particularly since he was almost certain to be elected. It would be both unwise and ungrateful to abandon him. It was at his own request, Haugen reminded La Follette, that Davidson had consented to run for the lieutenant governorship. Davidson would have preferred to remain state treasurer, but the bait of succession to the governorship had been held out to him. Despite his friendship and respect for La Follette, Haugen was a strong supporter of his fellow countryman.[28]

Davidson quickly gained support from many groups. As acting governor and old friend of many of the state officeholders, he was able to control the administrative machinery and enlist the support of the professional politicians. Many of the old stalwarts threw their strength to him in the hope of breaking up the progressive organization. Most of the state

The Magician

A cartoon by John T. McCutcheon in the *Chicago Daily Tribune* of December 29, 1911

THE NEW STATE CAPITOL, erected "without graft or waste."
Above, under construction, 1912. *Below,* recent aerial view.

press, including a majority of the large dailies, the country weeklies, and the foreign-language papers, were friendly to his candidacy. So also was Isaac Stephenson, who told La Follette he had "made a serious political blunder in bringing out Lenroot to oppose Davidson." The people of the state, thought Stephenson, were "fair minded" and would give Davidson his chance at the governorship. The expression was common that the people of the state did not want an "assistant dictator" in the governor's chair.[29]

Lenroot made a vigorous campaign and La Follette made a personal tour in his behalf, but Davidson won the primary election, the first under the new law, with relative ease and was elected in the general election in November. Apparently La Follette had greatly overrated his own ability to deliver votes to the candidate of his choice. Before the election he had predicted that Lenroot would win by fifty thousand votes; actually Lenroot was defeated by almost that margin. As a close friend later said, "La Follette had mistaken enthusiasm for himself for enthusiasm for Lenroot." Although somewhat strained by La Follette's attempt to dictate the choice of his successor in the primary struggle, there was no break in the progressive organization. Davidson gave no comfort to the stalwarts and continued to support progressive reforms. La Follette was generally recognized as the leader and spokesman of the party and regularly took a hand in state affairs. Friendly letters continued to pass between Davidson and La Follette, and the governor frequently consulted the senator on matters of policy and appointments.[30]

The departure of "Fighting Bob" La Follette from the arena of Wisconsin politics marked a major milestone in the history of the progressive movement in the state. The struggles that were closely identified with La Follette by the general public— the direct primary, the ad valorem taxation of the railroads, the establishment of the railroad commission, and the titanic fight to wrest control of the party machinery from the stalwarts —had all been decided and in large part written into the statute books. Presently the progressive Republicans embarked on a new series of broad social and economic reforms that were not intimately associated with La Follette's sponsorship. True, many of these later innovations, such as the reform of the tax structure by the Tax Commission, the intimate cooperation of the state and the University, and the state conservation program had had their beginnings under La Follette, but their more important effects belong to the later period. With the departure of La Follette a number of other progressive figures emerged as leaders in their own right and became associated with important reforms. While devoid of some of the sound and fury of the La Follette struggles, these later reforms and their sponsors are equally significant in the development of the pattern of progressivism in Wisconsin.

7 NILS HAUGEN AND THE TAX COMMISSION

★ ★ ★ ★ ★ ★ ★ ★ ★ ★ ★ ★ ★ ★ ★ ★ ★

IT IS NOT IMPROBABLE THAT THE KEY TO THE WHOLE SUCCESS OF the progressive reform program in Wisconsin lay in the role played by the state Tax Commission. Throughout the progressive era this body had a strong and pervasive influence, and its members participated in the planning and drafting of legislation in other fields. Strictly speaking, the progressives cannot claim sole credit for the establishment of the Tax Commission. It was already active before La Follette became governor and it continued to function as an important government agency after the progressive organization lost control of the state. But the progressive years were its years of growth and greatest influence in Wisconsin fiscal affairs. The philosophy of progressivism permeated the decisions of the commissioners and they did not hesitate to use the power of the state to shift the basis of taxation or to urge the use of public funds for broad social purposes. Hence the accomplishments of the Tax Commission were essentially progressive accomplishments and its contributions were vital to the success of the entire progressive program.

The need for a general reform of Wisconsin's tax system had been recognized by leading public men long before the advent of La Follette. As early as 1873, during the Granger period, the legislature had required the county registers of deeds to send annually to the secretary of state a record of "all sales of real estate" and it had considered establishing a board to collect statistics to facilitate the equalization of state taxes.[1]

These records later provided the basis for the "sales method" of tax equalization used by the commission. Agitation for a tax commission by K. K. Keenan, later temporary tax commissioner, kept the subject before the legislature throughout the nineties, but no further action was taken until late in the decade.[2]

In 1897, during Governor Scofield's administration, the legislature created a special temporary tax commission that studied the tax situation and submitted its findings to the governor. The commission's report indicated that public service corporations paid relatively less taxes than other classes of taxpayers and less than they would pay on an ad valorem basis. The commission found that there was so little sentiment in favor of an income tax that any discussion of the subject would be a mere waste of time.[3]

In addition to transmitting the report of the special tax commission, Governor Scofield proposed to the legislature that they establish an auditing and accounting system for all state funds. The lawmakers referred both recommendations to a new temporary tax commission charged with continuing the study, especially the investigation of corporate taxation.[4] This commission was to consist of one commissioner and two assistant commissioners to be appointed for ten years by the governor. This long tenure gave the commission a semi-permanent status that promised greater prestige and proficiency. The members were to be persons known to possess knowledge and skill in matters pertaining to taxation. The initial appointees were Michael Griffin, commissioner, and George Curtis, Jr. and Norman Gilson, assistant commissioners. Upon General Griffin's sudden death Governor Scofield made Judge Gilson commissioner and appointed William J. Anderson to fill his former place as assistant commissioner. This commission, composed of men of known ability and statewide reputation, was one of the first non-political, expert tax boards in the United States. Only Indiana and Massachusetts had previously set up a tax commission of professional character.[5]

Governor Scofield had long been interested in the broad aspects of the taxation problem. As early as 1898 he had advocated a general reform of the tax system and a permanent tax commission. On the problem of equalization he warned that the solution did not lie in merely raising the taxes of those who had been underassessed, but that a proportionate reduction should be made for those who had been paying more than their share. He was opposed to any scheme that would greatly increase taxes. It was equalization, he said, that interested taxpayers, not increased revenues.[6]

Other political leaders were also interested in the reform of the state's tax system. In 1899 John M. Whitehead, conservative state senator from Janesville and later stalwart candidate for governor, introduced the bill creating the temporary tax commission and sponsored legislation imposing ad valorem taxes on express companies, sleeping-car companies, freight lines, and equipment companies. The same legislature passed an inheritance tax law, which had been recommended by the special tax commission, and increased the taxes of life insurance companies. This rather substantial body of legislation justified to some extent the claims later made by one stalwart leader that the beginnings of tax reform had been a stalwart contribution which the progressives merely extended and popularized.[7]

The Republican state platform of 1900 endorsed the Tax Commission and predicted that its report would point the way to a reform and equalization of the state's tax policies. Throughout the harmony campaign La Follette praised the Tax Commission repeatedly and in his inaugural address urged the legislature to act on the commission's preliminary recommendations without waiting for its final report. The law, he insisted, "should discriminate neither in favor of nor against any class or interest." He pointed to the rise in the cost of state government in the past ten years and pledged himself to a more economical administration. "I believe it will be possible," he promised, "to effect a material saving to the State, without any injury to the public service, through a reduction in the number and a reorganization of the force of employees in the public service." [8] The subsequent rapid increase in state expenditures was in sharp contrast to the pledges La Follette had made as a candidate. As many other public figures have discovered, he found that campaign promises to reduce expenses were impossible to fulfill.

The *Report of the Wisconsin Tax Commission* for 1901 was awaited eagerly by both the governor and the legislature. The commissioners recommended that the license fees collected from the railways be increased and eventually replaced by an ad valorem tax, and that the license fees of street railway and telegraph companies be increased to a point that would bring their tax load more nearly in line with that of the average citizen. The commission boldly attacked the broad questions of authority and responsibility in tax assessments. It urged that assessors be given more power to enable them to reach a larger share of personal property and that at the same time they be held to a stricter accountability to some central authority. [9]

In spite of La Follette's full support of the Tax Commission's proposals, however, the legislative session of 1901 was almost barren of substantial achievement in the field of tax reform. The railroad tax bills went down in defeat as a result of the bitter political battle between the progressives and the stalwarts. Perhaps the most significant fiscal measure enacted was the one which made the Tax Commission a state board of assessment and defined its duties. Another act created the office of county supervisor of assessments and a third provided for the taxation of mortgages and mortgaged real estate. This last measure, called the Frost Act, was vetoed by La Follette on the grounds that it was loosely drawn, defective, and probably unconstitutional.[10]

The lawmakers directed the Tax Commission to continue its studies and make a complete report at the next session of the legislature. The administration forces embarked on a campaign to popularize the tax-reform program and to secure a legislature pledged to its enactment. During the same year, 1901, La Follette appointed his old friend Nils P. Haugen to fill a vacancy on the Tax Commission, giving that body an even more decidedly progressive cast than before.

Haugen had been one of the small group of original supporters of La Follette and was one of the key figures in the progressive victory of 1900. Not only did he enjoy prominence as a political leader among the Norwegians of the state but he had himself had an extensive political career. After graduating from the University of Michigan Law School in 1874 he had returned to Wisconsin and had served as railroad commissioner from 1882 to 1887. He had been a member of Congress for three successive terms during the years 1888 to 1894, having been the only Wisconsin member of his party who had not been unseated in the debacle of 1890. In 1894 he had been a candidate for the gubernatorial nomination but had suffered defeat because La Follette's support of him had provoked Philetus Sawyer to use his influence against him.[11] For several years thereafter he had held no political office, but he had been actively identified with the reform wing of the Republican Party and had repeatedly given assistance to La Follette in his early campaigns. Throughout this period he had been a close student of taxation and its social implications, and he came to the Tax Commission with a well-developed philosophy of the proper role of such a board and of his functions as a commissioner. Nominally he was the second assistant commissioner, but he soon became the dominant personality on the board and frequently imposed upon his colleagues his own concepts of the proper course of action.

Haugen was a tall, angular, somewhat phlegmatic man with sandy hair and ruddy cheeks—a Viking type of Norseman. Though outwardly gentle and easygoing, he could be blunt, outspoken, and incisive. Once he had arrived at a decision, he was not easily swerved from it. Closely identified though he was with the rise of Robert La Follette, he could not truly be described as a "follower" of "Fighting Bob," for he "wore the political collar of no man" and insisted on doing his own thinking. On occasion he could become bitingly critical of La Follette's policies and ambitions, and he did not hesitate to press his own views on either the governor or the other members of the Tax Commission. Upon becoming a member of the commission he gave that body a positive direction and purpose which became increasingly apparent with each report. And since Haugen served continuously for twenty years, his own philosophy of taxation tended to become that of the commission as a whole.[12]

The report that the Tax Commission made to the 1903 legislature embodied the results of four years of exhaustive study on the many different aspects of state taxation. Whereas the report of 1901 had suggested alternative methods of increasing the proportionate tax load of the railroads, the commission now definitely recommended a shift to the ad valorem system, which it estimated would yield almost a million dollars more annually than the gross earnings method. After a sharp struggle the legislature passed the ad valorem program as recommended, the tax commissioners, especially Haugen, playing a large role in the drafting of the final bill.[13]

The Tax Commission, in its 1901 report, also recommended the exemption of mortgages from taxation. La Follette had vetoed such a bill at the end of the 1901 session on technical grounds, and the new mortgage-exemption law, drawn to conform to the recommendations of the majority of the commissioners, was designed to meet his objections. It provided that mortgages should be taxed as an interest in real estate. The mortgagor was permitted to report his interest and that of the mortgagee as unencumbered real estate and assume all taxes. The purpose of the plan was to improve the bargaining position of the debtor or to require that the creditor assume part of the taxes. However, according to Dr. Thomas S. Adams, economics expert at the University of Wisconsin, the small borrower was still in a poor position in seeking loans. He was often forced to assume taxes with no reduction in interest. Haugen opposed this piece of legislation and later took great pleasure in preparing for Governor Davidson a message recommending its repeal. The legislature did not, however, repeal the act and the mortgage-tax situation remained unchanged until 1911, when the income tax law provided that the interest received by the mortgagee should be reported and taxed as income.[14]

The section of the Tax Commission's 1903 report dealing with the taxation of inheritances produced more satisfactory results. The commission recommended changes that would meet the objections of the Supreme Court to the 1899 law, which it had declared unconstitutional. The legislature promptly enacted the new measure and it was upheld by the high court in subsequent litigation. The inheritance tax proved to be a good producer of revenue, bringing in an average of almost $270,000 a year during the first five years the law was in operation. In 1912 the Tax Commission was placed in full charge of its administration and an inheritance-tax investigator was employed, under civil service, to counsel with the local officials and to represent the state personally in the cases of larger litigation.[15]

In accordance with the recommendations of the Tax Commission the legislature named the commissioners as a board of assessment to evaluate the properties of railroad sleeping-car companies, freight lines, and equipment companies and abolished the old ex-officio board.[16] Thus the commission assumed responsibility for all ad valorem taxes and proceeded, with the help of assistants, to evaluate the properties of these corporations and apply the tax rate of the general property tax to them as provided by law.

The commission in its report of 1903 boldly urged that all property be assessed at its true value. For many years underassessment had become progressively widespread until scarcely enough property appeared on the tax rolls to enable the officials to carry on the functions of government without resorting to confiscatory rates.[17] Haugen had strongly advocated that all property be assessed at its full value, and his view became the accepted policy of the Tax Commission. So vigorously did the commissioners, acting as the State Board of Assessment, apply this principle that local assessments increased from $648,000,000 in 1899 to $1,411,500,000 in 1905. During the same period state assessments approached sales value even more closely as they rose from $625,000,000 to $1,952,700,000. Under the ad valorem railroad bill the Tax Commission applied the rate of the state general property tax to the properties of the railroads. Haugen stoutly resisted all attempts to persuade the commission to reduce the assessment of railroad property directly or pad the total state valuation in order to reduce the mill rate. So sharply divided was the commission on this issue that Judge Gilson, its senior member, filed a dissenting opinion in each of the first two reports respecting the face valuation of railroad property. Even Governor La Follette, according to Haugen, feared that the initial step-up in valuation was too great and suggested that it be scaled down. In spite of this pressure Haugen and Curtis insisted on a constructive full valuation of all real estate, and increasingly this policy became standard.[18]

The purpose of the state assessment of property was twofold. Not only would it determine the rate of taxation to be applied to the corporations taxed under the ad valorem system but it would also afford a basis for the equitable apportionment of the state tax and provide a check on the competitive local undervaluation of property.[19] Fearlessly and almost belligerently the Tax Commission applied the "full value" principle in evaluating and assessing the railroad properties for 1904. The average rate at which the general property tax was levied in the state was determined to be $.0114403568. This was applied to the railroad properties as valued by the commission. The property of the Chicago and North Western Railway, for example, was valued at $71,500,000 and its tax was fixed at $817,985.51. Since the road had paid $628,753.85 as a license fee, a balance of $189,231.66 was declared due and was collected. Some of the smaller railroads, on the other hand, received refunds from their license fee payments.[20]

Theoretically the Tax Commission was to make the original assessment of all property subject to taxation in each county, but in practice this was not possible. The state assessments were of necessity based on the work of the local assessors, which was carefully checked and corrected. The principal device used in appraising the assessments of the local officers was the "sales method." Actual bona fide sales of real estate were listed and the ratio of assessed to true value determined. By applying this yardstick the commission was able to detect and adjust inaccurate assessments and undervaluations of local real estate. These records of the sales of real estate and livestock were supplemented by special reports of the state Department of Agriculture and University agencies. The "sales method" was not a new technique, but its application in Wisconsin was an important extension of the principle. It served as a valid check on local valuations and did much to standardize the valuation of all property in the state for purposes of taxation.[21]

A similar technique was followed in arriving at the physical valuation of the railroads. As a later member of the commission, Thomas S. Adams, described the procedure, the board used the "Michigan Appraisal" of 1901 as a model for the initial survey. A commercial valuation based on capitalization of earnings was first obtained from the company in a series of elaborate reports. Nils Haugen devised and applied a method for capitalizing railroad bonds. Adjustments were then made to cover depreciation, wear and tear, and "a thousand and one considerations such as the ordinary purchaser or buyer would take into account." The companies concerned were kept fully informed of the general procedure and were encouraged to present any facts bearing on the process of valuation.[22]

In 1905 the powers and duties of the Tax Commission were greatly expanded. The legislature placed under its authority the assessment of telephone companies, street railways, and all electric-light, heat, and power companies operated in connection with such railways. These utilities were to be taxed according to the ad valorem rate, which was to be computed by the Tax Commission in much the same way as it was computed for the railroads. At the same time the Tax Commission was made a board of review of local assessments in certain classes of appeals and was empowered to employ special assessors to make a reassessment of property in a district. It was authorized to require a report of expenditures from local governments and to prescribe a uniform system of accounting. The same legislature reorganized the Tax Commission on a permanent basis. Although it had been functioning as a permanent body for several years, it had been regarded technically as a temporary board. All the commissioners continued to serve, Haugen being appointed to the initial eight-year term.[23]

The functions of the Tax Commission were further broadened by the 1907 legislature. The Public Utilities Act of that year, which placed gas, water, electric-light, and telephone companies under the regulation of the Railroad Commission, charged this board to avail itself of the assessments and techniques already acquired by the Tax Commission and to cooperate in the task of valuation. The two boards shared the use of a single staff of engineers and each made use of the assembled data. Unnecessary duplication was thus avoided, and uniform valuations for tax assessment and rate determination were achieved.[24]

One important consequence of this legislation was that to a large extent the control of public utilities passed from the local governments into the hands of permanent and professional state boards. The Railroad Commission regulated the rates and services of all public service corporations, and the Tax Commission assessed the property and levied the taxes of all utilities in the state regardless of their location.

As a result of the fair and nonpartisan evaluation procedures of the Tax Commission the corporations of the state bore a fair but not disproportionate share of the soaring cost of state government. In fact, the railroads, whose spokesmen had protested violently against the "confiscatory rates," found that their taxes under the ad valorem system increased less rapidly than the state's tax receipts as a whole.[25] Some of the lesser corporations that were brought under the ad valorem system bore a relatively insignificant share of the tax load. One tax expert thought that the additional revenues from the sleeping-car, freight, and express companies were not enough to justify the increased expenses of administration and evaluation. Nevertheless the system insured fairness and gave the commission an exact knowledge of their taxable properties that was not possible under the gross receipts method.[26]

The progressive administration was slow to meet the long-standing need for a budget system and a centralized accounting department. At last in 1908 the legislature requested the Tax Commission to study the state's financial machinery with a view to its reorganization. The outcome was a special report on the finances of the state government which advocated consolidation of all the state's active funds for purposes of disbursement; a uniform classification of expenditures; a centralized audit system, under the direction of the secretary of state, for all state boards and commissions; and the establishment of a budget board charged with the duty of preparing appropriation bills and arranging for the payment of the state debt.[27]

While the Tax Commission was making this study a similar investigation was being conducted by the legislature's joint committee on finance. The committee, headed by Senator Albert W. Sanborn and Assemblyman Ray J. Nye, held public hearings and studied the problem from many angles and finally submitted its findings to the legislature in a special report. Its recommendations were similar to those of the Tax Commission and in addition it submitted model schedules for all departments, commissions, and agencies. On the basis of these reports the legislature drafted a comprehensive bill providing for annual budget estimates and a central accounting system to supervise the spending of the numerous state agencies.[28]

The terms of all the tax commissioners expired or fell vacant during the administration of Governor Francis E. McGovern, who thus had the duty of naming the new board. Nils Haugen consented to continue his service and was named chairman. Professor Thomas S. Adams was appointed to succeed Judge Norman Gilson, and Thomas E. Lyons of Superior replaced George Curtis.[29]

Perhaps the most troublesome problem facing the Tax Commission was the personal property tax. This long-established device for raising revenue, first enacted in 1873, was notorious for its inequality and the ease with which it could be evaded. The reforms in evaluation and assessment which did so much to equalize the general property tax were ineffective when applied to personal property. Not only did personal property tend to be grossly undervaluated, but the tax had the effect of discriminating against the rural areas in favor of the cities. The personal property of the farmer, such as farm animals, tools, machinery, harvested crops, and cut lumber, were easily discovered and assessed, whereas much of the property of the urban citizen, especially such holdings as stocks, bonds, and cash, might well escape the eye of the assessor.

These difficulties of assessment and collection persuaded many students of fiscal affairs in Wisconsin that the personal property tax should be replaced by some more equitable means of raising the needed revenue. Among the leaders of this movement was tax commissioner Haugen, who regarded the personal property tax as more or less unenforceable. In its place Haugen urged the adoption of a state income tax which would be simple to administer and difficult to evade and which would be borne chiefly by those most able to pay.[30]

The idea of an income tax was not new. Such a tax had been levied as a Civil War measure, and the federal government had enacted a short-lived law during the Cleveland administration.[31] Some of the older states had at one time or another experimented with an income tax, but most of them had later abandoned it as unprofitable. Of the states that were still imposing such a tax Virginia had had the greatest success, yet even there the income tax yielded only about a hundred thousand dollars a year, or approximately one-twentieth as much as the general property tax. The conclusion of most tax authorities was that the income tax was "unquestionably a failure," satisfying "neither the demands for justice nor the need of revenue." [32]

Nevertheless many legislators and administrative officials urged the adoption of a graduated income tax for Wisconsin, both as a measure to equalize tax burdens and as an opportunity to tap hitherto neglected sources of revenue. The first step was taken by the 1903 legislature, which approved a constitutional amendment authorizing a graduated tax on incomes, but because of a technical error the resolution had to be repassed in 1905. It was again approved by the 1907 legislature according to the constitutional requirements, and in a referendum held in 1908 the electorate adopted the amendment by more than a two-to-one majority.[33]

The way was now open for the enactment of an income tax law, but the legislature of 1909 showed little inclination to consider such a measure immediately. Even the Tax Commission failed to include specific recommendations for an income tax in its biennial report. In the interval between legislative sessions, however, both the Tax Commission and a "Special Recess Committee" of lawmakers gave careful consideration to the problem and drafted a bill embodying the best features of their findings. The legislature of 1911 promptly passed the measure with little change and almost no opposition. The framers of the bill made every effort to avoid the weaknesses that had crippled the income tax in other states. Largely because of the influence of the Tax Commission, one of the chief features of the new Wisconsin law was centralized administration. The assessors of income were to be appointed and removed by the Tax Commission. They were to be completely divorced from politics and were to be chosen from the civil service list.[34]

The graduated feature of the new law was very moderate. The rates ranged from one per cent per thousand dollars income to a maximum of six per cent on incomes in excess of twelve thousand dollars, with liberal exemptions and deductions. The new tax was designed to replace the old personal property tax, and taxpayers could credit their personal property tax payments against their income tax assessments, and thus actually were required to pay only the larger amount. Only ten per cent of the income tax was to remain in the state treasury; the balance was to be distributed among the local units of government, seventy per cent to the cities and towns and twenty per cent to the counties.[35]

The income tax was a success from the beginning. In the first full year of operation it produced three and a half million dollars in revenues—almost as much as the personal property tax. The cost of administering it was exceptionally low, less than two per cent of the taxes assessed. Governor McGovern attributed the success of the income tax in Wisconsin to the centralized administration of the Tax Commission. The failure in other states had been due to poor administration and careless collections. McGovern praised the new tax as one designed to distribute the burdens of taxation among those best able to pay and to exempt the poor man altogether from payment of taxes.[36]

In an address to the National Tax Association, Nils Haugen prophesied that Wisconsin's success with the income tax would lead to a revision of ideas concerning its feasibility. The successive reports of the Tax Commission emphasized that the income tax did actually tend to redistribute the tax load and compensate for the excessive tax burden which rural property had borne. The commission estimated that only five per cent of the farmers and virtually no farm laborers were paying income taxes. "If the income tax furnishes a proper measure of taxable capacity," concluded the commissioners, "farmers and those laborers subject to taxation have been greatly over taxed in the past." [37] The gratifying returns of the Wisconsin income tax did indeed inaugurate a new era in state taxation. By 1917 four states had followed Wisconsin's example and inaugurated a tax on incomes. By 1933 the number had grown to twenty-three.[38]

The effects of the income tax upon Wisconsin's economy precipitated a bitter controversy that continued for more than a decade. Admittedly the new tax weighed most heavily on the corporations of the state; in the first year of its operation two-thirds of the receipts were derived from corporations. As a result some firms preferred to locate in nearby states rather than in Wisconsin. In studying the effect of the income tax and other corporation taxes in the decade following 1912, the National Industrial Conference Board of New York found that Wisconsin was in an unfavorable position as compared with her neighbors. "This situation has had the effect," the board asserted, "of bringing into being certain devices whereby Wisconsin is very slowly becoming a state of branch factories." The Tax Commission, on the other hand, in a special report on the same subject denied that the tax had produced harmful results and cited statistics indicating that Wisconsin had progressed even more rapidly than her neighbors.[39]

Harold M. Groves, professor of economics at the University of Wisconsin and widely known tax expert, also made a study of the relation of taxes to the growth of industry in Wisconsin. In a paper entitled "Possibilities of the Income Tax," he cited statistics to demonstrate that, far from being crippled by the income tax, industry had grown more rapidly in Wisconsin than in any of the neighboring states except Michigan. In the fourteen years 1914–1928, Professor Groves pointed out, the value of manufacturing income in Wisconsin had increased by more than 255 per cent as compared with an average increase of 134 per cent in the United States as a whole. Most of the industries which had left Wisconsin had gone to states that also had state income taxes, and the total tax load carried by corporations in Wisconsin was neither markedly heavier nor markedly lighter than that borne by industry in Illinois, Michigan, or Indiana or most of the industrial states. It is difficult if not impossible to make any final evaluation of such conflicting claims, but no conclusive evidence has been produced to demonstrate that the Wisconsin taxpayer, either the in-

dividual or the corporation, was placed at any marked disadvantage as a result of the progressives' income tax program.[40]

As the progressives developed their fiscal policies the legislature steadily transferred power and authority from the local
units of government to the Tax Commission. This transfer
was accelerated by the tax commissioners themselves, who
frequently recommended, as they did in connection with the
administration of the income tax law, that the final authority
and responsibility be vested in them. The consolidation and
centralization of fiscal functions under the Tax Commission
accompanied a general rise in the cost of government, both
state and local. The steadily increasing number of services
performed by government on all levels created in turn a never-
ending search for new sources of revenue. The total cost of
government in Wisconsin more than doubled during the
period of the progressive regime from 1900 to 1913. The state's
revenues leaped from some five million dollars in 1900 to
more than fourteen and a half million in 1912.[41]

During this entire period of rapid growth of state expenditures, the function of the Tax Commission in regularizing and
equalizing the tax burden was of great importance to the
efficiency and well-being of the entire state.[42] The commission
also played an important role in the constant search for new
sources of revenue. In every report the commissioners surveyed
the field and recommended means of bringing additional
dollars into the state treasury. Without the help of the Tax
Commission as an agency of government and of the several
commissioners as individuals, the progressives might well have
been forced to abandon much of their reform program because
of lack of funds.

In short, the effectiveness of the Wisconsin tax reforms is
attributable primarily to the knowledge, character, and common
sense of the tax commissioners. They set a high standard of

professional and nonpartisan conduct which inspired confidence in their findings and valuations and increased their prestige among the people of the state. Under the guidance of the commission the legislature practically recast the tax laws of Wisconsin. The progressives took the initial steps toward shifting the bulk of the tax burden from general and personal property to corporate wealth and income. The principle of "taxation according to ability to pay" became an accepted part of the Wisconsin tax philosophy.

8 REGULATING THE LIFE INSURANCE COMPANIES

★ ★ ★ ★ ★ ★ ★ ★ ★ ★ ★ ★ ★ ★ ★ ★ ★

ANOTHER OF THE DISTINCTIVE REFORMS IDENTIFIED WITH THE progressive movement, not only in Wisconsin but throughout the United States, was the regulation of the life insurance companies. In attempting to bring these huge corporations under the control of the state the progressive leaders were extending the doctrine of public regulation and control, for until now the business of writing life insurance had been virtually unsupervised at any level of government. In fact, the growth of life insurance companies from modest corporations to giant trusts had been so rapid that they thrust themselves upon the attention of the public almost overnight as organizations in urgent need of regulation.

The business of writing life insurance in America had made phenomenal strides in the half century before the advent of the progressive era. For some years after the establishment of the first state-chartered company in 1843 the life insurance corporations had been modest in size, but by the close of the Civil War they had begun an expansion so rapid that at the turn of the century they were being described as "the first business of the land." [1] The center of insurance activity was the city of New York. There the four largest companies had their home offices and directed their regional agencies, which operated in almost all the states. Slightly smaller concentrations of insurance companies in Philadelphia, Boston, Newark, and Hartford also made these cities important insurance capitals. At the turn of the century the "old-line" companies located in these five Eastern cities were writing more then eighty per cent of the insurance carried in the United States.[2]

The growth of the insurance business was accompanied by the rise of great insurance tycoons. Most of the larger companies owed much of their expansion to the bold, aggressive, managerial leadership of their executives—John R. Hegeman and Haley Fiske of the Metropolitan Life, Henry B. Hyde of the Equitable Life, John A. McCall of the New York Life, and Richard A. McCurdy of the Mutual Life, each of whom left his characteristic stamp upon the entire insurance field. In the scramble to outdistance its competitors each of the major companies branched out and on occasion actively engaged in the operation of railroads, banks, and various utilities. The result was an amazing array of interlocking directorates which closely linked the life insurance business with most of the great industrial corporations of the country.[3]

Attempts at state supervision of the insurance business date back to the establishment of the Massachusetts Insurance Department in 1855 and a similar office in New York in 1860. There had been little effective regulation, however, for the state commissioners contented themselves with collecting statistics and reports, renewing licenses, and enforcing the general insurance laws. The New York laws were regarded as the most complete of the existing regulations and were accepted as a kind of standard for the insurance world. The fact that a company did business in the state of New York bespoke its soundness and stability.[4]

In Wisconsin the insurance field was dominated by one local company, the Northwestern Mutual Life Insurance Company of Milwaukee. This was one of the six largest insurance companies in the United States, and it competed successfully with the Eastern companies for business throughout the country. It wrote almost a third of all the life insurance policies issued in Wisconsin and paid about four-fifths of the taxes collected in the state from life insurance companies. Its only domestic competitors were two small companies incorporated in Wisconsin and the large Eastern firms such as the New York Life and the Metropolitan Life. But these had hardly begun to threaten seriously the local near-monopoly of the Northwestern Mutual.[5]

Long before the advent of La Follette and the progressives the state had eyed the insurance companies doing business in Wisconsin as a potential source of additional revenue. As early as 1868 the Northwestern Mutual had paid a state tax amounting to one per cent of its Wisconsin premiums. In 1899, during Governor Scofield's administration, the legislature levied a tax of one per cent on the company's gross income from all sources, which increased its taxes from about $29,000 in 1898 to more than $186,000 the next year. In addition a provision was enacted requiring out-of-state or "foreign" companies to pay one per cent of the gross premiums they collected in Wisconsin. This provision would have subjected the Northwestern Mutual to reciprocal or retaliatory taxes from other states, and the company promptly registered strong protest against so sudden and extreme an increase in taxes. In an able argument before the Tax Commission Vice-president Willard Merrill denounced as unjust the heavy burden the new tax would put upon the policyholders. The assets of a mutual life insurance company, he emphasized, should be considered not as a property subject to taxation in the same sense that the resources of an industrial corporation were, but as a "credit" or obligation which the company held in trust for its policyholders. He was especially vigorous in pointing out that the taxes the foreign companies would pay under the new law would total only a little more than twenty-five thousand dollars, but that the Northwestern Mutual would be subjected to about twice that amount in retaliatory taxes. If that amount of money must be raised, he said, it would be better for the state to impose the entire amount on the Northwestern and impose nothing on the outside companies doing business in the state.[6] The state administration, now headed by La Follette, was reluctant to take any action that would reduce the state revenues substantially, but it was not unmindful of the necessity of maintaining the well-being of this "golden egg-laying goose." When it became evident that the Northwestern Mutual would indeed have to pay heavy retaliatory taxes in other states as a result of the 1899 law, Governor La Follette and the 1901 legislature, hopelessly split on other issues, put aside their factional differences long enough to rush through legislation relieving the Northwestern Mutual of this threat. In so doing the lawmakers returned to the principle of basing taxes on gross annual premium receipts of the companies incorporated in Wisconsin. The domestic companies were taxed three per cent of such receipts. The foreign companies, as had been suggested by Vice-president Merrill, were to pay a nominal three-hundred-dollar license fee.[7] This pattern of taxation, despite repeated petitions by the Northwestern officials for revision, remained in effect until the end of the progressive era.[8]

The efforts to regulate the activities of the life insurance companies increased during the years of La Follette's administration. In 1903 Zeno M. Host, newly elected commissioner of insurance, attempted to force the companies to divide their surplus among the policyholders. The leading companies promptly contested the commission's ruling in the state courts and after more than two years of litigation won their case.[9]

Host was also the central figure in a spectacular case involving an investigation of the Prudential Life Insurance Company of New York, one of the oldest and most reputable of the old-line corporations. Charging that the control of the Prudential had been turned over to one of the New York trust companies, Host undertook a thorough investigation of its affairs at the home office. Using the threat to revoke its license to force compliance, Host transported a corps of bookkeepers, accountants, and clerks to New York to make the examination. For this the Prudential was required to pay $21,024, of which Host, a $3000-a-year state employee, received some $1,152 for twenty-seven days' work. Other employees received comparable amounts. So excessive did the charges for the investigation appear that both the Milwaukee and the New York press raised the cry of extortion. Technically Host was quite within the law, as he was authorized to employ actuaries and clerks to determine the value of policies.[10]

The Prudential paid the examination fee under protest and then brought suit in federal court to recover $20,314 from the commissioner, claiming that $710 was all that the law permitted Host to collect. After dragging through the courts for two years, the suit was eventually withdrawn at the company's request. In his report for 1904 Host expressed the opinion that the charges for such an investigation should be borne by the state and not by the company involved. To this the *Sentinel* added that such an investigation was not worth twenty-one cents to the Prudential, much less twenty-one thousand dollars. In reference to this and similar cases, John A. McCall of the New York Life charged that insurance executives were "badgered and harassed to death" in every state by the introduction of "blackmailing bills" and other practices.[11]

If the insurance executives had just cause to protest against the unfriendly attitude of many state officials, the public had even more justification for its suspicions of many of the activities of the great insurance companies. In their race for supremacy and fat profits many of the foremost companies all but forgot the primary reason for their existence. In a number of respects the policyholders were not well served. The percentage of losses they suffered from lapses and surrenders was unreasonably high. According to one insurance statistician, only 4.9 per cent of policy terminations resulted from death, whereas 93 per cent represented lapses.[12] The reports of many companies revealed violent fluctuations in new business, indicating that the overhead cost of placing more insurance in force had reached the point of diminishing returns. Although most experts condemned tontine and deferred dividend policies (semitontines), many companies, including the big four, continued to issue them, with the result that even larger surpluses were built up at the expense of policyholders. The heads of the insurance empires conducted themselves imperiously, gave scant opportunity for policyholders, even in mutual companies, to have a voice in management, and manipulated proxies to perpetuate themselves in office. Needless to say, the smaller companies followed the example of the insurance giants.[13]

Throughout the nation public attention was focused upon the life insurance companies by the sensational revelations made in 1905 by a New York legislative investigating committee. The formation of this committee was the result of a family quarrel among officers of the Equitable Life Assurance Society which reached the front pages of the press after charges and countercharges of fraud, unwarranted speculation, and excessive profit-taking had been tossed back and forth by the company's executives.[14] The committee was headed by state senator William W. Armstrong and employed as counsel the rising New York attorney Charles Evans Hughes.

The Armstrong Committee did much more than investigate the affairs of the Equitable Life. It directed a large part of its attention to a general examination of the foremost companies, the New York Life, the Metropolitan Life, and the Mutual Life. The affair took on the aspects of a murder trial, the press being represented by special writers, reporters, photographers, and cartoonists. Most of the insurance executives fared very badly at the hands of the calm, penetrating, bearded examiner; and the New York press boomed circulation by exploiting the exposure which resulted. *McClure's Magazine* published a dramatic article on the investigation by Burton Hendrick, entitled

"The Story of Life Insurance." Other periodicals printed similar sensational articles on abuses in the insurance business.[15]

The report of the Armstrong Committee made specific recommendations for the correction of the abuses it had uncovered, notably limitation of expenses on policies; prohibition of tontine insurance; standardization of policy forms; wider participation of policyholders in company elections; and a mandatory, complete annual report by every company. The next session of the New York legislature quickly enacted most of these recommendations into law.[16]

The Armstrong Committee's report caused a flurry of excitement throughout the country. Many states followed New York's example and examined the affairs of their insurance companies. One of the first states to do so was Wisconsin.[17]

In the fall of 1905, before the Armstrong investigation had been completed, La Follette called the Wisconsin legislature into special session and proposed, among other recommendations on a variety of matters, the reorganization of the insurance business in the state. He called for a thorough and impartial study of the question as a preliminary step to intelligent legislation. Insurance was of such great importance in the everyday lives of the people, he argued, that no step to protect their interests should be neglected. He was certain that with the exception of the transportation companies no class of corporations was more in need of careful and economical regulation than those which made a business of life insurance.[18]

La Follette called the recent New York investigation a "shocking disclosure of the demoralized business integrity of the country." The policyholders of at least three of the largest companies in the country, it had been revealed, had been systematically plundered by the operations of the officers of those companies. In fairness to the home-state companies, their policyholders, and the people of Wisconsin, he said, action must be taken that would preclude a repetition of the New York episode. He recommended that a committee be appointed with authority to summon witnesses, examine books, and investigate methods of doing business. It should report its findings to the governor, who in turn would transmit the report, with his own recommendations, to the next session of the legislature.[19]

The legislature promptly appointed a joint committee to examine the activities of the life insurance companies in regard to legislative lobbies, political contributions, methods of securing business and paying commissions to agents, the nature and conditions of their investments, and the manner in which the funds, securities, and other assets were safeguarded.[20] The joint committee was organized early in January, 1906, with Senator James A. Frear as chairman and Assemblyman Herman L. Ekern as secretary. The committee employed actuaries, attorneys, and clerks to assist it in its work. One of the actuaries, Miles M. Dawson, was a nationally known insurance expert who had played an important part in the Armstrong investigation.[21]

The committee confined its general examination to three companies, none of which had been investigated by the Armstrong Committee: the Northwestern Mutual, the dominant insurance company in Wisconsin; the Wisconsin Life Insurance Company of Madison, a small domestic company doing most of its business in the state; and the Union Central Life Insurance Company of Cincinnati, a moderate-sized conservative stock company which had a large number of Wisconsin policyholders.

The committee held sixty public sessions, during which witnesses were examined and official documents studied. It also sent questionnaires to practically all the companies transacting business in the state and from their answers gathered a vast amount of information. During the entire investigation the state commissioner of insurance, Zeno M. Host, participated in the proceedings and assisted wherever possible. The committee's report incorporating its findings and recommendations was submitted to the legislature by Governor Davidson in 1907.[22]

In regard to political activity and syndicate operations, the committee gave the three companies a clean bill of health. It found no evidence that they had contributed to any campaign fund or had been active in the election of any candidate. Nor was there any evidence, with minor exceptions, of any mis-appropriation of company funds for personal gain. But in respect to the internal management of the companies, methods of electing trustees, policy contracts, loan agreements, and similar aspects of insurance work the committee uncovered many questionable practices calling for "efficient, comprehensive, conservative, remedial legislation." [23]

The committee specifically questioned the practices of the Northwestern Mutual in conducting elections and in allowing non-policyholders to hold and vote proxies in its annual elections. More than half the proxy votes cast in the 1904 election had been cast by persons who were not policyholders. The company was managed not by its policyholders, as claimed in its literature, but by a self-perpetuating oligarchy. The committee also charged that the officers of the company received excessively high salaries and practiced nepotism to the detriment of the company's business. Three relatives of president Henry L. Palmer, for example, had been placed in excellent positions without regard to their fitness or experience.[24] Like most large companies the Northwestern Mutual had profited by an excessive number of lapses and surrenders during the past ten years. In some instances, certain policyholders appeared to have been discriminated against in favor of others. In the matter of efficiency and conduct of business, the committee had no complaint. The solvency of the Northwestern Mutual, the committee emphasized, was never in question. Every class of policies examined showed that the reserves set aside by the company were in conformity with the law and sound actuarial practice.²⁵

The Union Central Life Insurance Company of Cincinnati was cited by the committee as a conservative stock company which had a highly efficient and successful investment department that other companies might imitate with profit. Although salaries of officers were excessively high and there had seemingly been discrimination against policyholders during recent depressions, the company was judged sound and well run.²⁶

If the two large companies escaped from the investigation with only minor criticism, quite the opposite was true of the Wisconsin Life Insurance Company of Madison. The committee found there a "striking condition of incompetency and mismanagement on the part of some of its principal officers." The company had been reorganized four times in its eleven years of existence; the records showed no fixed salaries for the officers of the company; and its president, Rasmus B. Anderson, editor of the Norwegian-language newspaper *Amerika,* was evidently a dummy officer who had no knowledge of the company's affairs. The entire assets of the company, including the legal reserves, were insufficient to mature and pay all outstanding policies. This company, the committee concluded, was obviously insolvent.²⁷

The committee concluded its report with a series of recommendations. In regard to political activity it favored the enactment of laws requiring all insurance companies to file reports with the insurance commissioner detailing all bills they had favored or opposed, and listing all expenses for agents, counsels, lobbyists, and literature. Rebates given by any company official should be paid out of his own pocket, not out of policyholders' funds. The financial affairs of all companies should be given greater publicity, and lists of all policyholders in mutual companies should be available on request. With respect to elections the committee recommended that proxies be abolished, opportunity be given for the nomination of non-administration candidates, and the whole ballot be prepared and distributed among the policyholders in advance. The committee made specific recommendations regarding the limitation of expenses and the total cost of premiums. These proposals were incorporated in model bills accompanying the report.[28] The committee also urged that the insurance commissioner be vested with the necessary authority to compel sound procedures and eliminate insolvent companies unable or unwilling to put their houses in order.

Both major parties, in their 1906 platforms, urged that regulatory legislation be enacted to protect both the insurance companies and the policyholders.[29] Long before the legislature assembled in January of 1907 Governor Davidson, as well as the leading members of the Assembly and Senate, began to consider proposals for specific legislation.[30] Most of the members of the joint legislative investigating committee advanced to new positions of power and responsibility with the inauguration of the new administration. James A. Frear became secretary of state, George E. Beedle was elected insurance commissioner, Herman Ekern succeeded to the speakership of the Assembly, and Julius Roehr became chairman of the joint committee on banks and insurance.[31] These men were the leaders in the enactment of the legislation passed in 1907 for the regulation of insurance companies.

The joint committee on banks and insurance sponsored a comprehensive series of measures regulating the insurance companies, but individual members of the legislature likewise introduced bills on the subject. In all, more than seventy-five insurance measures were introduced during the 1907 session. Of these, only about one-third became law.[32] As several of the committee-recommended bills failed to pass, gaps were left in the regulatory pattern which had to be filled in by subsequent legislation. Of the measures passed the more significant were as follows: Misrepresentation while soliciting new business was prohibited, existing law was strengthened, and penalties for violations were provided. Companies were forbidden to discriminate against any individuals or class of policyholders. Companies were required to publish an annual statement, showing both gains and losses. Proxies were abolished. Contributions for political purposes were forbidden, and a report on all funds spent in lobbying was required. Companies were required to suspend business when liabilities exceeded assets. Salaries of top officials were limited to twenty-five thousand dollars a year. The surplus accumulated by mutual companies was to be distributed according to definite regulations. The rules for the election of directors of domestic companies were regularized. The amount of expenses that could be incurred was limited and reports of such expenses were required. The expenses of the company were restricted to the amount set aside for that purpose, and the loading of premiums for expenses was limited to one-third of the net single premium.[33]

Most of these measures became law with little or no opposition. Some of them had the approval of both the insurance companies and the consulting actuaries, who had recommended legislation patterned after the New York laws born of the Armstrong investigation. But the proposals to regulate the election of directors, to limit expenses, and to restrict the loading for expenses to a stipulated portion of the premium (and also, in fact, limiting the total premium) aroused the opposition of all the officials, agents, and consulting actuaries representing the insurance companies. Since these regulations were accompanied by a provision making violations punishable by a fine up to five thousand dollars and a jail sentence, this would make officials liable for criminal as well as civil action. It was only after a series of close and heated battles and considerable modification that their sponsors were able to force them through the legislature.[34]

While the insurance bills were under consideration the major companies exerted great pressure on the governor and various legislators to prevent the enactment of any restrictive legislation. The Northwestern Mutual urged Davidson to veto the bills restricting premiums and expenses on the grounds that foreign companies would withdraw from the state and that neighboring states would penalize the Northwestern Mutual with retaliatory legislation.[35] Miles M. Dawson advised Davidson to veto the "Ekern legislation," which he claimed would bring disgrace on the administration. The limitation of premiums and restriction of expenses, he warned, would justify the withdrawal of the major companies and leave Wisconsin an "insurance wilderness." The governor received telegrams from twelve of the old-line companies protesting against the enactment of the restrictive bills. Other prominent companies, including the Prudential, the Metropolitan, and the Travelers, joined in the protests and many threatened to withdraw from the state if these bills became law. Despite these warnings and threats Davidson signed the controversial measures and they became part of the insurance code, scheduled to go into effect the first of the next year.[36]

The *Milwaukee Sentinel* had strongly opposed the new insurance legislation and had regularly given prominent space to the objections of the insurance officials who were lobbying against the reforms. When most of the out-of-state companies felt obliged to carry out their threats to withdraw from the state the *Sentinel* reported each announcement almost gleefully and prophesied that retaliatory laws in the Eastern states would quickly bring the "socialistic" administration at Madison to its senses.[37] *The Insurance Field,* leading trade periodical of the insurance world, also viewed the Wisconsin legislation with distaste. The editor was quite in sympathy with the companies that had announced their intention to withdraw from the state and he predicted that Wisconsin would become the "finest and ripest field for wildcat companies in the United States." Even the pro-administration *Free Press* conceded that perhaps Wisconsin had moved too fast for its own good.[38]

Twenty-four companies decided to retire from the state rather than conform to the new regulations. As they had indicated in their earlier protests the officials of these companies objected most strenuously to the limitations of premiums and expenses and the drastic penalties provided for violations.[39] For example, the general agent of the Mutual Benefit Life, Frank L. Wilson, announced that his company could not operate if the laws were enforced. It was therefore withdrawing from the state, with the hope that retaliatory legislation and chaotic insurance conditions in Wisconsin would soon force the administration to repeal the objectionable laws.[40] A common criticism was that the Wisconsin insurance department had failed to interpret clearly just what the companies could or could not do under the new laws. The laws, charged officials of the retiring companies, had puzzled the commissioner as much as they had the companies and their counsels.[41]

In marked contrast to the attitude of these companies was the position of the New York Life and other out-of-state companies which expressed their intention of remaining in Wisconsin. "If the people of Wisconsin think they are wise laws," said the general agent of the New England Mutual, "then we think so too." A spokesman for the New York Life felt that the new legislation would work no hardship on the company. Attorneys for the company agreed that the New York Life would be able to use about as much of the first year's premiums for expenses as they had done before.[42]

At the invitation of the Association of Life Insurance Presidents, Commissioner Beedle and Assembly speaker Ekern journeyed to New York early in December of 1907 to explain the Wisconsin regulations. Grover Cleveland, president of the Association, had denounced as "vicious and unreasonable" the laws some states had passed, charging that they had been inspired by the "mean political ambition of petty demagogues." The insurance presidents listened to Ekern and Beedle, who read addresses on the Wisconsin legislation and answered questions on various aspects of the new laws. It was evident, however, that most of the officers had already determined upon their own course of action, for the *New York Tribune* commented that they appeared unconvinced.[43]

In an editorial on the Wisconsin insurance laws the *New York Tribune* observed that no particular class of companies was withdrawing and no particular class was staying. Those which were withdrawing alleged that to stay would entail large unreasonable expenditures on their part and that unjust restrictions would be placed upon their methods of doing business. Other equally prominent companies anticipated no difficulty in complying with the regulations. The editor of the *Tribune* was of the opinion that the policy of the New York Life and other companies that elected to stay and give the laws a fair trial was the wiser course.[44]

In enacting so comprehensive an insurance code the Wisconsin progressives were seeking to legislate in favor of the policyholders and the public rather than the corporations. This was in keeping with the progressive philosophy that business "affected with a public interest" should be regulated for the public good. Though the passage of the Wisconsin code brought protests from most of the companies and the withdrawal from the state of more than twenty of them, the new regulations were little more severe, if at all, than those of other industrial states. The Wisconsin insurance laws were generally comparable to those of New York and were even somewhat more liberal in some details, such as the limitation of expense of premiums.[45]

The withdrawal of most of the Eastern companies left some ten out-of-state corporations and two domestic companies, the Northwestern Mutual and the Wisconsin Life, to serve the needs of Wisconsin insurance buyers.[46] The out-of-state companies that remained included some of the largest and strongest of all the Eastern companies. The New York Life, the Metropolitan Life, and the Prudential all continued to do business in the state and altered their practices to conform to the new code. The Northwestern Mutual, which had opposed several of the new regulatory laws, took a moderate view of the overall effect they would have. In an address delivered to members of the Chicago Life Underwriters Association in 1908, George H. Noyes, general counsel for the Northwestern Mutual, explained that this insurance legislation was part of a nationwide campaign to stamp out the malpractices in the management of some of the country's largest and most influential corporations. Government supervision of insurance companies had been greatly neglected in the past and the Wisconsin measures were only designed to correct that situation. Any unfair or unworkable regulations doubtless would soon be modified. He pointed to the fact that only two of some twenty-seven bills that became laws were opposed by the Northwestern Mutual and that about fifty proposals, many of them ill-advised, had been defeated in the legislature.[47]

The chief complaint of the Northwestern Mutual was that neither the Insurance Commission nor the joint investigating committee had made a detailed study of the taxation of insurance companies. The Northwestern Mutual was forced to bear an extremely heavy tax burden in Wisconsin—an average of about a thousand dollars a day, or $367,726.01 for the year 1907. In the preceding ten years the company had paid nearly three million dollars in taxes, which had of course been passed on to the policyholders. This represented a higher rate of taxation than was imposed by New York, Minnesota, Pennsylvania, and other competing states.[48]

In his annual report for 1908 Insurance Commissioner Beedle gave a comprehensive survey of the Wisconsin insurance situation as it had been affected by the new regulations and the retirement of most of the out-of-state companies. In reviewing the arguments against the new Wisconsin code he pointed out that the policyholders had not benefited from the rapid increase in expenses of policies that had taken place in the past few years. Although eighteen companies had formally protested against the law limiting these expenses, seven of them continued to do business in Wisconsin without ill effects, and Wisconsin policyholders were able to buy insurance up to $5.50 per thousand cheaper than before the law was passed. The allowance of one-third for expenses, Beedle concluded, was extremely liberal. One of the withdrawing companies had objected that the provisions requiring a statement of deferred dividend accumulations was "unnecessary, unjust, unconstitutional and misleading," but the Northwestern Mutual had for years furnished this information both to the commissioner and to its policyholders without, apparently, impairing dividends.[49]

Commissioner Beedle noted the complaint of the Northwestern Mutual against "excessive taxes." The aggregate taxes paid by this corporation in the states in which it operated amounted to $803,252, which represented a tax rate of $.00344 on assets of $232,819,246, as compared with a rate of $.01151 paid by the railroads having about the same valuation. Theoretically, Beedle thought, it would be desirable to apply the ad valorem principle to insurance taxation. Most taxes in Wisconsin, he pointed out, were based on the value of the property. The insurance companies paid much less, in proportion to their holdings, than was collected from other property. But to put them on the ad valorem basis would invite retaliatory taxes against domestic companies, all of which were opposed to any action that would threaten their position in other states. In fact, the Northwestern had lobbied successfully in the 1907 legislature for the repeal of an act extending the three per cent premium tax to foreign companies. This act, passed in

1905 and scheduled to go into effect in 1908, would have cost the Northwestern Mutual an estimated three hundred thousand dollars a year in retaliatory taxes.[50] As a result the out-of-state companies continued to pay only nominal taxes in Wisconsin and the Northwestern Mutual profited from the reciprocal provisions of the law in other states.

The withdrawal from the state of most of the Eastern companies worked to the advantage of the companies that remained. The New York Life, which had suffered a slump in Wisconsin business in 1906 and 1907, wrote new policies amounting to almost two million dollars in 1909 and to more than three and a half million in 1912. The Metropolitan Life and the Prudential competed vigorously in the new field of industrial insurance and showed gains in the ordinary life field comparable to those of the New York Life. But by far the greatest advance was made by the Northwestern Mutual, whose new business in the state had leveled off in 1907 to about six million dollars a year. After the withdrawal of the twenty-four Eastern companies the Northwestern Mutual's new business jumped to more than eight million in 1909, nine and a half million in 1910, and thirteen and three-quarter million in 1912.[51]

Such a field of golden opportunity was too inviting to be left to a few great companies. Four new domestic companies were organized and did a substantial business. The Wisconsin Life reorganized in line with the directives of the commissioner of insurance and became a prosperous and reliable firm. Contrary to the hopes and expectations of the companies that had withdrawn from the state, the new insurance laws proved to be neither abortive nor unworkable. The state's revenues from life insurance taxes did not suffer the slump which had been forecast. After a slight decline in 1908 the tax receipts climbed again the next year to a figure above the 1907 level of $426,500. They continued to increase substantially every year and by 1914 exceeded $800,000. The rate of increase of tax receipts in the five years following the inauguration of the regulatory code was more than twice that of the five years preceding 1907. It was evident that there was no decline in the insurance business in Wisconsin; the policies simply were written by fewer companies.[52]

Far from relaxing the insurance code, the legislature constantly sought to strengthen the laws and to plug loopholes as soon as they appeared. The new laws of 1911 were largely of a technical nature, making no change in general policy. The 1907 regulations had prohibited the organization or admission of any new assessment life insurance companies. Finally, in 1911, the legislature ordered the valuation of the existing associations and the apportionment of their credits among the members. As a result all the remaining assessment companies either disbanded or withdrew from the state.[53]

In 1911 Herman L. Ekern, who as speaker of the Assembly had played a leading role in the enactment of the 1907 regulations, was elected insurance commissioner to succeed George Beedle. The legislature of that year, in an effort to make the post more highly professional, changed the status of the office from elective to appointive. Governor McGovern promptly reappointed Ekern, who continued to serve as commissioner of insurance until 1915.[54]

In a comprehensive review of life insurance in Wisconsin which Ekern presented in 1915 he pointed with pride to the successful application of the Wisconsin insurance code. No company organized in Wisconsin under the laws of 1907 had discontinued operation, and conditions surrounding the business of insurance were steadily improving. In regard to methods of solicitation, low premiums, and treatment of the policyholder, conditions were perhaps as good in Wisconsin as anywhere in the United States. Ekern also assumed credit for the belated abolition of the old three per cent premium tax paid by the domestic companies. Since it was impractical to impose

this tax upon companies from other states, it had resulted in
marked discrimination against the local companies. The legislature of 1915 had at last followed the recommendations of the
insurance commissioner and repealed the old statutes of 1899
and 1901 and placed domestic taxes on the basis of investments
alone. Ekern estimated that this act reduced the taxes of the
companies affected by about twenty per cent.[55]

This revision of tax policy met, in large measure, the arguments of the Northwestern Mutual officials, who since 1899 had
advocated a more moderate principle of taxation based on
investments rather than on premiums or total assets. As the
chief beneficiary of the new law, the Northwestern Mutual
saved about a hundred thousand dollars in taxes the first year.
This shift in the Wisconsin tax pattern removed a serious
discrimination against the Northwestern Mutual and enabled
it to compete with other companies, both in Wisconsin and in
other states, on even more favorable terms than before.[56]

The legislature of 1915 amended the insurance code to define
more specifically the limitation of expenses in premiums. The
change was little more than a gesture toward the companies
that had withdrawn in 1908, but it distinctly wrote into the
law, and hence made them defensible in the courts, the interpretations the commissioner of insurance had followed since 1907.
The Insurance Field voiced its approval of the changed wording
and predicted that it would enable the Eastern companies to
return to the state. The Mutual Life was the first to seize the
opportunity and announced that it would resume business in
Wisconsin immediately. The other leading companies followed
in short order. By the end of 1916 five of them had been read-
mitted and the others returned within a few years.[57]

During the period of the progressive regime the administra-
tion embarked on two adventures in state-sponsored insurance.
In 1903, in response to the recommendation of Governor La
Follette, a State Insurance Fund was created for the purpose

of insuring all state property against fire and other damage. The capitol fire of 1904, which occurred shortly after the inauguration of the plan, brought down a storm of criticism on the administration for leaving state property uninsured by commercial companies. The insurance fund borrowed from the general fund to meet the emergency and despite the condemnation was continued and augmented. The state insurance act was later amended to permit counties, cities, school districts, and library boards to insure the property under their control with the State Fund. This extension of the plan would, the commissioner of insurance estimated, enable 'he subsidiary units of government to effect a saving of approximately twenty-five per cent on the cost of insurance. The State Insurance Fund, which has been continued without major change since 1913, has proved to be actuarily sound and has resulted in a great saving to the state.[58]

In establishing the State Life Fund the progressives of Wisconsin borrowed one of the platform planks of the Social Democrats, who had been urging government insurance for years. The Fund stemmed directly out of the investigation of the Joint Committee on Life Insurance, which made a favorable report on the project in connection with its general investigation. Other groups, too, had studied the question, and interest was stimulated by the investigations of Professor John R. Commons and his associates into the possibility of a state system of workmen's compensation.[59]

After further study the legislature of 1911 set up the State Life Fund. The act provided that policies might be issued to residents or citizens of the state between the ages of twenty and fifty in multiples of five hundred dollars up to a maximum of three thousand dollars. It provided for medical examinations, loan and surrender values of policies, and annuity policies for those who desired them. The contemplated goal of the measure, explained Commissioner Ekern, was to provide "guaranteed insurance at cost, plus a slight contribution to the surplus." [60]

This experiment in government insurance attracted attention throughout the country. The insurance industry, not unnaturally, took a dim view of this incursion into its domain. *The Insurance Field* expressed regret that the state seemed determined to enter a field which fraternal and legal-reserve companies were better equipped to handle and predicted that insurance companies would be "amused" by it. The *Outlook*, on the other hand, viewed the experiment in state life insurance with comparative favor; it published a letter praising the plan and reported that Iowa was considering a similar one. [61]

Since the State Life Fund solicited no business and paid no agents, it was able to insure its policyholders more cheaply than the commercial companies. Its premium on a thousand-dollar twenty-year endowment policy, for example, was $43.83 as compared with $48.86 in the Northwestern Mutual and $49.33 in the New York Life. Its dividend rate was only slightly less than that of the Northwestern Mutual, and, alone of the insurance agencies, it allowed a cash or loan value on a policy during the first year it was in force. [62] Despite its low cost, however, State Life Fund insurance has never proved popular with the citizens of Wisconsin. Inasmuch as the prospective policyholder must take the initiative in applying for insurance and must conduct the entire transaction by mail, the Fund is not much publicized, and even today, after forty years of operation, its existence is unknown to a large proportion of the state's residents. But the importance of the State Life Fund does not lie alone in the number of policies it has in force. It constitutes a yardstick by which the commissioner of insurance and the legislature can evaluate the charges levied by the commercial companies. In other words, it provides a measure of what insurance, under the most favorable conditions, should cost. [63]

Thanks to the work of the Armstrong Committee, the joint committee of the Wisconsin legislature, and similarly constituted committees in other states, most of the abuses that were so general in the insurance industry at the turn of the century were remedied. Such practices as the unbridled competition for new business, the discrimination against policyholders, and the excursions of insurance companies into other fields of industry disappeared, and the responsibility of the insurance business to its policyholders and the public in general became generally recognized. In all this reformation of the insurance industry the Wisconsin progressives played a substantial part. Though the regulations they put on Wisconsin's statute books in 1907 were at the time characterized as radical and socialistic, succeeding years brought a general acceptance of the principles underlying that legislation. In less than a decade the companies that had withdrawn from the state so hastily were back, prepared to accept the Wisconsin code without major modifications.

The state's responsibility for the regulation of the insurance industry was part of the fundamental progressive philosophy of government, as was the regulation of the railroads and public utilities. The dire predictions that the public and the insurance business would be severely handicapped by the legislation of 1907 were not fulfilled. Instead it appears that the state, the policyholders, and the insurance companies have all thrived under the Wisconsin code.[64]

9 THE STATE AND THE UNIVERSITY

★　★　★　★　★　★　★　★　★　★　★　★　★　★　★　★　★

IN ALL THE STATES CARVED OUT OF THE ORIGINAL NATIONAL domain the state university has been closely identified with the parent commonwealth. This has been especially true of the University of Wisconsin. Born in the year of statehood, it steadily kept step with the growth of Wisconsin from a frontier region to a populous agricultural and industrial state. Situated in the capitol city, it was constantly under the scrutiny of the lawmakers and administrative officials, who, after an early period of indifference, were far from niggardly in their support of the institution at the other end of State Street. The University in turn, through its faculty and staff, accepted the responsibilities of this relationship and consciously organized the colleges of letters and science, law, and engineering with a view to the needs of the commonwealth.[1]

Of even greater service to the state has been the well-supported College of Agriculture. Here, under the leadership of Dean William A. Henry, Stephen M. Babcock, and others, a whole series of inventions, discoveries, and new techniques revolutionized dairy farming in the state. Before the turn of the century Dean Henry declared that just one of these discoveries had returned "annually to our people the whole cost of their Agricultural College."[2]

This relationship of the state and its university became even more friendly with the advent of the progressives under Robert M. La Follette. The interchange of ideas flowed more freely between Bascom Hall and the capitol, and the number of

University-trained young men in state service multiplied. The financial support given by the progressive legislature enabled the University to grow into a great institution of national and international reputation.

La Follette's personal relations with the faculty and student body were excellent. His own triumphs as a collegiate orator gave him a bond of kinship with the members of the various teams on the campus which he never lost. In the desperate struggle in the "Gymnasium Convention" of 1904 against the stalwart faction, University athletes formed a "riot squad," which stood ready to repel any strong-arm action by the stalwarts' followers and insure the successful organization of the state convention by the progressives. University students constituted a sizable portion of the crowd that jammed the spectator section and applauded the progressives as they beat down every conservative challenge and protest.[3]

La Follette was the first graduate of the University of Wisconsin to become governor of the state. As a student he had been profoundly impressed by the personality and example of President John Bascom. He absorbed Bascom's sense of moral and ethical values and his attitudes toward public affairs, especially the idea of devotion and service to the state. In later life he publicly attributed all that he had achieved to the inspiration he had received at the University.[4]

La Follette accepted without question the doctrine that "the purpose of the University was to serve the people," and he fostered its growth and expansion in every possible way. Under him and his successors the state government and the University were so closely allied that the latter became for a time an integral part of the progressive movement to reform the state's political and economic life.

As governor La Follette worked to advance this goal. By his own account, he "sought the constant advice and service of the trained men of the institution" in dealing with the difficult and complex problems confronting the state. He extolled the personal and mutually helpful relations that existed between the administration and the University, and frequently called in for conferences President Van Hise and Professor Richard T. Ely, John R. Commons, Paul S. Reinsch, Edward A. Ross, and others. He also organized the Saturday Lunch Club, which met regularly during the legislative sessions. Here he and some of the state officials met with the various members of the faculty to discuss on a direct and friendly basis the problems they had in common. Many progressive projects had their inception at this luncheon table. La Follette constantly urged the necessity of expanding the facilities and services of the University. "The state will not have discharged its duty to the University," he insisted, "nor the University fulfilled its mission to the people until adequate means have been furnished to every young man and woman in the State to acquire an education at home in every department of learning." [5]

Scholarship and the advancement of learning had been actively promoted in Wisconsin well before the progressive era. Presidents Bascom, Thomas C. Chamberlin, and Charles Kendall Adams, in particular, looked forward to the day when Wisconsin would take its place in the first rank of American universities. Each of them in turn had labored to improve its physical plant, augment its faculty, and broaden the scope of the curriculum. During Adams' presidency the new school of Economics, Political Science, and History had been established under the direction of Richard T. Ely, who had already gained recognition as head of the department of political economy at Johns Hopkins University. During the next decade Ely and historians Frederick Jackson Turner and Charles Homer Haskins, who were rapidly growing famous, lured graduate students in ever-increasing numbers from out-of-state circles.

The Adams administration also saw the testing of academic freedom at the sensational Ely trial in 1894. Here, as a result of a direct and open attack on Ely by the state superintendent of public instruction, Oliver E. Wells, the Board of Regents undertook a formal trial of the liberal-minded professor. The result was a complete vindication of Ely and the broad principle of academic freedom. The effort to establish state control and censorship over the subject matter taught at Wisconsin was specifically and completely repudiated. The regents' report on this affair was widely quoted and came to be regarded as a sort of Wisconsin Magna Charta. The eloquent declaration that constitutes the closing paragraph, including the famous "sifting and winnowing" phrase of President Adams, was later cast in bronze and placed at the entrance of Bascom Hall. There it has remained, the guiding star of the University; and no subsequent Board of Regents has had the hardihood to retract it.[6]

The tie between the institutions at the opposite ends of State Street was still further strengthened by the election in 1903 of Charles R. Van Hise as president of the University. It was more than a coincidence that the regents selected a personal friend of La Follette's, his classmate in the class of '79 and thus also a son of the University. Van Hise had a national reputation as a geologist and was an authority on forest reserves and the conservation of natural resources. He was also known as a friend of the progressive movement. Like La Follette he had come under the influence of John Bascom as an undergraduate and was eager to commit the University still further to the service of the state. He felt that the University should carry to the people whatever knowledge they could assimilate for their betterment along all lines. The only criterion should be whether the University was the "best fitted instrument" for the work. The investiture of Van Hise as president was the occasion for a Golden Jubilee, which was attended by many leading scholars from sister universities in America and distinguished representatives from Europe.[7]

In his inaugural address, which was a high point in the cele-
bration, Van Hise boldly called for vigorous expansion of
the University's activities along all lines of human endeavor. The
new president visualized an institution that would enable its sons
and daughters to pursue the study of any subject until they
themselves could contribute to it. Both then and later Van Hise
kept before the public the goal of a great university of national
reputation. He stressed that it should "develop, expand [and]
strengthen creative work at whatever cost." The opportunity to
work toward a great graduate school, he pointed out, was
unusually favorable at Wisconsin, where important beginnings
had already been made and all the colleges were on the same campus. He urged his colleagues to go on to higher goals until a
"university is built as broad as human endeavor, as high as
human aspiration." [8]

On the relationship of the University and the state Van Hise
noted the examples set in Germany and Austria, where "almost
every prominent professor" was an official adviser to the government. He saw in the University the agency, above all others, for
promoting the well-being of the state and urged that the administration make use of the faculty's special knowledge to solve its
practical and technical problems. "I am not willing to admit,"
Van Hise concluded, "that a state university under a democracy
shall be of lower grade than a state university under a mon-
archy." [9]

Increasingly, as the years passed, Van Hise urged the extension of the benefits of the University to all the people of the
state, through whatever channels might be suitable and in whatever fields they might find profitable. Van Hise was not only a
scholar and an administrator, but he was also a salesman. He
sought constantly to convince the people of Wisconsin that
state appropriations for the University had been "investments
which have been returned manyfold and will continue to be
returned in the future in even larger measure." He pledged

CHARLES R. VAN HISE

BALTHASAR H. MEYER

JOHN R. COMMONS

CHARLES MCCARTHY

Scholars in the Progressive Movement

Nils P. Haugen, Wisconsin Tax Commissioner 1901–1921

that the University would be "at the service of the state" and would "assist in carrying knowledge to the people" wherever they might be. This conviction was an integral part of his conception of the role of a state university in a democracy.[10]

As a result service to the state became a part of the established creed of the University. To be sure, this was not a reversal of policy but simply an expansion of an already established trend. Under Van Hise the idea of service became more explicitly an avowed part of the University's program. Between La Follette and his classmate there was cordial cooperation, and the governor frequently took occasion to laud the contribution the University was making in many fields. "In no state of the Union," La Follette observed in his autobiography, "are the relationships between the university and the people of the State so intimate and so mutually helpful as in Wisconsin. We believe there that the purpose of the university is to serve the people and every effort is made . . . to bring every resident of the state under the broadening and inspiring influence of a faculty of trained men." [11]

This service to the people of the state took many forms. Extension work, which had flourished at the University during the regime of President Chamberlin, had begun to languish at the turn of the century and by the time of Van Hise's presidency had almost ceased to exist.[12] Early in his administration Van Hise became committed to the expansion of the extension system as the agency to carry the University to the people. Legislative reference librarian Charles McCarthy, after conducting a survey of private correspondence schools, stated that the University had "facilities more ample" in every way and urged that steps be taken to develop its correspondence courses.[13] Once Van Hise had been converted to the extension program, he sought the best man available to administer the work. He persuaded Louis E. Reber, dean of the College of Engineering at Pennsylvania State College, to come to Wisconsin as director of the University's extension program. It was Reber who built the extension department into an effective statewide organization. By 1915 it had grown into an impressive group of co-ordinated branches: correspondence, lectures, debating and public discussion, and general information and welfare. Whatever the people wanted or could use, Dean Reber favored bringing to their doorstep, whether it was philosophy or sanitation, literature or labor relations. The activities of the extension division ran into the dozens, the courses offered numbering more than one hundred.[14]

Legislative appropriations to support the extension program kept pace with its growth. From $20,000 in 1907, the first year of Reber's administration, the fund rose to $214,525 in 1914. The program attracted attention throughout the nation, and numerous articles appeared in leading periodicals commenting favorably on the extension work. One writer extolled the system as meaning "better jobs, more pay and more intelligent work" for those participating. The extension division, she continued, aimed to create in all the people a "sense of their educational need and to satisfy that need." [15]

In the field of agriculture the University's record of cooperation with the state was even more impressive. As early as 1885 an Agriculture Short Course had been established by the Board of Regents, and the legislature had made provision for a series of annual farmer-institutes. Despite the dwindling interest in other phases of extension work, both the Short Course and the institutes had prospered and made steady progress. Frederick Jackson Turner, in discussing the University's extension program in 1893, credited these agencies with much of the progress the state had made in dairy farming, horticulture, and stock raising.[16] Under the progressive regime the funds for these activities were slowly but steadily increased, from $13,000 in 1900 to $20,000 in 1911. At the same time the scope of the courses was expanded to increase their appeal to more varied groups of the farm population. In 1903, for example, more than seven hundred farmers and farmers' wives (all over twenty-five) were enrolled in special short courses where the training was not bookish but consisted chiefly of demonstrations bearing on one subject which was taught intensively. The list of accomplishments of the College of Agriculture ranged all the way from scientific inventions and discoveries of insecticides to more businesslike bookkeeping procedures for the farm operator. The great revolution that took place in dairying and farming methods could be traced directly to the activities of the University.[17]

Throughout the progressive era the University also played a considerable role in the organization and coordination of the program of vocational and industrial education which the state put into operation in 1911. President Van Hise and Dean Reber had been active in the conferences and surveys that were the basis of the report of the Commission on Vocational Education. As a result of this report the legislature enacted a law setting up a State Board of Vocational Education. It was not directly under University control, but both the dean of the Extension Division and the dean of the College of Engineering were ex-officio members of its governing board. This program grew rapidly and offered a much-needed type of educational opportunity to Wisconsin youths who had already entered industry.[18]

These multifarious activities of the University spread general and special learning to every corner of the state. As Lincoln Steffens glowingly reported, Wisconsin had become "a realization of the idea of a university as a place where anybody can learn anything." And, he added, "anywhere." Leading periodicals published articles describing the popular aspects of Wisconsin's program, and several delegations came from other states to view it. One editor attributed the political experiments Wisconsin was making to the widespread activities of the University. Much of this praise may be discounted as the enthusiastic exaggerations of interested partisans, but the progress Van Hise made toward realization of his goal of "service to the state" was a significant achievement. Edward E. Slosson, writing in 1910, paid high tribute when he said, "It is impossible to determine the size and location of the University of Wisconsin. The headquarters of the institution is at the city of Madison and the campus has an area of about 56,000 square miles." [19]

This great growth of the functions and services of the University entailed a corresponding expansion of the operating budget and physical plant. With the same boldness and optimism that he had urged the University to extend its work in all fields, President Van Hise called upon the legislature to provide the "liberal support" that would enable the institution to become a great university of the first rank.[20]

During much of its history the University had been supported by a mill tax. This flexible support had been steadily augmented until by 1895 it totaled seventeen-fortieths of a mill for each dollar of assessed evaluation of the general property in the state. Many legislators had deemed this excessive and in 1899 the legislature repealed all mill levies for the University and replaced them with biennial appropriations from the general funds. Efforts to recover the mill tax failed in the sessions of 1901 and 1903, but Van Hise, on assuming the presidency, at once renewed the struggle. In his first report to the regents he urged that such a program would not only assure a steady income for the University but would expand with the prosperity of the state. In response to his pressure the last La Follette legislature enacted in 1905 a new mill levy of two-sevenths of a mill.[21]

The restored mill tax steadily increased the revenues of the University, since the state was experiencing an industrial boom. In addition to this assured income the University was granted separate appropriations for special purposes, such as the establishment of a medical school in 1907. The total receipts of the University rose from slightly more than six hundred thousand dollars in 1902–03 to more than three million in 1913–14. During the same period the enrollment had only a little more than doubled, increasing from 2,870 to 6,765.[22]

In the report he made to the regents in 1910 Van Hise presented a bold building program calling for the expenditure of almost a million dollars for buildings, another million for dormitories, and an addition to the State Historical Society building, which was housing both its own library and that of the University.[23] Such a program of physical expansion was already well under way, and by the close of his regime Van Hise had largely rebuilt the University's physical plant. In the fifteen years he served as president, Van Hise was instrumental in the construction of more than fifty structures at a cost of $2,384,480, almost as much as had been spent for construction during all previous administrations.[24]

Van Hise had a second valiant ally in his fight for a greater university in Governor Francis E. McGovern. The expansion program had continued uninterrupted during the governorship of James O. Davidson, but the close personal friendship which had existed between the University president and La Follette was lacking. McGovern, however, was also a son of the University—the second graduate to serve as governor—and a warm personal friend of Van Hise's. He gave almost unqualified support to the president's program of expansion. During his administration the University received generous appropriations, although the legislators exhibited an increasing disposition to earmark all funds for specific purposes and thus decrease the discretionary powers of the regents and the president. Nevertheless Van Hise, with the support of three successive progressive governors, had doubled the enrollment and the physical plant of the University while multiplying many times its facilities and offerings. The University's growth at this crucial time enabled it to fulfill its early promise and emerge as one of the great state universities of the country.[25]

Perhaps the most dramatic of the activities of the University during the progressive era was the participation of its faculty and staff in the public affairs of the state. In retrospect La Follette declared that "in order to bring all the reserves of knowledge and inspiration of the University more fully to the people," he had made it a policy "to appoint experts from the University wherever possible upon the important boards of the state." Van Hise, in his inaugural address, urged the state to follow the German example and make use of the special knowledge of the University faculty in solving the problems of government. As he frequently remarked in his public addresses, his aim was to make the University "the instrument of the state in its upbuilding." [26]

In view of the nature of the reform legislation enacted by the progressives it was only logical that University personnel should be asked for technical assistance. The tax reforms and the regulation of railroads presented problems in mathematics and economics rather than politics. The organization and administration of the Industrial Commission called for the services of persons trained in labor relations, statistics, and sociology. The primary election law and the civil service legislation were practical adaptations of basic principles being taught by political scientists.

In the solution of all these problems the University played an important part. La Follette later observed that it would be difficult to "overestimate the part which the University had played in the Wisconsin Revolution."

A great number of persons served both state and University in some significant capacity, either simultaneously or successively. Charles McCarthy listed forty-six people who were serving both the University and the state in 1911. In a popular article published in 1909 Lincoln Steffens stated that forty-one

professors were serving in sixty-six state offices. President Van
Hise led by virtue of his membership on five different boards.[27]

Even a casual study of the most representative reform agencies instituted by the progressives reveals how significant a part
the University faculty played in their organization and administration. Balthasar H. Meyer, professor of economics, served for
six years as the first chairman of the Railroad Commission before resigning to accept a similar position with the Interstate
Commerce Commission. Thomas S. Adams served as a member
of the Tax Commission without relinquishing his teaching duties in the department of political economy. The staff of expert
engineers who served both the Railroad Commission and the
Tax Commission included Professors William D. Pence, who
served as chief engineer, John G. D. Mack, and Halsten J.
Thorkelson, all of the University College of Engineering. Professor John R. Commons and Charles McCarthy largely drafted
the law setting up the Civil Service Commission, and Professor
Samuel Sparling of the political science department served as
its first chairman. Commons also helped conduct investigations
for the Industrial Commission, assisted in drafting the technical
portions of the bill which were designed to meet the requirements of previous court rulings, and served as a member of the
commission during its first years. Both Frederick E. Turneaure,
dean of the College of Engineering, and William O. Hotchkiss,
instructor in geology, were logical choices for the new Highway Commission which was set up in 1912 and which expanded
rapidly in the years following. President Van Hise and Dean
Edward A. Birge were active members of both the State Board
of Forestry and the Conservation Commission. Indeed there is
hardly a phase of the progressive movement in Wisconsin in
which one or more members of the University faculty did not
perform some significant function or serve in some important
capacity.[28]

Other faculty men rendered technical and professional advice on specific occasions. Professors Richard Ely, Paul Reinsch, Frederick Jackson Turner, and Edward A. Ross and various members of the medical staff all contributed ideas and advice in their special fields. The interchange of information between the institutions at the opposite ends of State Street seemed to be mutual, continuing, and often quite informal. The influence this association had upon the social and economic philosophy of such young progressives as Herman Ekern, Irvine Lenroot, John J. Blaine, John M. Nelson, and William T. Evjue can only be surmised. The University in turn was profoundly affected by the social and economic reforms of the progressive movement. State officers such as reference chief Charles McCarthy and chief forester Edward M. Griffith lectured at the University without additional compensation. The influence of the Wisconsin scene upon the thinking of the faculty can be illustrated by Frederick Jackson Turner's generalizations on the influence of the midwestern state university upon the rapidly changing pace of American life.[29]

Of all the projects resulting from the close association of the University with the state administration, none was of more lasting influence than the Legislative Reference Library, which came to be linked in the popular mind with the University. The only connection between the two institutions, however, was one of spirit, the Legislative Reference Library being a quite independent state agency of entirely separate origin. This unique institution was an outgrowth of the Free Library Commission, which had been established in 1895. The membership of this commission, largely ex-officio, consisted of the president of the University, the state superintendent of public instruction, the superintendent of the State Historical Society, and two members appointed by the governor. Under the efficient administration of its first secretary, Frank A. Hutchins, the commission stimulated a statewide growth of public libraries, developed traveling libraries with great success, and coordinated the work of the University in training librarians with the demands of the libraries in the state. These achievements brought prestige to the commission, and it became a permanent part of the state's board and commission system.[30]

When the new building of the State Historical Society was completed in 1900 and its library removed from the capitol, the legislators were left without reference materials to consult in drafting legislation. To fill this need the legislature of 1901 authorized the Free Library Commission to establish and maintain in the state capitol a working library for the use of the legislature. It was to be as complete as practicable and include all the important public documents of Wisconsin and other states as well as the standard works of reference. To take charge of this "Department of State Documents" the commission appointed Charles McCarthy.[31]

McCarthy was one of those gifted mortals who are capable of creating a man-sized job for themselves where no job at all previously exists. He was an ardent champion of causes, and his boundless enthusiasm and personal influence made him a significant factor in the passage of much of the progressive legislation of his day. McCarthy had come up the hard way. After working his way through Brown University he had come to Wisconsin to take graduate work in history and political science under Frederick Jackson Turner, Charles Homer Haskins, Paul S. Reinsch, and others. Here in 1901 after the usual years of study he received his doctorate. He had been a capable student and the recipient of several honors, yet his professors hesitated to recommend him for either an academic career or the diplomatic service. His forthrightness, indifference to tradition and custom, and a ruggedness and lack of polish in speech seemed incongruous in these more formal callings.[32] Fortunately for both McCarthy and the state the position under the Free Library Commission became available. With typical energy he built the Department of State Documents into the first true

Legislative Reference Library in the United States and, incidentally, gained a widespread reputation as one of the foremost legislative consultants in the country. For his success he himself gave chief credit to the University of Wisconsin: "I, a wandering student, seeking knowledge, came knocking at the gates of the great University of Wisconsin, and it took me in, filled me with inspiration, and when I had left its doors, the kindly people of the state stretched out welcoming hands and gave me a man's work to do." [33]

The "man's work" did not become apparent immediately. In creating the reference library the legislature provided only fifteen hundred dollars for the first year's service. McCarthy was listed on the payroll as a "document cataloguer" at a modest salary. But he was not content simply to supervise general reference materials for the legislators. He collected all the available information on the two burning issues of the day, primary elections and railroad taxation. He indexed all the bills proposed in the previous session of the legislature and procured copies of similar bills that had been introduced in neighboring states. He set up a clipping bureau so that the information on a given subject would be immediately available. After the 1902 elections he sent a circular letter to members of the legislature inquiring how he could assist them in the coming session and urging them to call upon the Legislative Reference Library for any service it could render. He offered to gather information on any subject and make it available in concise form. More than a hundred requests poured in at once, and when the lawmakers assembled they found McCarthy ready and eager to help them. In fact, he would go into the corridors and invite the legislators to inspect the library and make use of its facilities. Before long he and his assistants were helping the members of the legislature draft their bills, and a "bill-drafting department" was established in a room set aside for this service.[34]

McCarthy was careful to insist, both in public and in private, that the services of the drafting department were technical and clerical in character. He sought to avoid the charge that he was drawing up legislation on his own responsibility or imposing his ideas upon the legislators. To safeguard himself against such accusations he posted and enforced a series of rules for the guidance of his drafting-room assistants:

No bills will be drafted in the Reference Room. A separate Drafting Room and a separate force have been provided. No bill will be drafted, nor amendments prepared, without specific detailed written instructions from a member of the legislature. Such instructions must bear the member's signature. The draftsman can make no suggestions as to the contents of the bills. Our work is merely clerical and technical. We cannot furnish ideas. We are not responsible for the legality or constitutionality of any measures. We are here to do merely as directed. As this department cannot introduce bills or modify them after introduction, it is not responsible for the rules of the legislature or the numbering of sections either at the time of introduction or on the final passage.[35]

Much of the progressive legislation of La Follette's administration was drafted in the Legislative Reference Library. Until 1907 no special appropriation was made for the bill-drafting service, but in that year the legislature, taking cognizance of the growth of the library's functions, boosted the annual appropriation to fifteen thousand dollars and gave McCarthy the title of "Chief, Legislative Reference." Throughout the remainder of the progressive era McCarthy and the Legislative Reference Library continued to play an important role in the planning and drafting of the social and economic legislation passed during the administrations of Governors Davidson and McGovern. McCarthy also served on various commissions and took part in the inner councils of the progressive organization.[36]

La Follette, too, spoke and wrote highly of McCarthy's contributions, but he evidently did not consider the brawny Irishman one of his intimate associates. When he made use of McCarthy and the legislative reference service, which was often, he apparently did so through intermediaries. The drafting of the bill setting up the civil service system illustrates the general procedure and La Follette's rather indirect methods.

After "Fighting Bob" was re-elected in the bitterly contested campaign of 1904 he sought to carry his demand for efficient state administration to its logical conclusion by enacting a sweeping civil service act. For the details of such a bill he turned to John R. Commons, University professor of economics and recognized authority on labor relations, and requested him to draw up a comprehensive measure. Commons at once called on McCarthy and the Legislative Reference Library and before long he was provided with "everything that one would need" for the purpose. McCarthy collected the existing laws and pending bills of other states, material on the federal government's experience with the national civil service law, pamphlets and articles on the subject, and bills previously introduced in the Wisconsin legislature. All these were assembled and condensed so that Commons and his assistants could find what they wanted in a minimum of time. In a matter of weeks, with the help of McCarthy, Professor Commons was able to produce a civil service bill which even its critics conceded was well drawn.[37]

McCarthy made the Legislative Reference Library available to all government officials. He was willing to frame a bill on any subject for any legislator. In 1913 he even drafted for a conservative Republican member a bill to abolish the Legislative Reference Library itself. The bill was laughed out of existence and its author twitted unmercifully when it was discovered that it had been prepared in McCarthy's drafting room.[38]

Despite the precautions McCarthy had taken it was inevitable that he and the Legislative Reference Library should be charged with exerting undue influence over the process of lawmaking. Opponents dubbed his office a "bill factory" and branded him a "super lobbyist." Professor Commons, in an article written for the *Review of Reviews,* examined some of the charges. The

Legislative Reference Library was in fact, he said, a "bill factory." But it was one operated by the state, not private interests. Whereas in the past lawmakers had gone to interested lawyers to frame their bills, they now went to a "legislative expert" who was much better equipped to meet their needs. McCarthy's conscientious enforcement of the "drafting room rules" and the file of signed requests for bills which he kept went far to refute such charges against him.[39]

The success of the Legislative Reference Library soon prompted other states to inquire about its organization and to send representatives to Madison to study it at first-hand. Evidently they were impressed with what they saw, for legislative reference libraries were established in increasing numbers. California, which began its library in 1905, borrowed not only the idea and plan but hired McCarthy's assistant, Ernest Bruncken, to supervise it for them. By 1910 fifteen states had copied the Wisconsin system, and legislation had been introduced, pushed by John M. Nelson of Wisconsin, to establish a similar service for the federal lawmakers. Most of these new positions were filled by men who had worked in the Wisconsin Reference Library or been trained in legislative reference work at the Wisconsin Library School, a branch of the University. McCarthy, preferring to remain in Wisconsin, declined a proffered position in the new federal reference service.[40]

The defeat of the progressives in 1914 brought an avowedly hostile governor into power. Emanuel Philipp had campaigned against both the University and the Legislative Reference Library. The increased taxation, the Wisconsin system of regulatory commissions, and the interest of the state in social and labor legislation were all charged to the genius of McCarthy. As soon as the legislature of 1915 convened a bill was introduced to strip the library of most of its functions and discharge its director. In the hearings on the bill McCarthy defended both himself and the reference service with great vigor and effectiveness. He pointed out that the library had acquired great prestige in other states and had been widely praised for its contributions to the scientific drafting of Wisconsin's laws. He hotly denied that he had exerted undue influence over any lawmakers or had written his own views into any proposed legislation. The result was that all efforts to weaken the Legislative Reference Library or to discharge its director came to naught, and McCarthy emerged from the struggle stronger than ever. As time passed, Governor Philipp, whom even his severest critics conceded to be an able and honest man, came to recognize the worth of the "bill factory." He even became a warm personal admirer of McCarthy and sought his advice on many occasions.[41]

No further efforts were made to cripple the Legislative Reference Service or to muzzle its chief. Appropriations remained at their former level or were increased during wartime to meet rising costs. McCarthy continued as chief of the reference service until shortly before his death in 1921. Throughout Philipp's administration the "bill factory" continued to function effectively and to draft administration measures for conservatives as expertly and efficiently as it had done for the progressives. This portion of "The Wisconsin Idea" has remained a permanent part of present-day legislative machinery.

The increasingly important influence of the University extended to all branches of state government. The number of college and university graduates in public service steadily increased until it reached, during McGovern's administration, a high point that was not to be equaled again for almost twenty years. A comparison of the personnel of the state legislature in 1901 and in 1913 illustrates the extent of this shift from non-college to college-trained government officials. In 1901 the Senate included fourteen college-trained men as against nineteen without college training, and the Assembly twenty and eighty, respectively. Twelve years later the Senate boasted twenty college-trained men and the Assembly thirty-three. In the Wisconsin congressional delegation and the executive branch of the state government the proportional increase of college-trained personnel was equally significant. The fact that two of the three governors of the progressive era were graduates of the University did much to foster cordial and intimate relations between the University and other departments of the state government. At the same time the opportunity for college-trained young men to enter useful public service tended to become identified with the progressive cause.[42]

The part that the University of Wisconsin played in the public affairs of the state attracted the attention of the entire country. There was hardly a popular American magazine that did not devote at least one article to the Wisconsin experiment and its relation to the University. William Hard glowingly reported in the *Outlook* that the influence of the University covered a wide area, from "civil service to stallions." Frank Stockbridge called it "a University that runs a state," an institution that had "applied the scientific method to legislation." In an article for *La Follette's Magazine* Lincoln Steffens rated Wisconsin higher in "political intelligence" than most other areas of the United States. He credited the successful outcome of the drive for "representative government" to the University, which had played a major part in the "democratization of knowledge" and been instrumental in the development of a "community brain" in Wisconsin.[43]

Of more lasting influence than any of these popular writings was the volume published in 1912 by the arch apostle of "The Wisconsin Idea," Charles McCarthy. It seems altogether fitting that this book, which supplied an epithet for the progressive movement in Wisconsin, should have reached the public at the high tide of progressive success, in the "Progressive Year." McCarthy's *The Wisconsin Idea* is essentially a declaration of faith in the democratic process. In it he describes how the major progressive reforms were accomplished by a union of "soil and seminar," a union that made use of the best brains and talents wherever they could be found, in the state and elsewhere. Though uncritical and at times inaccurate, *The Wisconsin Idea* has remained the basic account of the Wisconsin story, vibrant with faith in the future and in the ultimate triumph of democracy.

It was inevitable that such widespread activities on many fronts should have aroused much hostile criticism. The close personal friendship of La Follette and Van Hise and the positive role played by many members of the University faculty in drafting legislation tended to align the attackers and defenders of the University in accordance with the stalwart-progressive split. As a result the whole program of the University was drawn into the maelstrom of factional politics which swirled about the heads of Robert La Follette and his followers.

Criticism of Van Hise and his fiscal policies began almost as soon as he became president. Ex-Regent Elisha Keyes derided the request Van Hise made in 1905 for a special deficiency appropriation from the general fund as springing from the "utter folly of an inexperienced president," and charged that the whole University had been "subjected to gross mismanagement." The *Wisconsin State Journal* protested against any such juggling of the state's funds and intimated that the University's accounts were hopelessly snarled. The legislature took account of these rumors and during the special session of 1905 set up a special subcommittee to investigate the affairs of the University. The resulting probe and report, however, gave the University's management a clean bill of health, and for the moment overt criticism subsided.[44]

Periodically the same cries of extravagance, waste, and mismanagement were heard again. To these was added the charge that the University and its faculty were engaged in politics. The conflict over the proper role of faculty members in politics be-

came a personal and bitter one when President Van Hise and
Regent Granville D. Jones found themselves on opposite sides
of the water power controversy. The progressive press vocifer-
ously defended the University against all critics and in so doing
connected the institution in the minds of most readers with the
paper's own policies and program.[45]

The last progressive-controlled legislature, that of 1913, met
this continuing criticism with a resolution calling for a thorough and detailed examination and investigation of the affairs
of the University by the State Board of Public Affairs. The
board engaged the services of two expert investigators, William
H. Allen of New York and Eugene C. Branson of the University
of North Carolina, to make detailed surveys along specific lines;
Allen was to examine the efficiency of teaching and educational
methods, and Branson was to study the College of Agriculture.
After more than a year's work the board's report, comprising
almost a thousand pages of comments, exhibits, appendices, and
conclusions was forwarded to the legislature. Since the regime
of the progressives and Governor Francis E. McGovern expired
at the end of the year, it fell to the incoming conservatives
under Emanuel Philipp to study the report and take action
on it.[46]

With respect to the charge that the University was engaging
in politics, the State Board of Public Affairs agreed that it was
doing so "insofar as students, faculty members, regents are in
politics as individuals," but that this represented only an exercise of "their rights to independent thought and action as individuals and citizens"; the board had received no information
to show "that the University of Wisconsin as an organization is
or has been in party or factional politics," and no charge had
been made "that officials of the university have organized or
attempted to organize the university at any time in favor of any
individual, faction or party." [47]

The report proper was objective and friendly in tone. It presented an imposing array of facts and figures which could be used with profit in the formulation of a long-range program for the University. But the report by William H. Allen, printed as a separate section or appendix, called forth prompt, angry rebuttal by the University faculty. The "Allen Report" consisted of a vast compilation of arbitrary criteria for judging efficiency, detailed criticism of each portion of the University's program that did not conform to these criteria, and thirty-six exhibits ranging from the organization of the Board of Regents to errors in the catalogue. The sum and substance of Dr. Allen's observations was that much was wrong and little right about the University of Wisconsin. Despite his assertions of friendly cooperation with the University, the tone of his report and the implications it contained were frankly hostile. The faculty defended the general efficiency of the University and launched a vigorous counterattack questioning Allen's examining methods, his survey techniques, and his general fitness to undertake such a project. At the request of the faculty the State Board signified no formal acceptance of the Allen Report but instead published its own general report, in which it included, side by side, without comment, both the Allen Report and the faculty's replies.[48]

Nevertheless the Allen survey was a valuable weapon in the hands of those who were determined to reduce the University's pretensions to national rank, and to terminate its independent role in the public affairs of the state. The failure of the progressives to agree on a gubernatorial candidate in the summer of 1914 had resulted in the nomination of Emanuel Philipp and reopened the old stalwart-progressive factional fight. The conservatives concentrated much of their fire on the University as "a wheel of the progressive movement," and the whole question of the status of the institution became a burning political issue.[49]

As a candidate Philipp had pledged himself to pare down

the expensive University establishment and to integrate the entire educational system on a businesslike basis. The opponents of the University flocked to his support in increasing numbers. For various purposes they proposed that the expenses of the University be reduced to fit the actual needs of the state. Charles P. Cary, state superintendent of schools, in a letter to *The Survey,* expressed fear that the people of Wisconsin would soon have a "university state instead of a state university." Many citizens urged Governor Philipp to make drastic cuts in the whole University organization. One irate businessman even attributed the lack of growth of northern Wisconsin to the policy of the University, which, he charged, "owns the state." [50]

Among the proposals of the new administration was one for the creation of a "central board" to control and integrate all branches of the state's educational system from the elementary and high schools to the state normal schools and the University. Philipp had advocated such a board during his campaign as a means of increasing efficiency and bringing the University into line with the actual needs of the state's citizenry. As a serious and open-minded student of the plan, Philipp gathered information from many of the most prominent educators in the country. He studied carefully a survey of such boards that had been made by President Frank L. McVey of the University of North Dakota. He conferred with President Van Hise in an attempt to find ground for agreement and even made use of the University's political science department to secure technical information and advice on the subject.[51]

But no such plan was instituted by the legislature. President Van Hise vigorously opposed any reorganization that would destroy the independence of the University or place it under the control of unsympathetic and narrow-minded administrators. The board that was eventually established was a mere shadow of the one originally proposed and placed little check on the independence of the Board of Regents and the president.

In the midst of the controversy Philipp slowly veered around to the position of a friend of the University. He had been obviously hostile during his campaign, but his careful study of the many-sided work of an institution of higher learning, and of its goals and aspirations, converted him into a staunch supporter of Van Hise. The president in turn recognized in the governor an able, intelligent, and conscientious executive. As a result the two men were able to work together effectively for the advancement of the University during the years before Van Hise's death in 1918.

Indeed the threat to the University posed by the conservatives made no important change in the pattern of growth which had taken shape before 1914. The activities of the faculty as technical and expert advisers on government did, however, decline. No longer were University professors frequently seen going in or out of the state capitol. As John R. Commons commented in his autobiography, he, and other faculty members, would have been willing to serve the conservatives, but he was "never called in except by Progressives." [52]

10 McGOVERN AND THE SERVICE STATE

★ ★ ★ ★ ★ ★ ★ ★ ★ ★ ★ ★ ★ ★ ★ ★ ★

AS THE PROGRESSIVE ERA DEVELOPED IN STATE AND NATION THE movement toward what Charles A. Beard called a "Social Democracy" gained momentum.[1] The political reforms, which had placed power more directly in the hands of the electorate, and the new tax measures, which greatly increased the revenues of the state, enabled a progressive administration to embark on more ambitious social and economic ventures to promote the "general welfare." Characteristic of this trend was the movement for the conservation of natural resources. Even more widespread was the drive for the "conservation of human resources," which envisioned the use of the state's power to improve the condition of the worker in industry. This pattern of broadening social aims was similar on all levels of government from the municipality to the nation.

The question of labor legislation, which had been discussed since the Civil War, had become even more acute during the first decade of the twentieth century. On both state and federal levels, however, most of the efforts to improve the worker's condition had been nullified by the judiciary. The prevailing philosophy of the Supreme Court, defending an extreme interpretation of "judicial review," "freedom of contract," and "due process of law," ran counter to the ideals and aims of most progressive-minded people throughout the country. The state of New York, for example, had seen its legislation limiting hours of employment for certain types of workers declared invalid by the United States Supreme Court. A federal statute recognizing the rights of workers to bargain through labor unions met the same fate at about the same time. To the usual difficulties faced by legislators in drafting bills on social and economic subjects was added the problem of achieving a phraseology that would survive the scrutiny of laissez-faire-minded jurists.[2]

In Wisconsin the enactment of labor legislation was rendered still more urgent by the weed-like growth of its metropolitan areas. Whereas the population of the state as a whole increased by only a modest 12.8 per cent in the decade from 1900 to 1910 and some counties even declined in population, the industrial areas of the state were growing much more rapidly. The state's largest city, Milwaukee, expanded by thirty-one per cent during the ten-year period.[3] The rapid industrialization of the state was also mirrored in the annual output of manufactured products, which increased during the decade from $360,000,000 to almost $600,000,000. This growth of the urban and industrial population brought with it a variety of new and complex problems calling for legislative action.[4]

The social philosophy of the progressives called for action to improve the condition of the industrial workers in the metropolitan areas. If industrial accidents were too numerous, if the bargaining power of the individual worker was ineffectual, if conditions of employment were depressing, the state should correct these evils. La Follette himself had long been an ardent champion of the rights and dignity of the common man. In the Senate he had advocated the passage of an employers' liability act and a law limiting the hours of continuous service of railroad employees. He urged the state to intervene in behalf of the working man and to establish additional commissions of experts to deal with this problem as "our social and industrial life grows daily more and more complex." [5]

Governor Francis McGovern was also eager to use the power of the state to regulate industrial activity. He urged the legislature to enact laws and set up civil institutions that would "secure and maintain desirable conditions in the daily lives and occupations of men." The people could not live on the framework of government, he insisted; they demanded control over the "economic conditions under which they earn their living." [6] If the state could be used by special-interest groups for their own selfish advantage, as was being pictured by the "muckraking" journalists, then it would be equally feasible to make the state serve the people and advance their interests against the seekers of special privilege. Regulation by commissions was already a successful part of Wisconsin government. During McGovern's administration the principle was extended into the fields of social and industrial legislation, marking the high tide of the progressive movement in Wisconsin.

The Wisconsin progressives had boldly declared their labor program in the state Republican platform of 1910. They denounced the use of the injunction against labor unions and pledged their efforts to secure a classification that would exempt unions and similar associations from persecution under the anti-trust laws. They were specifically pledged to work for workmen's compensation and minimum wage laws. "Losses occasioned by bodily injuries in industrial accidents," proclaimed their platform, "should be borne by the industry rather than by the disabled wage-earner or his dependents." They pledged immediate enactment of employers' liability laws and the creation of a system of workmen's compensation. They proposed a study of occupational diseases to provide information for subsequent legislation and they set forth the doctrine that "excessive hours of labor of children and women are a menace to the health, intelligence, and industry of the state." In short, they proposed to enact such labor and factory legislation, and make such provisions for the health and well-being of the workers, as would place Wisconsin on a level with the most progressive states in the union or any foreign country.[7]

In the 1910 election the progressive Republicans again won by an impressive majority and the new legislature prepared to redeem the party's campaign pledges. It was the boast of progressives in later years that the 1911 legislature carried out every one of these promises. At the opening session Governor McGovern called attention to the human waste that was taking place in the industrial world and urged that the responsibility for accidents and disabilities be placed squarely where it belonged, on the shoulders of industry itself.[8]

For a decade the agitation for workmen's compensation legislation had been growing more insistent, both in Wisconsin and elsewhere. There was increasing recognition that the system of employers' liability based on suits at common law was a failure. A few states, including Maryland, Montana, and New York, had passed compulsory compensation laws only to have them declared unconstitutional. A federal statute providing for employers' liability on railroads had been declared void, but in 1908 Congress had succeeded in passing a similar law that was acceptable to the court.[9]

In Wisconsin the State Federation of Labor led the first organized efforts to secure an adequate workmen's compensation law. As early as 1905 it had urged legislation to provide for "liability of employers for injury to health, body or life." With the example of the federal statute and the efforts being made in other states the Wisconsin trade unions made steady progress in attracting the attention of the entire state to the need for an effective workmen's compensation act. By 1909 a large part of the progressive-minded people in Wisconsin, employers as well as workers, had recognized the need for a comprehensive system of accident compensation for industrial workers.[10]

The Social Democrats had agitated for years for the enactment of a workmen's compensation law. One of their number, Frederick Brockhausen, had introduced bills on the subject at each session of the legislature, only to see them rejected in committee or postponed. When eventually the bill backed by the administration was introduced in the legislature of 1911 the *Social-Democratic Herald* of Milwaukee followed its course with interest and the twelve Socialist assemblymen supported it on every roll call.[11]

The legislature of 1909 had named a special committee to make a study of the problem of industrial insurance. This committee, headed by Senator Albert W. Sanborn, investigated the existing systems of workmen's compensation in various European countries and in several states. The chief hurdle to be surmounted in drafting a feasible plan was the problem of constitutionality.[12] The committee sought assistance from the leading students of social legislation at the University and held a series of meetings at which representatives of the State Federation of Labor and members of the Merchants and Manufacturers Association of Milwaukee were given an opportunity to offer suggestions on the form such legislation should take. The committee proposed that employers be given the option of coming under the new law or not as they chose. As a means of persuading them to come under it "willingly," it proposed to abolish, by legislation, the principal common-law defenses which had hitherto prevented an injured worker from securing adequate compensation through the courts. Thus the employer would no longer be able to escape payment of damages by claiming "voluntary assumption of risk by the employee" or "contributory negligence by a fellow servant." The measure recommended by the committee set up a system to provide compensation in all cases where an employee suffered an injury growing out of his employment, provided such injury had not been caused by wilful misconduct. The law was to be administered by a three-man Industrial Accident Board.[13]

The workmen's compensation bill was passed with only nominal opposition in substantially the form the special committee had recommended. The State Federation of Labor endorsed the act in its semiannual convention and the Milwaukee Merchants and Manufacturers Association, which was accused by the Socialists of trying to sabotage the measure, appeared to be quite friendly to the passage of a moderate law.[14]

The act tended to make employers more safety-conscious. It was "good business" to promote "accident prevention" rather than to rely simply on "accident compensation." The actual writing of insurance to provide for compensation was handled in a variety of ways. The larger corporations were permitted to set up their own systems of "self-insurance." Employers were also allowed to form their own "mutual companies" for insuring their collective establishments. Of these, the Employers' Liability Mutual Insurance Company of Wausau, Wisconsin, has become the best known.[15]

Although the Workmen's Compensation Act deprived employers of two of their traditional common-law defenses, only a minority of employers elected to come under the law. In 1913 the legislature reversed the admission procedure by assuming that all employers who had not filed notices to the contrary had elected to come under the act. The legislature of 1913 also abolished the common-law defense of "worker's contributory negligence," the third of the principal defenses employers had traditionally used. As a result of these changes most of the employers came into the system at once. By 1914 the commission estimated that more than ninety per cent of all accidents reported were covered by compensation. The number of cases settled rose rapidly from 846 in the first year to 8,496 in 1914, and the amount of benefits paid from $60,000 to $851,000.[16]

The legislature of 1911 also made some progress toward solving the problems created by the presence of women and children in industry. Laws were passed limiting hours of labor for minors, establishing minimum health standards, and giving the state control over apprenticeship contracts. Women in industry were declared to be in need of special protection, and a schedule of hours and working conditions was set up. They could not be employed in occupations deemed "harmful or injurious" to their health or on terms that were "prejudicial" to their general welfare. Two years later the legislature placed women in industry under the protection of the Industrial Commission, which was given authority to formulate and enforce a code of minimum hours and wages that would insure their health, safety, and welfare.[17]

The capstone of the progressives' labor legislation was the creation, later in the 1911 session, of the Industrial Commission. To this agency was entrusted the enforcement of the numerous factory regulations that had been enacted over the years and the supervision of the laws relating to women and children. It was authorized to devise and publish safety codes, which should have the force of law, for the various industries. It also took over from the Industrial Accident Board, which had only begun to function, the administration of the Workman's Compensation Act.[18]

The commission was also charged with the supervision of safety and sanitation in every place of employment except those of agriculture and domestic service. Instead of listing numerous machines and devices to be safeguarded and practices to be avoided, the new law expressed the will of the legislature in the most general way, simply declaring it to be the duty of the employer to safeguard the life, health, and safety of the employees and entrusting the enforcement to the Industrial Commission.[19]

Governor McGovern, following the example that had been set in the appointment of previous Wisconsin commissions, sought the best experts available for the new board. He appointed Charles H. Crownheart, attorney of Superior, as chairman; Joseph D. Beck, previously state commissioner of labor; and John R. Commons of the University of Wisconsin.[20] Commons, already a nationally known authority on labor and industrial problems, had played a large part in the drafting of the

law creating the Industrial Commission. It had been a cooperative task which utilized the research of some fifty University
students, who had charted the industrial laws and experiences
of all available countries and summarized their findings for the
legislative committee. In general the measure reflected Commons' social philosophy that labor legislation should provide
only for the broad basic pattern of regulation and leave the detailed investigations and decisions to the commission existing
for that purpose.[21]

The drafters of the act establishing the Industrial Commission, like the authors of the Workmen's Compensation Act,
faced the difficult problem of writing a strong and efficient law
that would meet the approval of the courts. Unless a practice,
service, or value was "reasonable" in the eyes of the courts, it
was unconstitutional; and the definition of "reasonable" tended
to become "average," "ordinary," or "usual." To take the usual
standards of safety or responsibility as a criterion would not
greatly improve the situation. The commission ultimately devised a definition of reasonable safety that overcame these difficulties: "The term 'safe' or 'safety' as applied to an employment or a place of employment . . . shall mean such freedom
from danger to the life, health, safety, or welfare of employees
or frequenters . . . as the nature of the employment or public
building will reasonably permit." To this definition and its
application may be attributed much of the success of the Industrial Commission. "Reasonable conditions" were interpreted to
mean the best that existed in actual practice, which allowed the
commission to strive for higher standards. The high court
found the law unassailable and gave its approval to this broad
delegation of authority to the Industrial Commission.[22]

In the performance of its inspection functions the Industrial
Commission replaced the old Bureau of Factory Inspection,
whose deputies had been accused of extensive political activity
during the early years of the progressive era. No longer would

the factory inspector visit a plant, view the conditions, and issue remedial orders on the spot. He would simply submit his report to the commission, which would assume the responsibility of issuing orders and securing compliance.[23]

The formulation of a satisfactory safety code for any given type of factory was worked out pragmatically by the commission. After the factory inspector, now called a deputy, made his report on unsatisfactory conditions in a plant the commission would designate a subcommittee to draw up a tentative proposal for correcting the situation. Public hearings on the proposed code would be held, after which the commission would revise and complete the administrative order, which would then be issued with the force of law. The work of the committee on boiler safety furnishes an excellent illustration of this process. The commission called in a manufacturer of boilers, a manufacturer who used boilers in his business, an insurance company's inspector of boilers, an employee who operated boilers, and a deputy of the commission who had had boiler experience. This group worked out a tentative "boiler code," which was "the best that the nature of the industry would allow." After holding public hearings on the proposed regulations the commission issued the code as an order. In subsequent litigations the court upheld it.[24]

The legal position of the commission was strengthened and safeguarded by the legislature. Borrowing a section from the act establishing the Railroad Commission, the law provided that a litigant could introduce no evidence in court that he had not presented before the commission. If he did so, the case was returned to the commission, which would consider the new evidence. The law also provided that suit must be brought against the commission not at whatever local justice's court a disgruntled employer might choose, but in the Circuit Court of Dane County, which gave preference to this type of case. From here it could be appealed directly to the state Supreme Court. Although the legislature could not legally prevent the court from pursuing its own investigations and arriving at its own definitions, in practice the methods of the commission accomplished just this. The employment of experts representing the various interests involved and the submission of their findings at an open hearing of interested persons made the orders of the commission prima facie reasonable and placed the burden of proof on the plaintiff. In fact, the employer who resisted the acceptance of a safety code approved by his fellow employers was regarded as "unreasonable" by the court.[25]

It was this authority and prestige which, in effect, made the Industrial Commission "a fourth branch of the government." Professor Commons in a review of the first two years of its work viewed the commission as "combining, but not usurping, the work of the three other branches. It is a legislature continually in session, yet the power of the legislature is not delegated. It is an executive, sharing with the governor the enforcement of laws, but also enforcing its own orders. It is a court, deciding cases that the judiciary formerly decided, but not assuming the authority of the courts." [26]

The commission sought constantly to promote accident prevention along with the administration of accident compensation. It was Commons' belief that "a workmen's accident law, if properly drawn, would cost nobody anything." By interesting both the employers and the committees representing the employees in promoting safety campaigns and inducing the employers to hire safety experts, the commission succeeded in sharply reducing the rate and severity of industrial accidents. The companies found it cheaper to employ safety experts and conduct safety campaigns than to hire detectives and lawyers to protect them in court.[27]

The scope of the Industrial Commission's authority was steadily extended. At the time of its creation public employment offices, four in number, were placed under its supervision, and by an act of 1913 the private employment offices were added. The public offices were cooperative agencies, for which the local county, town, or city government furnished suitable quarters and the commission provided the personnel and supervision. In reorganizing the free employment offices the commission enlisted the services of an advisory committee representing both the manufacturers and the trade unions. As a result both groups were satisfied with the objectivity and fairness of the official who conducted the office and were more disposed to use his services.[28]

The legislature of 1911 enacted two comprehensive laws governing child labor. An apprenticeship law regularized the system of indentures and provided that each indenture should include a statement of the trade to be taught, the number of hours to be spent in work and in instruction, the proportion of time to be spent in each phase of the work, and the compensation, which was to include a fifty-dollar bonus upon completion. The Industrial Commission received copies of all apprenticeship contracts and supervised the program.[29]

The companion piece to the apprenticeship law was the act providing for industrial and continuation schools. All cities of five thousand population were required to maintain a daytime vocational school, and all boys and girls under sixteen having work permits were required to attend school five hours a week for at least six months a year. The Industrial Commission enforced school attendance if this duty was not otherwise assigned and also issued permits. The system of industrial education was in a sense completed with the acquisition by the state of Stout Institute, a private institution which for many years had been engaged in training instructors in vocational education. The State Board of Industrial Education, also established in 1911, directed the instructional aspects of this program and organized all elements into a complete system of vocational training.[30]

This comprehensive program of industrial legislation delegated to the Industrial Commission broad powers over the fields of industrial accidents, safety and sanitation in factories, conditions of labor for women and children, public and private employment offices, and apprenticeship regulations, and gave it partial responsibility for the program of vocational education. Thus the Industrial Commission took its place alongside the Railroad Commission and the Tax Commission as a major agency for the regulation of the activities of the commonwealth. It was with pardonable pride that Governor McGovern wrote that the 1911 legislature "did more for the cause of workingmen than has ever been done before in any American state at a single legislative session." [31]

None of the numerous problems that faced McGovern and his administration in 1911 presented greater difficulties, both legal and practical, than the conservation of natural resources. Conservationists throughout the country were urging that a program be set up to safeguard natural resources, and the public generally associated conservation with progressive policies. On the national scene President Theodore Roosevelt and Gifford Pinchot, head of the Forestry Service, had effectively propagandized the country in favor of state and federal forest reserves, water-power sites, and mineral deposits. In 1907, in his annual message to Congress, Roosevelt had elaborated upon the problems of conservation and had urged Congress to extend and enlarge the national forests and public parks. The next year, at the instance of the president, a Conference of Governors was held at the White House which was attended by numerous officials of the national government, the governors of thirty-four states, and representatives of the other twelve. Out of this conference emerged the National Conservation Commission, which in 1909 issued a report on the nation's resources that has become a landmark in conservation history. Most states followed the federal example and set up state conservation

FRANCIS E. McGOVERN

JOHN J. BLAINE

IRVINE L. LENROOT

HERMAN L. EKERN

Leading Young Progressives

La Follette after the Close of the Progressive Era

From an oil painting by Seymour M. Stone
in the possession of the State Historical Society of Wisconsin

commissions to handle the natural resources within their boundaries.[32]

The problem of conservation was especially acute in Wisconsin. The long-continued exploitation of the state's lumber resources had left a large section of the state denuded of timber, unfit for agriculture, and in danger of becoming a permanently barren waste. Even the state park system, which had been started in 1878, had been thrown open and in 1897 sold to the lumber interests. Many of the state's leading politicians—Philetus Sawyer, Edward Scofield, Isaac Stephenson, Joseph Babcock, and others—were identified with the lumber industry and were unsympathetic toward any program for the establishment of an extensive system of state forest reserves and state-controlled mineral and water resources. Nevertheless the beginnings of a conservation program were made before Governor Scofield left office in 1901. The report of the Commission on Forestry which had been appointed by the previous legislature recommended the creation of a State Board of Forestry and the adoption of a program to prevent forest fires.[33]

Robert La Follette had been an ardent champion of conservation since his days in the House of Representatives. As governor he was instrumental in the establishment of a State Department of Forestry headed by State Forester Edward M. Griffith. Under the direction of this board some hundred and fifty thousand acres were purchased for a forest reserve and subsequent administrations steadily enlarged it. During the same period the state acquired many of the parks in the present system, including a section of Door County, the Wisconsin Dells, and Devil's Lake.[34]

During the administrations of Governors Davidson and McGovern the legislature exhibited great interest in the problems of conservation. In 1909 it appointed a joint committee on "Water Powers, Forestry and Drainage," headed by Senator Harlan P. Bird. This committee made extensive tours of the northern half of the state and studied every aspect of the problem. In the report it submitted to the legislature in 1911 it asserted that the prosperity of the entire state was in large measure dependent upon the reforestation of the northern part. To achieve this end it recommended the establishment of a conservation commission, the formation of an adequate forest patrol system, and a policy of cooperation with the neighboring states and the national government. To finance the reforestation program the committee recommended a tax of two-tenths mill to be added to the general levy. With respect to water power it favored a system of indeterminate franchises which should include a franchise rental that would be used for conservation work. The committee was by no means unanimous, however, on the control of water-power sites, and a minority report on the subject was offered by Senators Paul Husting and Henry Krumrey. Fearing that water power would be monopolized in Wisconsin, they urged that the state declare specifically that the use of water in navigable streams for power, developed under a franchise from the state, was a public use and all energy should be subject to the control of the state for the greatest public good. Husting and Krumrey would have based franchises to water-power users on this assumption, subject to revocation on breach of contract.[35]

The State Conservation Commission (a temporary and largely ex-officio body) also considered the subject of water-power franchises in its report of 1911. The majority report, expressing the views of University President Van Hise, combined the essential elements of the two reports from the legislative committee. The general proposition that water power and the energy derived therefrom are properties of the state was implicitly accepted. The commission urged establishment of a permanent board to issue water-power franchises, which should be either indeterminate contracts or definite leases and should carry a rental charge.[36]

The whole issue of water power was squarely drawn in a minority report of two members of the commission, George A. Whiting and William Irvine, who denied that the state had any right to interfere with private property or the liberty of a citizen. They cited the case of *Huber v. Merkel*, in which the court had forbidden the state to interfere in the private use of artesian wells. In short, they contended that water-power rights belonged to the person who owned the land along the bank and the state had no authority to interfere with his use or abuse of his property. "The only way to conserve water power," they said, "is to use it" and this the private owners were doing.[37]

The legislature of 1911 followed the recommendations of the majority of both the legislative committee and the Conservation Commission and enacted a comprehensive series of laws designed to conserve the natural resources of the state. A permanent Conservation Commission was established, part ex-officio and part appointive, to enforce the new laws and aid in formulating principles of conservation policy which would serve as a guide for future legislation. As the initial appropriation was only a thousand dollars and the members received no compensation except for expenses, the Conservation Commission was forced to call on other agencies for their cooperation in securing needed information.[38]

The legislature recognized the pressing need for a long-range program to reforest the northern part of the state. It provided funds for this purpose and placed the project under the supervision of the State Board of Forestry. An act was also passed making it a misdemeanor for any person to injure or destroy any natural resource.[39]

The Conservation Commission was fortunate in having for its chairman such a person as University President Charles Van Hise. Van Hise was not only an outstanding administrator and educator but also a geologist of great ability and a conservationist of national reputation. He was frequently consulted by

President Roosevelt and Chief Forester Pinchot, and his scholarly monograph on *The Conservation of Natural Resources in the United States* was used as a standard reference work throughout this period.[40]

The legislation on water-power sites was also based on the majority reports of the temporary Conservation Commission and the legislative committee. The issue of public versus private rights in water-power cases had been hotly debated in the press and was dramatized in spectacular fashion by the "John Dietz Battle of Cameron Dam." Within the University's administrative family President Van Hise and Regent Granville D. Jones exchanged hotly indignant letters over the matter.[41] The Water Power Act embodied the general progressive philosophy that the state had prior rights and interests in the use and conservation of water power and that holders of water-power franchises must conduct their business in the public interest. The act provided that sites should be leased for twenty-year periods and vested in the Railroad Commission the authority to grant franchises and to charge both a fee and a yearly rental. The contract should be terminated if the corporation violated the terms or spirit of the act or if the state at some future time chose to enter the public-power field directly.[42]

The conservatives at once attacked both the reforestation and the water-power measures in the courts. In a far-reaching decision handed down in January, 1912, the State Supreme Court found the water-power law unconstitutional in that it deprived the owner of both property and liberty. "The right of the riparian owner to use the water for developing power," said the court, "is a private right." The progressive administration tried to salvage something from the wreckage, but the Water Power Act of 1913 only partly protected the state's interest in the navigable rivers, and no effective law to recapture such water-power sites for public use was passed for another decade.[43]

The reforestation program fared no better. After three years of litigation the Supreme Court found that no "public purposes" were served by the collection of taxes and use of state funds as provided in the act of 1911, and that hence it was unconstitutional. Justice John B. Winslow, in a concurring opinion, held that the "reforestation of large areas" did not represent "works of internal improvement within the meaning of the constitution" and that therefore the state could not authorize the expenditure of state funds for such a project.[44]

The decisions of the high court voided much of the conservation legislation enacted by the McGovern administration. In 1915, during the tenure of Governor Philipp, a measure acceptable to the courts was passed by the legislature, but it was not until 1924 that the work of reforestation was resumed on a large scale.[45]

The legislature of 1911, following the recommendations of the governor, created a third major public service agency, the State Board of Public Affairs. This board was charged with such diverse duties as supervising the state budget and the budget director, compiling a scientific study of the state's resources, and making a series of surveys on a variety of topics. It also served as a clearinghouse for news and as a semiofficial news agency for the several departments. Such a bureau had been urged upon McGovern by various prominent citizens, including John R. Commons, who had recommended an agency of this kind to the governor on the basis of his work with the Milwaukee Bureau of Economy and Efficiency. The State Board of Public Affairs was composed of both ex-officio and appointive members, the governor acting as chairman. Other members were Secretary of State James A. Frear, Senator Albert W. Sanborn, Assemblyman Ray J. Nye, William H. Hatton, John Humphrey, and William H. Hanchett.[46]

For a body composed of busy public officials and active men of affairs serving without remuneration the State Board of Public Affairs showed enormous energy and initiative. Within four years it completed an impressive series of surveys, almost twenty in all, on many aspects of the state's life and activities, including agricultural conditions, public finance, education, and prison labor.[47]

Many of these investigations had far-reaching effects. The survey of the University resulted in a fight for the reduction of its budget and the creation of a central board of education. The investigation of the accounts and records of public agencies produced a general reform of budgetary practices in the state's subdivisions. The board's examination of the cost of state printing revealed that the rapid increase of these expenditures —to $258,000 in 1914—was due largely to "waste and inefficiency." On the basis of these several investigations the board concluded that it would be possible to effect immediately a saving of at least four hundred thousand dollars in the conduct of the business of the state: a hundred thousand in the cost of state printing, another hundred thousand in the operation of the normal schools, and two hundred thousand in the operation of the University.[48]

The board's comprehensive report on cooperation and marketing, published in 1912, also had long-range results. This survey followed the enactment of a law in 1911 permitting the formation of agricultural cooperative associations and exempting them from prosecution under the anti-trust laws. To determine the relative advantages of various types of farm cooperatives the board directed research into numerous aspects of the subject. In its report it devoted separate sections to cooperatives in Denmark and other European countries, cooperative credit, municipal markets, and distributive or store cooperation. It urged adoption of a program that would help the farmer to help himself and suggested that it could be integrated with the extension department of the University.[49]

On the basis of this report Governor McGovern proposed to the legislature of 1913 that it set up a Marketing Commission to do for the farmer what the Industrial Commission was doing for the workingman. Unfortunately the split in the progressive ranks had become so pronounced by this time that any recommendation of the governor's was at once opposed by La Follette's supporters in the legislature, and this project, too, had to be postponed until the progressives returned to power eight years later.[50]

The McGovern administration established still another commission of experts, one designed to implement the idea of a "Service State." The advent of the automobile had emphasized the need for a public highway program, and in 1908 the voters had approved a constitutional amendment to remove the constitutional barriers to the expenditure of state funds for such internal improvements. Acting upon the recommendations of the governor, the legislature set up a State Highway Commission and passed the first state-aid highway-construction law. The Highway Commission was organized under civil service rules with three full-time and two part-time ex-officio members. J. A. Hazelwood of Jefferson served as chairman. Before McGovern left office the annual appropriation for the state's highways had been increased to over a million dollars.[51]

The first years of McGovern's administration might well be termed the flowering period of the progressives in Wisconsin. Under his leadership the legislature of 1911 enacted into law a large number of important projects. Its labor legislation alone, crowned by the creation of an Industrial Commission, would have been a major accomplishment for any legislature. Much of the reforestation and water power legislation was soon declared invalid, but the work done was along sound lines and later bore fruit. The highway law was widely used as a model in other states, and the cooperative marketing plan later proved to be of permanent importance. The State Board of Public Affairs, with its supervision of the budget and accounts, had long been needed. The series of surveys it made did much to improve the efficiency of the rapidly expanding state government. Its disclosure of widespread waste, inefficiency, and extravagance called timely attention to the evils bred by an unchecked bureaucracy, and in so doing perhaps hastened its own liquidation.[52]

By 1912 the Wisconsin state government was a vastly different structure from what it had been at the turn of the century. Instead of the eight elective state offices that appeared on the ballot in 1900 there were now only five. Candidates for the office of state superintendent of public instruction had been placed on the nonpartisan ballot to be elected along with the judges. The Railroad Commission and the Insurance Commission had become appointive, and a dozen other commissions and boards were in operation as integral parts of the state government. Together they performed many of the functions formerly carried on by the executive department.[53] It was not without cause that one conservative complained that Wisconsin now had a government by commission. But in general these commissions performed their duties efficiently and served the people of the commonwealth well. By 1912 Wisconsin had advanced a long way toward the progressives' goal of a "Service State."

11 THE SPLIT IN THE PARTY

★　★　★　★　★　★　★　★　★　★　★　★　★　★　★　★　★

HARDLY HAD THE PROGRESSIVES COMPLETED THE BUILDING OF THEIR
political organization when a series of conflicts and dissensions
threatened to disrupt the whole edifice. Many basically unsympathetic groups and elements had been welded together to promote the comprehensive reform program that came to be known
as Wisconsin progressivism. Old Populists, idealistic crusaders,
practical reformers, University intellectuals, social planners,
professional officeholders, ambitious youngsters, Scandinavian
and farming groups, and a disgruntled multimillionaire had
combined to rout the old political forces and take over the entire machinery of the state.

The cohesive force that had brought together these dissimilar
elements was, of course, La Follette. His appeal to the independent and marginal voter greatly strengthened the organization. He had the personal devotion of a great number of his
supporters, old and young alike, and to a large segment of the
organization his word was law. Yet "Fighting Bob" was a unique
combination of zealot and practical politician. The conflict of
these opposing aspects of his character was often apparent. After
at last gaining complete control of the party's political machinery, he championed the installation of the direct primary, which
made it difficult, if not impossible, for him to control the state
elections. After building up an impressive patronage organization he inaugurated a civil service system that prevented any
other progressive leader from gaining any real control of the
electorate. In retrospect it appears that the zealot in him gained
ground as he grew older, provoking him to violent breaks with

old friends who dared to disagree with him on issues and policies. Yet La Follette never lost his great personal popularity among the voters of Wisconsin. In every election, regardless of the office he was seeking, he could always be assured of the support of his home state.

In 1906 the contest for the governorship between Irvine Lenroot, backed by La Follette, and incumbent James O. Davidson had strained the progressive organization and for a time threatened to split its ranks permanently. But Davidson held out an olive branch to his erstwhile opponents, and La Follette supported him in the general election.[1] Harmony prevailed once more among the progressive Republicans, and Davidson continued in office for two full terms, during which the progressive program was steadily advanced and La Follette cooperated cordially with the state officials on matters of policy and patronage. But the elements of discord were present and were soon to become apparent on another issue.

The sudden resignation of John C. Spooner from the United States Senate in 1907 found the progressive forces in disagreement over the choice of a successor. Several progressive politicians expressed a willingness to be drafted for the honor, but most observers expected Isaac Stephenson to claim the seat as compensation for his contributions to the party cause. This he did in a public announcement in the *Milwaukee Free Press* and in numerous letters to his friends.[2]

Perhaps the best qualified person available for the senatorship was Congressman Henry Allen Cooper of Racine. Cooper had had long experience in the House of Representatives and had taken a prominent part in shaping progressive legislation. But in spite of the entreaties of many of his supporters Cooper refused to take any part in the race, testily commenting that he would not compete against Stephenson's money. Congressman Esch and Governor Davidson likewise refused, in the face of many letters from friends, to campaign actively for the seat.[3]

Stephenson conducted a vigorous campaign among the legislators and he was easily the leading candidate for the appointment, his chief opposition being Irvine Lenroot and William H. Hatton. According to Stephenson, La Follette had assured him of his support and promised to do all he could to assist in his election. When the legislature failed to agree on a successor to Spooner, a deadlock ensued. At length Stephenson proposed to his opponents that they withdraw from the contest for the short term, agreeing that he would not be a candidate to succeed himself in 1908. But Lenroot and Hatton refused and the deadlock went on until, eventually, the aged lumber baron secured a majority of the votes and was declared elected.[4]

On the day after the election, as Stephenson recalled, La Follette telegraphed his congratulations and at once wrote him a most cordial letter, addressing him as "my dear Senator." Upon Stephenson's initial appearance on the floor the senior senator presented him and his credentials to the presiding officer and then escorted him to his seat. Throughout that session of Congress La Follette was continuously helpful and the two distributed patronage on a friendly basis.[5]

But as the time approached for the nominations for the full senatorial term, La Follette's attitude changed markedly. He evidently thought that the Marinette millionaire, having been given the title of senator, should now retire and allow some younger and more truly progressive spokesman to represent the people in Washington. Stephenson, however, had no intention of relinquishing the high position he had been so long in attaining. He felt under no obligation to Hatton, who had refused the arrangement he had proffered in 1907. Besides, he was not yet eighty, his eyes and memory were still good, and he prided himself on his grasp of details. He was indignant when opponents spread rumors that he was old and senile.[6]

Several avowedly progressive candidates, among them Hatton, Congressman Esch, and Francis E. McGovern, then district attorney at Milwaukee, campaigned vigorously for the party's senatorial nomination during the summer of 1908. "Uncle Ike," although he made only a few speeches, built up a most efficient organization to promote his re-election. By the simple procedure of opening a suite of offices in Milwaukee, employing several assistants, and hiring a corps of clerks, he effectively propagandized the entire state. Large amounts of space in the country papers were purchased, and no stone was left unturned to reach every voter. The opposing candidates were swamped under the sheer weight of Stephenson's campaign literature and the efficiency of his organization.[7]

The preferential senatorial primary gave Stephenson a plurality of almost ten thousand votes and he carried thirty-nine of the state's seventy-one counties. According to the terms of the primary law, the legislature was pledged to support the winning candidate. Thus Stephenson should be assured of re-election. As soon as the legislative session began, however, John J. Blaine, state senator from Boscobel, moved that the senatorial primary be investigated. The resulting inquiry disclosed that the nominee had spent an enormous amount of money in his campaign. Stephenson candidly admitted that the nomination had cost him about $107,000. This, he agreed, was an excessive amount of money, but he had started late and had had severe handicaps to overcome. The investigators were unable to find any tangible evidence of fraud, and on March 4, 1909, the legislature re-elected Stephenson to the Senate.[8]

La Follette had been highly critical of Stephenson's campaign. In the newly established *La Follette's Magazine* he charged that Stephenson had spent liberally of his huge fortune "bribing and corrupting" a sufficient number of electors of the state of Wisconsin to secure his nomination. He urged a thorough investigation to protect the good name and honor of the state.[9]

Although Stephenson had been vindicated and declared duly elected by the state legislature, the United States Senate undertook an independent investigation of its own. Eventually, after more than two years' delay, it confirmed Stephenson's election by the rather narrow margin of 40 to 34, La Follette voting with the minority to declare the seat vacant.[10]

By this time Stephenson had become very bitter against La Follette and his henchmen. He later charged that the very progressives who had eagerly accepted large contributions from him to promote their own campaigns had been the most violent in denouncing his expenditures in his own behalf. Stephenson also found himself involved in a libel suit as a result of the attack the *Free Press* had made on Charles Pfister in 1905. The case eventually cost the paper several thousand dollars, which he, personally, had to provide. La Follette in turn tended to belittle any contributions made by "Ike" to the progressive cause. He announced that he would welcome any "statement or revelation" of the amounts that had been spent in his behalf.[11]

In later years the two senators from Wisconsin usually found themselves on opposite sides of the controversial questions that came before Congress. Stephenson became more conservative and tended to vote with the regular Republicans, and in state affairs he became a leading member of the anti–La Follette bloc. Needless to say, "Uncle Ike" completely closed his coffers to the progressives. By this time the party's widespread popularity and long tenure in office had lessened its dependence on Isaac Stephenson, but his disaffection was nevertheless a serious blow to the prestige and power of the progressive Republicans and to La Follette.

One result of Stephenson's election to the United States Senate and the subsequent investigation was a general demand for a tightening of the laws governing election expenditures. The progressive Republican platform of 1910 advocated an effective corrupt practices act, one that would restrict expenditures to a stipulated amount and to specified purposes; require publicizing and accounting of such funds; and provide "rigorous penalties" for violations, including imprisonment and disqualification of the candidate.[12]

The legislature of 1911 promptly enacted a measure embodying these proposals. In their eagerness to eliminate the use of great wealth in election campaigns the lawmakers made its terms so stringent and the penalties for violation so drastic that they subsequently embarrassed themselves. The act was effective in limiting campaign expenditures during the remaining years of the progressive era, but the politicians eventually found successful means of circumventing its restrictions.[13]

La Follette had gone to the United States Senate in 1906 with the anticipation that he would be allowed to take a substantial part in the program of reform being carried on at the national capital. He had looked forward to receiving the wholehearted cooperation of President Roosevelt, whom he had admired and praised when the latter became chief executive. But from their first meeting the two men became increasingly antagonistic, and soon La Follette was openly voicing his criticism of the president's methods and policies. He sought to lead his fellow legislators along the road he had traveled in his home state. He argued that Congress should begin an immediate valuation of the country's railroads as a preliminary step to shifting their taxes to an ad valorem basis. He would have no dealings with the conservative congressmen who were allied or friendly with the large corporations.[14]

Roosevelt, on the other hand, was willing to go only so far as he could with the public's support. He did not hesitate to work with the corporationists in the Senate and much preferred a "half-loaf" to none. He regarded La Follette as too much the radical and zealot, too much the idealist to work effectively in the atmosphere of compromise and party politics. Yet so long as Roosevelt was in the White House the two reformers continued to give the appearance of working in harmony; not until later did their deep-seated mutual antipathy become apparent.[15]

La Follette had been extremely resentful of the treatment he had received upon his entrance into the Senate. In his *Autobiography* he described this portion of his career in a chapter entitled "Alone in the Senate." He soon associated himself with a small group of progressive extremists who became known as "insurgents." It irritated La Follette exceedingly when his colleague from Wisconsin, Isaac Stephenson, refused to take any part in the drive to reform the United States.[16]

When Roosevelt retired from the presidency in 1909, La Follette would have been glad to succeed him. Neither the national political leaders nor the metropolitan press, however, seriously considered him as a possibility, and, with Roosevelt's approval and blessing, the nomination went to William Howard Taft. La Follette stifled his disappointment with an eye to the election four years hence. His intimate associates, however, were keenly aware of his feeling of frustration and resentment over being rejected for Taft. Haugen later recalled that when he told Bob he had "discovered no demand for his candidacy," La Follette was piqued and ceased to invite him to "sit in" at the conferences on strategy. In Congress, on the Chatauqua platform, and in his periodical La Follette embarked on a crusade expounding the cause of progressivism. His eye was on the election of 1912, which he was convinced would be the "progressive year." [17]

The fight of the "insurgents" in Congress and the countrywide speech-making of La Follette and others dramatized and popularized the progressive cause. Many of the reformers agreed that it was time to form a permanent organization. Accordingly La Follette drafted a "Declaration of Principles" and a constitution for the organization of a league, and submitted it to some of his colleagues for their approval. As a result, early in January, 1911, "The National Progressive Republican League" came into formal existence at La Follette's home in Washington. The constitution adopted declared the object of the league to be "the promotion of popular government and progressive legislation."

It advocated the direct election of senators, direct primaries for all elective officials, direct election of delegates to national conventions with some provision for enabling the voter to express his choice among the candidates, amendments providing for the initiative, referendum, and recall, and a thoroughgoing corrupt practices act. Thus La Follette provided himself with a concise and advanced platform upon which to wage his campaign. Most of the avowed progressive reformers joined the organization and pledged their support. But one name was notably absent. Theodore Roosevelt, although he expressed his sympathy with the movement, declined to be identified as one of the League's members.[18]

Wisconsin progressives played a leading part in La Follette's campaign for the presidency. Many astute political observers were of the opinion that the nomination could easily go to La Follette, especially if Roosevelt remained in retirement. Clubs boosting "La Follette for President" sprang up in most Wisconsin towns and cities and in many neighboring states. Former Secretary of State Walter Houser became his campaign manager. His lieutenants solicited campaign funds, and Governor Francis McGovern spoke and wrote in favor of his candidacy. In October, 1911, the first installment of La Follette's autobiography appeared in the *American Magazine*. His supporters hoped this would start a boom that would lead to his nomination and election. As he had so often done in his state campaigns, La Follette had begun his active campaigning well before the other candidates had organized. He proposed steadily to increase the tempo, to speak in every Northern and Western state, and to enter every presidential primary until the very day of the convention.[19]

Despite this vigorous campaigning many leading progressives throughout the country had private doubts whether La Follette could capture the nomination from Taft. Roosevelt, by his very silence, encouraged many of his old friends to hope that he would re-enter the political arena. True, most of the lesser progressives had become members of the National Progressive Republican League and were committed to promoting the candidacy of "Fighting Bob." They could not desert him, even for Roosevelt, without cause. Nevertheless many sincere supporters of the progressive cause were uneasy. Like William Allen White, they found that the "grim, unsmiling" La Follette aroused little enthusiasm in their home states. Old Roosevelt cronies like Frank Knox of the *Chicago News* and Gifford Pinchot, late of the Forestry Service, personally urged "T. R." to take over the movement.[20]

Through December and January the ex-president vacillated. He protested that he was "not a candidate" but carefully avoided any unequivocal statement that, like General Sherman, he would not accept the nomination under any circumstances. But as the torrent of mail urging him to accept the nomination continued to pour in, he began to consider issuing a new statement which would make him available for a "draft." As late as January 16, 1912, he explained at length to Frank A. Munsey why he had declined to add anything to his "I am not a candidate" statements. But two days later he expressed his willingness to make a statement for publication in reply to a proposed joint letter from a group of Republican governors urging him not to refuse the call of the people to carry forward the fight for progressivism.[21]

Even after the wheels had thus started to turn and his friends had begun to create an organization, Roosevelt still hesitated. In a letter to William Allen White he said he thought it would be better "not to make a public statement" after all and in another letter he protested that he certainly would "not be a candidate." By early February, however, he was certain that a statement would be the "only right course" and he was prepared to toss his hat into the ring. "La Follette," Roosevelt confided to an old friend, "has done first rate work in Wisconsin but does not size up for the national field any more than Chase or Seward sized up for it." [22]

While the supporters of Roosevelt were seeking an excuse to draft their idol and other progressives were anxiously looking for evidences of growing popular support of their cause, "Fighting Bob" La Follette himself unwittingly shattered his own presidential hopes. Throughout the winter of 1911–12 he had carried on his campaign in numerous speeches in the East and Middle West. His exertions, along with the strain imposed by his youngest daughter's critical illness, had brought him close to the point of exhaustion. From the beginning of his career he had constantly driven himself to the point of collapse in almost every campaign, and it was perhaps inevitable that he should at last suffer the consequences. [23]

While he was still far below par physically the Periodical Publishers Association invited him, because of his national prominence as a progressive leader, to make one of the principal speeches at its annual banquet to be held in Philadelphia on February 2, 1912. Other speakers were to be Woodrow Wilson, governor of New Jersey, Detective William J. Burns, and neurologist S. Weir Mitchell. The banquet was planned as a social and intellectual gathering, and presumedly no comprehensive campaign orations were expected. [24]

It appears that La Follette made at least three major errors of judgment before he even rose to speak. Considering his physical condition and the illness in his family, he should probably have declined the invitation when it was first tendered. If he had felt that he must accept it, he should have planned to make only a brief speech about some facet of the progressive movement. Even if he had prepared a lengthy oration, his long political experience should have led him, in view of the situation, to switch to a brief talk. La Follette did none of these things. By the time he was introduced at ten o'clock the other speakers had finished and the audience was restless and about ready to go home. La Follette himself, having arrived late, had not eaten at all. Yet he spoke, or attempted to speak, for almost two and a half hours; his printed speech ran to thirty-five pages.[25]

The press reported that apparently La Follette had broken down completely. La Follette and his managers promptly denied this and denounced the "sensational and false reports" as propaganda of the Roosevelt followers.[26] Congressman Henry A. Cooper, however, one of La Follette's closest political friends, who had been present at the affair, was so disturbed by La Follette's behavior that he scribbled on the back of his invitation a memorandum describing what took place:

It was a shocking scene. He lost his temper repeatedly—shook his fist—at listeners who had started to walk out too tired to listen longer,—was abusive, ugly in manner.—Stopped many times to shout at men walking out. From the very outset his speech was tedious, inappropriate (for a banquet occasion like that) stereotyped, like too many others of his was extreme in matter and especially in manner. The editor of both bureau [s] (Philadelphia) said to me "Mr. Cooper, this is shocking—too bad. What ails him?" John Hannan, La Follette's secretary, came over to me after I had moved into the center of the room and with a dejected, disgusted look said softly to me—"This is terrible—he is making a d——d fool of himself." It ends him for the Presidency.[27]

Cooper thought that La Follette had "killed himself politically" by this speech. Possibly his fortunes were already beginning to decline, but it was this Philadelphia debacle that caused even his most loyal friends and supporters to give up. As William Allen White commented, "We stopped insisting on La Follette delegates to the national convention, and let nature take its course."[28] On the morning of February 2, 1912, La Follette had been a leading progressive candidate for the Republican nomination. By midnight he had by his own actions shattered his national support. Only the Wisconsin organization remained completely loyal thereafter.

But La Follette refused to retire from the race even after Roosevelt formally entered the campaign on February 24, 1912. In a biting editorial in his magazine he denounced those who were deserting him and turning to Roosevelt. After a short rest he resumed the contest. He campaigned vigorously in Nebraska but lost the state by an overwhelming vote to Roosevelt. He managed to carry North Dakota and lost South Dakota by only a narrow margin. In his speeches and articles he took increasingly advanced and radical ground. In most of his utterances he seemed to concentrate his fire on Roosevelt, whom he characterized as a "professing progressive" whose record failed to fulfill his promises. Taft he usually ignored as one having no principles worthy of discussion.[29]

The progressive organization in Wisconsin gave vigorous and continuous support to La Follette's candidacy, even after it became evident that his was a lost cause. Governor McGovern spoke and wrote in his behalf, urging the extension of Wisconsin's reforms to the rest of the nation, and he and other state officers contributed liberally to the campaign chest. For delegates at large to the national convention, the Wisconsin electors named McGovern, Andrew H. Dahl, Walter L. Houser, and Alvin Kletzsch. All of them, as well as a full slate of district delegates, were pledged to support La Follette.[30]

La Follette was especially bitter over the desertion of the Pinchot brothers and Medill McCormick, Chicago publisher. These men, he charged, pretended that they were shifting to Roosevelt because La Follette had withdrawn or would withdraw shortly. He was hostile to any suggestion that the progressives should withdraw from the Republican Party and form their own organization. The Sawyers and Paynes, he reminded his readers, would have been more than glad to see him bolt.[31]

As the date for the Republican national convention approached, the question that perplexed most of the Wisconsin delegates could be phrased "After La Follette, what?" To be sure, they were completely and wholeheartedly loyal to "Fighting Bob." But all except his blindest partisans recognized that his political fortunes had declined and that he had little chance, except in the event of a deadlock, to win the nomination. All the delegates were strongly opposed to the renomination of Taft. Governor McGovern received many congratulatory notes when he sent a blistering reply to the appeal of Republican chairman William Barnes Jr. that he support Elihu Root as the "regular" candidate for temporary chairman. He denounced Root as a "standpat tory" and warned that if the politicians ignored the wishes of the people they would convict the party and invite defeat in November.[32]

Many Wisconsin citizens expressed similar views to the delegates. Typical of these communications was a letter from Augustus C. Umbreit, Milwaukee lawyer, to Governor McGovern. Umbreit favored La Follette and was confident that the Wisconsin delegates would support him as long as he had any chance of winning, but he hoped that when the time came they would vote for "some progressive candidate" who could secure the nomination. Roosevelt supporter Cassius E. Gillette of Philadelphia protested to Walter Houser against La Follette's policy of campaigning against Roosevelt rather than Taft. He demanded that all progressives join in opposing the organization of the convention by "conservatives and reactionaries." Any other procedure, he warned, would be playing politics to the detriment of the progressive cause.[33]

In the meantime the practical problems involved in translating the popular progressive sentiment against Taft into progressive support at the convention gave Roosevelt and his lieutenants increasing concern. In the states where the delegations were chosen by preferential primaries Roosevelt ran well ahead, amassing 278 votes to Taft's 46. He fared less well, however, in the machine-dominated state conventions. Long before convention time it was recognized that the vote would be exceedingly close and that control would probably hinge on the initial organization of the convention and the personality of the chairman.[34]

The choice of Roosevelt and his chief advisers for this key position was Governor Herbert S. Hadley of Missouri, a strong supporter of the Rough Rider who had been one of the signators of the joint letter urging Roosevelt to become a candidate. Hadley was urged to make the strenuous fight for the chairmanship against Root and the stalwarts. Hadley, however, proved reluctant to undertake the contest and eventually declined to do so. Roosevelt's mind then turned to Governor McGovern of Wisconsin, whom he had already considered as a likely prospect for permanent chairman. In a letter to Hadley "T. R." expressed his willingness to "support any good La Follette man such as Governor McGovern or Gronna, for instance, against Root." [35] The strategy of the Roosevelt forces would be to offer no candidate for the chairmanship themselves, but to support the La Follette candidate, almost certainly McGovern, and thus combine the strength of all progressives against Taft and the conservatives. McGovern was a personal friend of the ex-president's and had assured him of his support when and if La Follette's candidacy should "become hopeless." Only thus could the Roosevelt supporters hope to prevent a split in the progressive ranks and win the chairmanship and with it the control of the convention.[36]

Sometimes before June 12 his Wisconsin friends began maneuvering to have McGovern named temporary chairman of the national convention. The strategy was to have him, as the nominee of all the progressive forces, oppose Root, the choice of Taft. By that date McGovern was already at work on the speech which he would deliver if he was elected. On June 13 McGovern's fellow delegate, Alvin P. Kletzsch, wrote that "with proper maneuvering, we ought to have no difficulty in getting the Roosevelt forces to join with us in putting you in the chair."

Kletzsch thought that McGovern had an exceptional opportunity and felt certain that the North Dakota delegation would join in placing his name in nomination.[37]

The Republican national convention of 1912 came to order on June 18. National Committee chairman Victor Rosewater had planned the initial proceedings with great thoroughness. The control of the convention hinged on some seventy-two delegates who were claimed by both the Taft and the Roosevelt forces. The National Committee "temporarily" seated the Taft faction and in so doing loaded the convention with enough pro-Taft delegates to give him a clear though narrow majority. It appeared that the only chance of wresting the control of the convention machinery from the administration was to elect a progressive as temporary chairman. Perhaps a dynamic, popular drive by all the progressive elements, supported almost certainly by the galleries, might have stampeded enough Taft delegates to throw the chairmanship to McGovern. But the progressive forces were never given an opportunity to gamble on this bold political stroke. Henry F. Cochems of Wisconsin placed McGovern's name in nomination and a delegate from North Dakota made the seconding speech, but before the movement could gain much momentum it was blasted with dramatic suddenness.[38]

As the convention date had approached, La Follette had vented his spleen increasingly against Roosevelt and had ignored Taft. He felt that he had been used as a "stalking horse" for the Rough Rider and had been tossed aside when the progressive movement had shown strength and promise of success. Consequently he was determined not to ally himself with the Roosevelt forces for any purpose. Following orders from his chief, campaign manager (and delegate) Walter Houser arose on the floor of the convention and heatedly disavowed McGovern's candidacy for the chairmanship. The nomination of the Wisconsin governor for chairman, he told the convention, was not in the interests of Senator La Follette. He ended his dramatic speech on a semi-hysterical note. "We make no deals with Roosevelt," he shouted. "We make no deals with Taft. . . . Let no man think that Bob La Follette has traded with anyone. . . . We make no trades." [39]

The drive for a united progressive front collapsed on the spot. The emotional reaction of the convention to this internal split among the progressives was a far more potent factor than the loss of the Wisconsin delegates who joined Houser in refusing to support McGovern. As all semblance of unanimity among the progressives vanished, the potential crusading appeal of their cause evaporated. The well-oiled Taft machine proceeded to roll over the opposition, elect Root as chairman, and triumph by substantially identical margins on every issue. On the first presidential ballot Taft received a clear majority with 561 votes. But 344 of the 451 Roosevelt delegates sat glumly by, refusing to take part in the proceedings, and the faithful—twenty-six delegates from Wisconsin, ten from North Dakota, and five from South Dakota—continued to cast their votes for La Follette until the end. [40]

The Chicago convention split the progressive group in Wisconsin into warring factions. McGovern received stacks of telegrams and letters approving the course he had followed at Chicago and an almost equal number denouncing him for his "disloyalty" to La Follette. A particularly terse and pointed note from three Milwaukee progressives read, "We the undersigned know of a law office for rent." Even more ominous for McGovern was the silence of the leading progressive lieutenants. Herman Ekern, John M. Nelson, Irvine Lenroot, and John J. Blaine, who had frequently conferred with him before the convention, now refrained from discussing with the governor any matters concerning the campaign. [41]

McGovern and his friends sought to defend his course against the attacks of La Follette and his personal followers. The *Mil-*

waukee Free Press featured an interview with delegate A. W. Prehn, who thought that Houser had made a grave mistake in scuttling the combined efforts to put McGovern in the chair. "None of the Wisconsin La Follette Men," he claimed, "are in any position to question McGovern's devotion to progressive principles or his loyalty to Senator La Follette." McGovern in his reply to the "office-renting Milwaukeeans," angrily denied that he became the "messenger" of Houser when he accepted election at the head of a La Follette ticket. He had the right to promote progressive interests and La Follette interests as he deemed wise. "My course," he contended, "was the only plan by which the Wisconsin delegation could remain neutral—to vote for a La Follette man for temporary chairman." He charged that the defeat of the progressives would affect everyone in the party. It would doom the Republicans to defeat in November, would leave the party in the control of the machine politicians, and hence would result in the loss of all the La Follette principles.[42]

La Follette, in his magazine, had denounced the efforts of McGovern and his friends to unite the progressives in opposition to Taft. He referred to McGovern as the Roosevelt candidate for the chairmanship and praised Houser's speech of denunciation, which he said had "thrilled the convention." He and his supporters went to work to tighten his personal control of the progressive machinery in Wisconsin. The names of the local progressive clubs were changed to La Follette Progressive Clubs. In all his utterances La Follette stressed the "fight for progressive principles, policies and candidates." He encouraged his followers to concentrate on sending men with progressive principles to Congress, where, he said, they would hold the balance of power. He attacked Congressman John J. Esch of the Seventh District, who had come out for Roosevelt, claiming that his record was not the record of a true progressive. In Esch's place he favored his own henchman Andrew H. Dahl. On the presidential race La Follette was vague and indefinite. His periodical carried numerous articles praising Bryan and Wilson for their progressive principles, and some thought he would support the Democratic candidate. But he urged the Wisconsin progressive Republicans to remain within the party, and he was especially insistent that they give no aid or comfort to the Progressive Party. "Don't bolt," was his admonition.[43]

McGovern, on the other hand, leaned toward the Progressive candidate. Many of his friends advised him to come out for Roosevelt; some even urged him to hitch his own candidacy for re-election as governor to the National Progressive Party. Others, such as University regent Granville D. Jones, reminded him that anything he did would give serious offense to La Follette and his supporters; he advised McGovern to stay in the party and support the regular nominee, thus keeping the state's party lines intact. During the entire summer McGovern was noncommital about the national race, but eventually, after much urging, he announced that he would support the "Progressive candidate for President and not the reactionary one." [44]

McGovern was unopposed in the state gubernatorial primary and, despite La Follette's displeasure, was renominated to succeed himself. In the general election he was opposed by the conservative Democrat John C. Karel and the Social Democratic nominee Carl D. Thompson. La Follette had little choice but to support McGovern. He publicly admitted that he had "a deep and lasting resentment" against McGovern for his actions at Chicago but appealed to all progressive voters to support him in this vital election. A vote for McGovern would be "a vote for the progressive movement." *La Follette's Magazine* carried an article by California's Senator John D. Works urging all progressives to vote for Wilson. La Follette probably did not vote for Wilson himself, but he doubtless preferred the Democratic candidate to either Taft or Roosevelt. The voters of Wisconsin evidently took him at his word.[45]

In the presidental race Wilson carried Wisconsin by a plurality of approximately thirty thousand, Roosevelt running a poor third. McGovern won re-election by a margin of only twelve thousand votes, but at that he and Karel both ran ahead of their parties' presidential candidates. There was undoubtedly a wide variety of "scratched tickets" among the ballots. Some of the progressives voted for Wilson and McGovern, some conservative Republicans for Taft and Karel. Probably most of the "Bull Moose" supporters went down the line and voted for McGovern also. At least some of the more rabid of La Follette's followers "cut the head of the state ticket." Nevertheless McGovern ran slightly ahead of the other Republican candidates. *La Follette's Magazine* presented the results as a "rebuke" to McGovern for affiliating himself with the Roosevelt candidacy. The *Free Press* vigorously denied this, pointing to McGovern's popular total as the largest given any candidate for any office in the election.[46]

La Follette's supporters proceeded to strengthen their own control of the Republican organization throughout the state. New La Follette Progressive Clubs were formed and old ones purged of pro-McGovern members. Their purpose, so the governor's friends charged, was to control the election of the junior senator in 1914. In the 1913 legislature the battle was also carried on between the two factions of the progressive Republicans. Charging that insurance commissioner Herman Ekern was campaigning for an anti-McGovern candidate for the speakership of the Assembly, McGovern summarily removed him from office. Ekern took the case to court and eventually won reinstatement.[47]

The legislature of 1913 was markedly hostile to the governor. Unlike its predecessor it contributed little to the progressive reforms, but it did much to harry and embarrass the executive. Even in social affairs the split was noticeable. The flood of responses which "declined with regret" an invitation to the governor's reception amounted almost to a boycott.[48] The personal relations of La Follette and McGovern were broken entirely. The governor had "no influence or communication" with the senior senator, he told a correspondent who had inquired about his endorsement of an application for a federal appointment. So bitter did the intraparty feud become that Charles McCarthy was prompted to write La Follette a letter of warning. "Your name," he said, "has been used and is being used by little and ambitious men to foment a war between factions in this State which nobody can profit by except the force of evil in the long run. . . . They are on the brink of defeating good legislation in order that he [McGovern] may not gain in any way by the passage of such legislation." [49]

In a further effort to frustrate McGovern the legislature considered a motion, made by a follower of La Follette, to recess the legislature until January, 1914, and then reconvene. This would have caused pending legislation to be laid over and would have enabled the lawmakers to sit during the 1914 election season. Fortunately for the state budget, this proposal was eventually rejected, and after a few weeks of further delay the legislature adjourned. McGovern summed up his view of the situation in a letter to one of his younger supporters. "All my present troubles," he related, "are due to my Bull Moose declaration of last year and my progressive friends must have patience until the battle is fought out to the end. Our Senior Senator has assumed the role of dictator here; and until the question of whether we are political serfs or free men is finally settled here in Wisconsin, no other issue can receive much consideration." [50]

The election of 1914 brought the climax of the bitter strife within the progressive ranks. Despite the active opposition of La Follette, McGovern won the Republican senatorial primary. His Democratic opponent was the popular Paul Oscar Husting, who had first attained prominence in the investigation of Senator Stephenson's campaign expenditures a few years before. In the primary race for the gubernatorial nomination La Follette's candidate, Andrew H. Dahl, ran against William H. Hatton, who had the backing of a majority of the other progressive Republicans. Emanuel Philipp, long-time stalwart leader, was backed by the conservatives. In the election the progressive vote was split almost equally between Dahl and Hatton, and Philipp, whose supporters had been in eclipse for a decade, won a bare plurality and became the Republican nominee.[51]

The nomination of Philipp demonstrated the complete failure of the "second-choice" primary law that La Follette had devised to meet just such a contingency as had developed. Had they acted logically the voters who cast their first-choice ballots for either Hatton or Dahl would have designated the other as their second choice. When these second-choice votes were counted the progressive in the lead would easily have overtaken the stalwart Philipp and received the nomination. Instead, most of the voters either scattered their second-choice votes aimlessly among the several minor candidates or left the second-choice space blank. This so-called "Mary Ann" law had been derided by Philipp and other conservatives as complicated and meaningless. Evidently to a majority of Wisconsin voters it was both. It was repealed soon thereafter.[52]

In the general election the progressive Republicans swallowed their distaste for their old enemy, and Philipp won over Democrat John Karel. An independent progressive, John J. Blaine, who ran without organized party backing, was swamped. McGovern lost to Husting by less than a thousand votes. The press attributed his defeat to La Follette's personal animosity. Not only did the progressives lose both the governorship and the senatorship, but no less than ten constitutional amendments, which had been approved by two consecutive legislatures, were defeated. The progressive organization, which had climbed to power under La Follette from 1900 to 1904, broke ranks and suffered eclipse as a result of their intraparty split and subsequent defeat. La Follette succeeded in defending his Senate seat in 1916, but it was not until after the World War that the progressives regained control of the state.[53]

The trail of "Fighting Bob" La Follette, in his climb to national fame and prestige, was strewn not only with his political opponents but also with many of the colleagues who had helped him win his earlier political battles. Davidson, Stephenson, and McGovern, and later Irvine Lenroot, loyal supporters of the progressive cause though they had been, were all read out of the party by the implacable senior senator. Even his relations with his closest friends, Henry Allen Cooper and Nils P. Haugen, cooled for a time during his career.[54]

Robert Marion La Follette, by virtue of his contributions to the state and to the nation, won recognition as a statesman of first rank. Not only was he responsible for a large number of constructive achievements, but he was the conscience of the Republican Party. But he was also excessively ambitious, and his ambitions would not permit him to brook any opposition. Nils P. Haugen regarded his presidential ambitions as especially unfortunate for himself and for the party. When it became apparent that there was no reasonable hope for victory, Haugen thought, he became a "carping critic" of each and every administration and was entirely incapable of team work.[55]

It is not unlikely that by the time of the Chicago convention of 1912 La Follette was regarding himself as a martyr to the cause of reform. As a martyr he was completely unwilling to make the political compromises that were necessary for the success of the party. The principle for which he battled was more important to him than the achievement of the substantial "half-loaf" which McGovern and others thought attainable. As a result the progressive Republican Party of Wisconsin, in spite of its popular appeal to the electorate and its many able and vigorous leaders, broke into warring factions and was ousted from power after almost a decade and a half of rule.

12 THE BALANCE SHEET

★ ★ ★ ★ ★ ★ ★ ★ ★ ★ ★ ★ ★ ★ ★ ★ ★ ★

THE PROGRESSIVE MOVEMENT IN WISCONSIN AFFECTED, DIRECTLY or indirectly, every institution and every person in the commonwealth. The progressive philosophy envisioned the use of the state as an instrument of reform, and many activities that had once been the concern only of those directly involved, now came under the supervision of the state. This expansion of the state's functions to safeguard the social well-being of its citizens and the conscripting of experts to help devise and administer the reform policies were integral parts of the "Wisconsin Idea."

Fundamental to the progressive philosophy was the movement to remove all barriers separating the elected official from the direct control of the voters. The primary election law of 1903, the second-choice primary law of 1911, and the preferential primaries for president and United States senator were all steps toward this goal. The progressives fully expected to cure the ills of democracy by more democracy, and they were sure that once direct voting procedures were established the "will of the people" would indeed be "the law of the land." [1] But the people proved surprisingly susceptible to demagoguery and the techniques of the professional politicians. The vagaries of the electorate were often unpredictable, even to so astute a campaigner as La Follette himself.

Nevertheless the direct primary was a marked advance. The growth of cities, improvements in communications, and greater experience in political affairs had given the voter a certain political maturity that made him dissatisfied with the system of indirect elections. The caucuses and conventions that had served an earlier generation very well had become identified with secret deals, machine politics, and bossism. The techniques and methods of the progressive campaigns, in contrast, called for intelligent and mature consideration of the issues by the voter. La Follette's practice of limiting his discussions to a few significant proposals also tended to encourage the citizen to study at least these issues seriously. Thus the progressive campaigns were a form of adult political education. The device of the "roll call," also popularized by La Follette, tended to make the voters more critical of their officials, who in turn became more concerned about their public records. This technique has become a favorite weapon of liberal and reform leaders on all levels of government throughout the country. The roll call has been used frequently by the national executive as a means of purging reactionary opponents.

In this movement to carry the elections to the people the Wisconsin progressives played a leading role. Wisconsin's direct primary law was the first to establish a comprehensive system of direct nominating elections in the United States. The pattern of this legislation and the progressives' campaign techniques were widely followed in other states and became a standard part of the nation's political machinery.[2]

The system of commissions of experts was the progressives' solution of the problems created by the pyramiding of industry and the congestion due to urban growth—problems too complex to be met by legislation alone. The Wisconsin system was by no means the earliest employment of the commission principle, but its use as a means of regulating corporations, public service and others, tended to identify it especially with the progressive movement in Wisconsin. The success that was achieved was largely attributable to the individual ability and judgment of the initial appointees. Here La Follette set a high standard, which was adopted by his successors. Under the leadership of such men as Balthasar H. Meyer, Nils P. Haugen, Herman L. Ekern, and John R. Commons the several commissions won the public confidence that was necessary for the general acceptance of their decisions and orders. As a result of the Wisconsin experience the commission has been widely accepted as a normal arm of the state.

The Railroad Commission was charged with many complex duties and functions. Not only did the commission regulate the rates and services of the railroads in the state, but it supervised public utilities, street railways, power projects, and securities as well. Since most of these corporations were "affected with a public interest," and many of them were partial or complete monopolies, the need for effective state supervision seemed self-evident to the progressives. Indeed the previous records of some of them would indicate that the public interest did require such supervision. Many of the difficulties confronting the Railroad Commission stemmed from the essentially interstate character of some of the public service corporations. For example, the most careful supervision of its activities in Wisconsin did not prevent the Chicago, Milwaukee, St. Paul and Pacific Railway from becoming insolvent and going into receivership in 1925. Yet, in general, the Railroad Commission performed its duties well—so well, in fact, that the conservative administration which followed the progressive downfall in 1914 continued and extended its functions.

The enactment of a comprehensive insurance code and the creation of an appointive, non-political, one-man insurance commission placed Wisconsin among the most advanced states in the field of insurance regulation. It is true that much of the initial friction could have been prevented if the state administration had adopted a more conciliatory attitude toward the insurance companies, and the companies had given greater evidence of cooperation. It is probable that if the controversial statutes had been drafted with more care and moderation, the

withdrawal of the Eastern companies might have been prevented. Yet Wisconsin did not suffer from this so-called radical
legislation. The ultimate general acceptance of the code and the
fact that, as Herman Ekern reported, no company licensed under the laws of 1907 went into receivership testified to the merit
of the insurance laws.

The establishment of the Industrial Commission was a bold
attempt to bring the resources and authority of the state to
bear upon problems born of the industrialization and urbaniza-
tion of certain areas. The growth of the labor population produced demands for legislation to improve and safeguard the
condition of the industrial worker. The progressive Republicans had, from La Follette's first election in 1900, attracted a
large share of the labor vote, and they continued to hold this
support through most of the period of their ascendancy despite
the rise of a radical, class-conscious party in the metropolis. The
union of the shop with the soil and seminar of the progressive
tradition produced a labor code that attracted favorable attention throughout the country. The Industrial Commission of
Wisconsin, the first comprehensive administrative board in the
labor field, regarded itself as a social agency charged with the
duty of insuring a fair deal to labor. In the fields of workmen's
compensation, safety inspection, women and children in industry, employment offices, and industrial education the commission set a standard of administrative excellence that other
states sought to emulate.[3] Somewhat less effective have been its
efforts to settle strikes and lockouts. In the early years of its
existence it appears to have lacked both the funds and the desire
to intervene in the arbitration of industrial disputes. It also
appears that in setting up a schedule of fixed payments for industrial injuries the commission inadvertently acted against the
interest of workers who might have had an excellent case under
common law. Nevertheless the overall condition of labor in Wisconsin under the Industrial Commission compared favorably

with that in other parts of the country. In taking steps in 1911 to intervene in the terms and conditions of industrial employment, the progressives placed Wisconsin among the leaders in the field of labor legislation.

Perhaps the key to the whole progressive program was the Tax Commission. The equalization of the general property tax throughout Wisconsin was an achievement that many other states have since used as a model. So effectively and judiciously was the system of ad valorem taxation carried out by the commission that it was widely copied throughout the country and the principle was borrowed by the federal government. The tax commissioners also made notable contributions to the theory and philosophy of taxation. The reports they issued during the progressive era rank high in the field of tax literature. Especially significant was the role the commission played in the enactment and administration of the first successful state income tax. In adopting the principle of "ability to pay" the commission took a most important step in the modernization of the tax structure. Here again the leadership of the Wisconsin progressives was attested by the fact that a number of other states hastened to enact income tax laws after viewing the success of the Wisconsin experiment.

This mass of constructive legislation had an enormous influence upon other states and upon the federal government the full extent of which cannot be measured. Governors Davidson, McGovern, and Philipp received many inquiries from governors, legislators, and others about the effectiveness of various Wisconsin innovations. Delegations from other states visited Wisconsin to view the working of the progressives' laws, boards, commissions, and institutions.[4] La Follette and other Wisconsin leaders participated in campaigns to introduce reforms in neighboring states. In Congress La Follette, Henry A. Cooper, John M. Nelson, and John J. Esch worked unceasingly to get the principles and ideals of Wisconsin progressivism written into federal law. Conversely, Wisconsin progressives were also greatly influenced by other reform movements, particularly those in Colorado and Oregon.[5]

The influence of Wisconsin progressivism was extended also by the exceptional publicity it received in the national press. La Follette's autobiography was carried serially in the *American Magazine*. A surprising number of periodicals devoted long articles to Wisconsin's achievements, most of which were glowing in their praise and largely uncritical. Equally laudatory and uncritical were the principal books on the movement, *The Wisconsin Idea* by Charles McCarthy and *Wisconsin: An Experiment in Democracy* by Frederick C. Howe, both of which appeared in 1912. The Wisconsin progressives may well have received more publicity than was desirable for their own good. Very little of it was objective, unbiased, or analytical, and too much of it suggested that the reforms approached perfection. As a result the conservatives became even more bitter in their opposition to the progressive reforms and were disposed to consider the innovations more radical than they actually were. The ultimate reaction was perhaps more pronounced than it otherwise would have been.

The presence of a strong and growing Social Democratic Party in the state aroused much speculation over the possibility of a union of the two groups. But there was never any real alliance between the progressive Republicans and the Milwaukee Socialists. On many specific issues, especially labor issues, they were able to work together, but such agreements were only temporary. Perhaps the conflicting personalities of Robert La Follette and Victor Berger prevented any lasting agreement. However that may be, the growing Socialist strength cut deeply into the progressive Republican majorities in most industrial areas, and basically the two groups remained antagonistic. Although the Social Democrats had achieved an excellent record for efficient and forward-looking administration in Milwaukee, the state progressive Republican organization cooperated in the "nonpartisan" bloc that ousted them from the City Hall in 1912 after only two years in office. The strong showing Emil Seidel made in 1914 in the United States senatorial race probably cost Francis McGovern the vote of his home city and with it the election.[6]

Comprehensive as was the program of the Wisconsin progressives, there were many reforms that were popular in other states which they either ignored or failed to write into law. In many states woman suffrage was an important part of the progressive program, but Wisconsin did not adopt this reform until the enactment of the Nineteenth Amendment. True, La Follette was eager to extend the franchise to women, and a constitutional amendment for the purpose was submitted to the people in the 1912 election, but in the tangled presidential and state balloting it was overwhelmingly defeated. The next year McGovern vetoed a resolution to resubmit the amendment and thus terminated for the time being the drive for woman suffrage in Wisconsin.[7]

Wisconsin also failed to adopt the initiative, referendum, and recall, which were features of progressivism in Oregon. Resolutions favoring these innovations were approved by the legislature and placed in the ballot in 1914, but were defeated by a large majority.[8]

One of the bitterest defeats suffered by the progressives was the rejection by the State Supreme Court of their efforts to establish an effective water-power and reforestation program. On the whole the progressives' legislation fared rather well at the hands of the courts, but the water-power decisions led to agitation to reorganize the judiciary and make the amending process easier. La Follette himself, in a series of editorials in his magazine, led the attack on the court, calling it a "judicial oligarchy." But the high court maintained its equanimity, and proposals for the recall of state judges and a simplified amending process were lost, either in the legislature or at the polls in the progressive debacle of 1914.[9]

There were also certain significant by-products of the progressive movement in Wisconsin that doubtless were unforeseen. Among these were the revelations, by the State Board of Public Affairs, of bureaucracy, waste, and extravagance in the state government. Despite the high character of most of the officials in key positions and their sense of public responsibility, the rapid increase in government offices and expenses had led to waste and inefficiency. It was not strange that within a decade after the progressives' rise to power, responsible citizens were clamoring for relief from the ever-growing bureaucracy.[10]

An inevitable consequence of the establishment of state commissions with wide powers was the transfer of many functions of government from the local unit to the state. The tendency of the Tax Commission to extend its control over the collection of taxes reduced the authority and importance of local officials. The drive for uniformity, equalization, and efficiency was accomplished only at the expense of the independence of the town and county governments.

In spite of the progressives' campaigns against monopoly the administration unwittingly fostered monopoly in the process of regulating many public service corporations. Because the Railroad Commission lacked a yardstick for measuring unit costs, it tended to guarantee a fair return and profit regardless of the efficiency or inefficiency of the operation of a power plant, waterworks, or street railway. The physical evaluation of properties was only a partial check against inefficiency and the trend was toward higher rates to compensate for rising costs.

The cooperation between the progressive administration and the University was not an altogether unmixed blessing. The close tie between members of the faculty and many phases of the progressive program rendered it inevitable that the University should also be seriously affected by the reaction that set in after

1914. In subsequent years the University has frequently been greatly disturbed by major shifts of administration at the state capitol.

The progressive reform drive was perhaps too ambitious and too thoroughgoing to be completely assimilated into the governmental framework in the short space of a decade. The political history of Wisconsin since 1914 has been characterized by oscillations which appear to have been more violent than comparable shifts of administration in neighboring states. The bitterness of the progressive-stalwart fight is still apparent in some quarters, despite the honor in which the name of Robert M. La Follette is held.

The story of the development of Wisconsin progressivism before 1914 is of course only the first chapter of the history of the state's progressivism. After the debacle of 1914 the stalwart Emanuel Philipp held the governorship for three terms, during which time advances in social and economic welfare were relegated to a secondary place. In 1920 the pendulum of political fortune swung again to the progressives when John J. Blaine, who had first attracted public attention as a state senator in the Stephenson investigation, succeeded to the governor's chair. Under him the program of progressive reform was resumed along the lines charted by La Follette. During all this time "Old Bob" had continued to hold his Senate seat, and in 1924 he carried the state's electoral vote in his campaign for the presidency on an "Independent and Progressive" ticket.

Blaine's administration was followed by a second conservative reaction, but with the coming of economic depression in 1930 and the inauguration of the New Deal the progressives once more gained the ascendancy. For more than a decade the "Cubs of the Old Lion," Philip F. and Robert M. La Follette Jr., dominated the political life of Wisconsin. It was during this time that the progressive movement at last became the Progressive Party as the younger La Follettes led their followers into a third party. The 1940's saw the triumph of the conservatives once more and the retirement of both the junior La Follettes to private life. It seems likely that the pattern of alternating conservative and progressive upheavals will continue, with varying violence. In every such upheaval the shadow of "Fighting Bob" La Follette and the original, fundamental progressive movement in Wisconsin will play a significant role.

Taken as a whole the progressive regime in Wisconsin provided the people with good, if expensive government. During fourteen years surprisingly little graft was revealed on any level, and no key figure was involved in a financial scandal. The commissions of experts performed a much-needed public service in controlling and regulating the rapid industrialization of the state. Under the influence of the "Wisconsin Idea" the state administration was widely accepted as a friend of the common man. Wisconsin became famous as a leader in the fields of economic and social reforms. These accomplishments were the work of no one man but of a large corps of talented leaders. It would be difficult to estimate the contributions made by such men as Nils P. Haugen, Francis E. McGovern, Charles McCarthy, Herman L. Ekern, Charles R. Van Hise, John R. Commons, Thomas S. Adams, William H. Hatton, and John J. Blaine.

But after credit has been duly apportioned the student of the rise of the progressive movement in Wisconsin must return to Robert M. La Follette. It was he who first led the progressives from defeat to victory. It was he who perfected the progressive machine and completed the overthrow of the conservative organization. Again, it was La Follette who first brought Wisconsin progressivism to national attention and made it an effective part of a larger movement. The program of the party bore the stamp of his personality more than any other. The ideals and prejudices, the powers and weaknesses, the triumphs and failures of Robert M. La Follette were reflected in the progressive movement in Wisconsin.

NOTES TO THE TEXT

NOTES TO THE TEXT

★ ★ ★ ★ ★ ★ ★ ★ ★ ★ ★ ★ ★ ★ ★ ★ ★

1. THE SOIL OF PROGRESSIVISM

[1] Benjamin Parke De Witt, *The Progressive Movement* (New York, 1915), vii.

[2] See John D. Hicks, *The Populist Revolt* (Minneapolis, 1931), Appendices A to F.

[3] *The Twelfth Census of the United States*, 1900 (Washington, 1901–02), Vol. 1, Pt. 1, p. lxxxiii; Vol. 7, pt. 1, p. liv.

[4] The key leaders in the Republican organization in the eighteen nineties were Henry C. Payne, Milwaukee streetcar magnate and national committeeman, and Philetus Sawyer, Oshkosh lumber baron and one-time United States senator. Sawyer was long recognized as the political boss of the state, but associated with him in positions of power were such men as John Coit Spooner, railroad lawyer and United States senator, Isaac Stephenson, multi-millionaire lumberman, and Payne. The party strongholds were centered in the German wards of Milwaukee, where the machine henchmen were able to deliver the vote almost as a bloc. The Democratic machine, though far less powerful and seldom in power except on the local level, was organized along similar lines. See Dorothy Ganfield [Fowler], "The Influence of Wisconsin on Federal Politics, 1880–1907," in the *Wisconsin Magazine of History*, 16:10 (1932); Lincoln Steffens, *The Struggle for Self-Government* (New York, 1906); Bayrd Still, *Milwaukee: The History of a City* (Madison, 1948), 308 ff.

[5] *Wisconsin Blue Book*, 1901, p. 655; *Laws of Wisconsin*, 1874, Ch. 273; 1876, Ch. 97; Balthasar H. Meyer, *Railway Legislation in the United States* (New York, 1903), 167; *Wabash, St. Louis and Pacific Railway Company v. Illinois*, 118 U. S. 557 (1886); *San Mateo County v. Southern Pacific Railroad Company*, 118 U. S. 394 (1886); William Z. Ripley, *Railroads: Rates and Regulation* (New York, 1912), 456–486; Isaac Stephenson, *Recollections of a Long Life* (Chicago, 1915), 213–214.

[6] The national average increase from 1890 to 1905 was 20.8 per cent and the urban increase 36.8 per cent. *United States Census*, 1900, Vol. 1, Pt. 1, p. lxxxviii.

[7] *Ibid.*, Vol. 8, Pt. 11, pp. 952–954.

[8] The agricultural statistics are for the year 1899. *Ibid.*, Vol. 5, Pt. 1, p. cxxii; Vol. 8, Pt. 11, p. 951.

2. LA FOLLETTE AND THE ELECTION OF 1900

[1] *Wisconsin Blue Book,* 1899, pp. 354–355.

[2] "Republican State Platform, 1898," in the *Wisconsin Blue Book,* 1899, p. 711. The inheritance tax law was declared unconstitutional in 1902. See *Black v. State,* 113 Wis. 205. It was later (1903) redrawn, repassed, and upheld by the Supreme Court. *Laws of Wisconsin,* 1903, Ch. 44; *Nunnemacher v. State,* 129 Wis. 190 (1909).

[3] Roswell Miller to Elisha W. Keyes, November 11, 1891, in the Elisha W. Keyes Papers, and Ellis B. Usher to John J. Esch, March 13, 1900, in the John J. Esch Papers, in the State Historical Society of Wisconsin.

[4] La Follette was born in 1855 in Dane County about twenty miles from Madison and had grown up on a farm amid the most modest surroundings. After attending the local grammar schools he worked his way through the state university, holding a variety of jobs, including that of editor and publisher of the campus paper. At this time the family fortunes were at such low ebb that he was obliged not only to support himself but to help support his mother and sister also. Short, and at that time thin, La Follette nevertheless became a campus leader and speaker. In his senior year he won both state and interstate contests in oratory and on his return from his final triumph was given a hero's welcome by his fellow students. Even at this early age La Follette displayed the qualities—ambition, tenacity, mental capacity, and forthrightness—that were to carry him far in national life. See Robert M. La Follette, *La Follette's Autobiography: A Personal Narrative of Political Experiences* (Madison, 1913); also Belle Case La Follette and Fola La Follette, *Robert M. La Follette* (2 vols., New York, 1953).

[5] La Follette, *Autobiography,* 19.

[6] "Speech in the House of Representatives," in the *Congressional Record,* 49 Congress, 1 Session (1886), 2780; "Speech upon being re-elected to the United States Senate," in the *Wisconsin Assembly Journal,* 1911, p. 118; La Follette, *Autobiography,* 28.

[7] The Sawyer–La Follette incident of 1891 is famous in Wisconsin's political history. In his *Autobiography,* pages 143–150, La Follette denounced the offer as a bribe. For other accounts of the controversy see the *Milwaukee Sentinel,* October 28, 1891; Horace Rublee to Jeremiah M. Rusk, November 3, 1891, in the Jeremiah M. Rusk Papers, in the State Historical Society of Wisconsin; Philetus Sawyer to Keyes, November 1, 1891, in the Keyes Papers; and Nils P. Haugen, *Pioneer and Political Reminiscences* (Evansville, Wisconsin, 1930), 118.

[8] Payne to Keyes, July 10, 1896, Jerome A. Watrous to Keyes, August 14, 1896, La Follette to Theodore Kronshage, December 14, 1899, and Ira B. Bradford to Keyes, July 8, 1897, in the Keyes Papers; William D. Hoard to La Follette, January 30, 1900, in the Robert M. La Follette Papers, in the State Historical Society of Wisconsin.

[9] Keyes was often in error in his forecasts and interpretations, but he presents an interesting example of stalwart reaction to the events of this period. See his letter to Spooner of January 25, 1900, in the Keyes Papers. La Follette charged that Keyes was opening his mail for the purpose of dis-

covering his intentions. See La Follette to Rodney A. Elward, March 18, 1900, in the La Follette Papers, and the *Milwaukee Sentinel,* March 26, 1900.

¹⁰ Usher to Esch, March 24, 1900, in the Esch Papers.

¹¹ *Milwaukee Sentinel,* March 9, 30, 1900. When Sawyer's death was announced one of La Follette's henchmen wrote gleefully, "The old devil is dead. Isn't this the opportunity we have long sought?" H. S. Comstock to La Follette, April 2, 1900, in the La Follette Papers.

¹² T. M. Purtell to Nils P. Haugen, March 23, G. V. Borchsenius to Haugen, April 9, and George F. Cooper to La Follette, May 19, 1900, in the Nils P. Haugen Papers, in the State Historical Society of Wisconsin; La Follette to George P. Rossman, April 9, and to Stephenson, April 14, 1900, in the La Follette Papers; La Follette, *Autobiography,* 229; Emanuel L. Philipp, *Political Reform in Wisconsin* (Milwaukee, 1910), 28; Stephenson, *Recollections of a Long Life,* 212; Stephenson to Keyes, September 24, 1898, in the Keyes Papers.

¹³ Henry Casson to La Follette, January 16, and La Follette to Gilbert E. Roe, March 21, 1900, in the La Follette Papers; Usher to Esch, March 13, 1900, in the Esch Papers; La Follette, *Autobiography,* 228; Keyes to Spooner, March 28, and to H. O. Taylor, April 9, 1900, in the Keyes Papers; Babcock to James O. Davidson, July 2, 1900, in the James O. Davidson Papers, in the State Historical Society of Wisconsin. See also "Sketch," unpublished manuscript by Harry W. Barney, Babcock's secretary, concerning this campaign, in the Joseph W. Babcock Papers, in the State Historical Society of Wisconsin.

¹⁴ La Follette to William D. Hoard, May 3, Roe to La Follette, March 28, and La Follette to Albert R. Hall, May 2, 1900, in the La Follette Papers. Baumgartner failed to oust David Rose from the mayor's seat in the Milwaukee city election, which was regarded as a discouraging but not disastrous setback for the La Follette forces. *Milwaukee Sentinel,* April 11, 1900; Keyes to R. J. Flint and to Rose, April 4, 1900, in the Keyes Papers; La Follette to Kronshage, March 16, 1900, in the La Follette Papers.

¹⁵ "State Press Notes," in the *Milwaukee Sentinel,* 1900: April 11, p. 4; April 27, p. 2; April 28, p. 5; May 4, p. 4. La Follette promised fair play for the brewing and railroad interests and agreed to remain aloof from the coming senatorial race. In return Gill and Philipp undertook to see Marvin Hughitt of the Chicago North Western. They got no promise of funds from him, only his agreement to "stand non-committal" for the time being. Later La Follette had a personal conference with Hughitt. Memorandum of Emanuel L. Philipp, April 25, 1900, in the Emanuel L. Philipp Papers, in the State Historical Society of Wisconsin; William D. Hoard to La Follette, April 30, La Follette to Murphy, May 3, and Babcock to La Follette (2 letters), May 4, 1900, in the La Follette Papers.

¹⁶ La Follette to Haugen, May 7, 11, 12, 16, and Hall to Haugen, May 7, 1900, in the Haugen Papers; La Follette to Babcock, May 2, 1900, in the La Follette Papers.

¹⁷ *Bee* (Phillips, Price County), May 9, 1900; *Advance* (Soldier's Grove, Crawford County), April 27, 1900; quoted in the *Milwaukee Sentinel,* May 4, 1900, p. 4.

[18] Pamphlet *Announcing La Follette's Candidacy for Governor,* a copy of which is in the library of the State Historical Society of Wisconsin; *Milwaukee Sentinel,* May 17, 1900, p. 4; *Hudson Star Times* (St. Croix County), May 18, 1900; *Fond du Lac Commonwealth,* May 18, 1900.

[19] La Follette, *Autobiography,* 232; Keyes to Spooner, May 21, 1900, in the Keyes Papers; Usher to W. H. Mylrea, June 30, 1900, in the Usher Papers; La Follette to Thomas H. Gill, May 12, 1900, in the La Follette Papers.

[20] Letters to Keyes from John M. Whitehead, May 17, Fred Dennett, May 18, and James J. McGillivray, June 6, 1900, in the Keyes Papers; La Follette to Arthur Pugh, June 4, 12, 1900, in the Arthur Pugh Papers, in the State Historical Society of Wisconsin.

[21] A. M. Jones to Keyes, May 22, Keyes to Quarles, May 22, and Quarles to Keyes, May 25, 1900, in the Keyes Papers; Henry C. Adams to La Follette, May 2, 1900, in the La Follette Papers; Bradford to Esch, June 18, 1900, in the Esch Papers.

[22] *Milwaukee Sentinel,* May 31, 1900; Davidson to O. G. Munson, June 16, 1900, in the Davidson Papers.

[23] Keyes to William H. Stennett, June 3, 1900, in the Keyes Papers; *Milwaukee Sentinel,* May 30, 1900; La Follette to James A. Stone, May 3, 1900, in the Stone Papers; La Follette to Babcock, May 10, 1900, in the La Follette Papers.

[24] Granville D. Jones to James A. Stone, July 6, and Stone to Jones, July 7, 1900, in the Stone Papers; Usher to Judge C. M. Webb, June 11, and to W. H. Mylrea, June 30, 1900, in the Usher Papers; P. A. Orton to Keyes, June 7, 1900, in the Keyes Papers.

[25] *Ashland Daily Press,* June 2, 1900; John C. Gaveney to Esch, June 20, and William C. Donovan to Esch, June 26, 1900, in the Esch Papers; La Follette to Haugen, May 25, 1900, in the Haugen Papers; Keyes to Bradford, May 27, 1900, in the Keyes Papers.

[26] *Milwaukee Sentinel,* June 24, 27, 30, 1900.

[27] *Ibid.,* June 27, 1900.

[28] *Oshkosh Northwestern,* June 28, 1900; *Appleton Evening Crescent,* June 27, 1900; *Milwaukee Sentinel,* June 28, 1900. See also the comments of the state press quoted on page 4 of this issue of the *Sentinel.*

[29] Hiram D. Fisher to Keyes, April 4, 1909, in the Keyes Papers.

[30] *Milwaukee Sentinel,* June 28, 1900.

[31] *Ibid.,* July 1, 2, 1900; *La Crosse Daily Republican and Leader,* July 3, 1900; La Follette to Haugen, July 7, 1900, in the Haugen Papers; Babcock to Davidson, July 2, 1900, in the Davidson Papers.

[32] Spooner to Payne, May 7, to F. A. Dennett, May 19, to S. W. Campbell, June 17, and William H. Phippi, July 9, 1900, in the John C. Spooner Papers, in the Library of Congress; Usher to Lute W. Nieman, July 12, 1900, in the Usher Papers; P. A. Orton to Keyes, June 7, Keyes to Esch, June 15, and Keyes to Gaveney, July 7, 1900, in the Keyes Papers; *Milwaukee Sentinel,* July 6, 7, 1900.

[33] *Milwaukee Sentinel,* July 25, 26, 1900.

[34] Usher to E. T. Wheelock, July 13, 1900, in the Usher Papers.

35 *Milwaukee Sentinel,* August 9, 10, 1900.
36 *Wisconsin Blue Book,* 1901, pp. 690–691.
37 *Milwaukee Sentinel,* August 11, 1900; *The Eagle* (Marinette, Wisconsin), August 18, 25, 1900.
38 *Milwaukee Sentinel,* September 10, 20, 1900.
39 *Wisconsin Blue Book,* 1901, pp. 699–700.
40 F. W. Walker to Haugen, October 16, 1900, in the Haugen Papers; W. H. Rosenstengel to Davidson, October 11, and G. M. Burnham to Davidson, October 24, 1900, in the Davidson Papers; W. L. Houser to Esch, October 1, 1900, in the Esch Papers.
41 *Milwaukee Sentinel,* November 4, 1900.
42 La Follette to Haugen, August 21, 1900, in the Haugen Papers; James A. Stone to La Follette, July 5, and to George E. Bryant, November 8, 1900, in the Stone Papers.
43 *Wisconsin Blue Book,* 1901, pp. 266, 328–336.
44 The general goodfellowship which existed among erstwhile political enemies was quite evident during the post-election lull. La Follette took a much-needed rest at West Baden Springs in Indiana to recover from the strain of the campaign. There he basked in the sunshine and bathed in the hot springs in company with Babcock, state senator George Burrows, Hiram D. Fisher, Keyes, and others from the Wisconsin and Chicago area. Keyes returned well pleased with the prospects of a friendly and peaceful administration. In a letter to William H. Stennett, counsel for the Chicago and North Western Railway, Keyes praised the change in Bob's outlook and his evident desire to cooperate with all elements of the party. The ex-boss was well pleased with the results of the election and the new governor. See Hoard to Keyes, November 22, and Gaveney to Keyes, November 23, and Keyes to George B. Burrows, December 1, to Gaveney, December 1, and to Stennett, November 7, 1900, in the Keyes Papers.

3. BLOCKED BY THE STALWARTS

1 *Wisconsin State Journal,* January 7, 8, 1901; *Milwaukee Sentinel,* January 8, 1901.
2 *Milwaukee Sentinel,* December 14, 1900, January 8, 1901, p. 7; *Wisconsin Blue Book,* 1901, pp. 728–772.
3 *Wisconsin Assembly Journal,* 1901, pp. 16–48; La Follette, *Autobiography,* 243.
4 *Laws of Wisconsin,* 1891, Ch. 439; 1893, Ch. 7, 249; 1895, Ch. 288; 1897, Ch. 366; 1899, Ch. 341; *Wisconsin Assembly Journal,* 1897, p. 246; *Milwaukee Sentinel,* March 10, 1894, March 21, 1898; Philipp, *Political Reform in Wisconsin,* 23.
5 Ernst Christopher Meyer, *Nominating Systems* (Madison, Wisconsin, 1902), 83–93.
6 For an account of the beginning of this literature of exposure see Cornelius Regier, *The Era of the Muckrakers* (Chapel Hill, North Carolina, 1932).

[7] *Milwaukee Sentinel,* February 23, 1897, March 13, 1898, July 30, 1900, p. 5; *Wisconsin State Journal,* August 4, 1900; other newspapers quoted in the *Milwaukee Sentinel* of November 16, 1900, p. 4. The year 1901 marked a new high in enthusiasm for the direct primary throughout the country. In no fewer than nineteen states measures similar to the Stevens bill were introduced in the state legislatures. Most of these either failed of passage or were drastically modified before passage. Perhaps the most comprehensive of those passed was the measure enacted in Minnesota. Here, where a primary law affecting Hennepin County (Minneapolis) has been in effect since 1899, the legislature extended the system to provide for the statewide compulsory nomination of all except state officers. See Meyer, *Nominating Systems,* 94–96; also John A. Fairlie, *Direct Primaries in Minnesota (Publications of the Michigan Political Science Association,* Vol. 6, No. 1, Ann Arbor, 1905), 55.

[8] *Wisconsin Assembly Journal,* 1901, p. 127; *Wisconsin Senate Journal,* 1901, p. 119. E. Ray Stevens and George P. Miller were the respective authors of the two bills, a combined version of which was popularly known as the Stevens bill. *Milwaukee Sentinel,* January 16, 19, February 6, 1901.

[9] *Milwaukee Sentinel,* January 5, 18, 1901. The *Wisconsin Blue Book* in reprinting the Republican platform used both words with "recommend" in parentheses. Both groups produced copies of the original convention platform to support their claims. *Wisconsin Blue Book,* 1901, p. 670; La Follette, *Autobiography,* 267.

[10] Philipp, *Political Reform in Wisconsin,* 31, 32, 41; Keyes to H. A. Taylor, February 28, 1901, in the Keyes Papers.

[11] La Follette, *Autobiography,* 244–245.

[12] *Milwaukee Sentinel,* February 10, 12, 1901. The conservatives, led by Pfister, Spooner, and Philipp, were regularly called stalwarts, and the followers of La Follette became known as "half-breeds" or progressives.

[13] La Follette, *Autobiography,* 252; Philipp, *Political Reform in Wisconsin,* 40; Keyes to Spooner, February 13, 1901, in the Keyes Papers.

[14] *Milwaukee Sentinel,* February 24, 27, 1901; March 2, 1901, p. 4.

[15] *Wisconsin Assembly Journal,* 1901, pp. 583–589, 626–627; *Milwaukee Sentinel,* March 6, 14, 22, 1901; La Follette to Cooper, February 16, 1901, in the La Follette Papers; Keyes to R. J. Flint, February 11, 1901, in the Keyes Papers.

[16] *Milwaukee Journal,* February 22, 1901; quoted in the *Milwaukee Sentinel* of March 2 and March 5, 1901; Keyes to H. A. Taylor, March 18, and to Mrs. Lillie Law Finch, March 26, 1901, in the Keyes Papers; La Follette to Irvine L. Lenroot, June 25, 1901, in the La Follette Papers; *Wisconsin Senate Journal,* 1901, p. 830; *Milwaukee Sentinel,* April 12, 1901.

[17] *Wisconsin Assembly Journal,* 1901, pp. 1022, 1116–1118; *Milwaukee Sentinel,* April 26, May 3, 4, 1901.

[18] *Wisconsin Senate Journal,* 1901, pp. 1026–1035; *Milwaukee Sentinel,* May 11, 1901.

[19] *Wisconsin Senate Journal,* 1901, pp. 1061–1063; *Milwaukee Sentinel,* April 15, 1901; Philipp, *Political Reform in Wisconsin,* 48.

[20] La Follette, *Autobiography*, 258–266. It is significant that Emanuel Philipp, who after 1904 assumed the leadership of the stalwarts, conceded a few years later that the Hagemeister bill was not a workable measure and that La Follette had been justified in vetoing it. Philipp, *Political Reform in Wisconsin*, 40–50.

[21] Guy Edward Snider, *The Taxation of Gross Receipts of Railways in Wisconsin* (*Publications of the American Economic Association*, 3d Series, Vol. 7, No. 4 [1906]), 30. The best examples of railroad commissions having genuine regulative powers before 1900 are those of Texas, Iowa, Minnesota, and Illinois. All were similar in that they had authority to fix rates, correct abuses, and exercise general control over the railroads in their respective states. However, their powers had been curtailed by adverse federal court rulings such as *Chicago, Milwaukee and St. Paul Railroad Co. v. Minnesota*, 134 U. S. 418 (1889) and *Reagan v. Farmers' Loan and Trust Company*, 154 U. S. 362 (1894). See Meyer, *Railway Legislation*, 173–184, and Frank H. Dixon, *State Railway Control* (New York, 1896), 194–195.

[22] *Wisconsin Assembly Journal*, 1895, pp. 106, 780; Philipp, *Political Reform in Wisconsin*, 168; La Follette, *Autobiography*, 212–217; *Wisconsin State Journal*, April 10, 1898. In shipping a milk cow from his home in Oconto to Madison, Scofield used a complimentary frank from the Railway Express Company to avoid payment of shipping costs. It touched off anew the fight against the railroads' practice of granting special privileges, and Scofield's cow became famous as a symbol of such privileges. The anti-pass law of 1899 applied only to political officeholders, but it was amended in 1905 to include the general public. *Laws of Wisconsin*, 1897, Ch. 340; 1899, Ch. 206, 357; 1905, Ch. 486.

[23] See above, page 18; La Follette, *Autobiography*, 236–237.

[24] *Wisconsin Blue Book*, 1901, p. 690.

[25] La Follette, *Autobiography*, 238–239.

[26] *Report of the State Tax Commission*, 1901, pp. 107, 111, 162; La Follette, *Autobiography*, 244.

[27] *Wisconsin Assembly Journal*, 1901, p. 144; Assembly Bills, No. 164A (January 30, 1901). For details of physical evaluation see the next chapter, pages 50–52.

[28] *Wisconsin Senate Journal*, 1901, p. 237; *Wisconsin Assembly Journal*, 1901, p. 114; Keyes to J. W. Fosey, January 24, to William H. Stennett, January 20, and to Albert J. Earling, February 2, 1901, in the Keyes Papers.

[29] *Milwaukee Sentinel*, March 11, April 21, 1901.

[30] Philipp, *Political Reform in Wisconsin*, 153, 213; La Follette's "Message to the Legislature," in the *Wisconsin Assembly Journal*, 1901, pp. 16–48; La Follette, *Autobiography*, 257–266.

[31] *Wisconsin Assembly Journal*, 1901, pp. 1080–1088; *Milwaukee Sentinel*, May 3, 1901; *Wisconsin State Journal*, May 2, 1901.

4. CURBING THE BOSSES AND THE RAILROADS

¹ Interviews with John M. Nelson, June 16, 1948, and Fred R. Zimmerman, July 10, 1951.

² See Philipp's "Autobiographical Sketch" in the Philipp Papers, in the State Historical Society of Wisconsin; La Follette to Keyes, March 1, 1910, and Carl P. McAssey to Keyes, August 13, 1906, in the Keyes Papers.

³ See letters from Taylor and Casson to Keyes, especially Taylor to Keyes, June 9, 1902, and Casson to Keyes, March 6, 1906, in the Keyes Papers; Dorothy Ganfield [Fowler], "The Influence of Wisconsin on Federal Politics, 1880–1907," in the *Wisconsin Magazine of History*, 16:10–25 (1932); *Congressional Directory*, 1903, pp. 213, 230.

⁴ La Follette to Cooper, November 5, 1902 (telegram), January 19, December 23, 1904, November 27, 1905, in the Cooper Papers; La Follette to Cooper, February 16, 1901, in the La Follette Papers; A. M. Brayton to Henry C. Campbell, September 21, 1910, in the Esch Papers; John M. Nelson to Keyes, December 23, 1907, in the Keyes Papers.

⁵ H. C. Adams to Grant Thomas, December 21, 1903, and letters to Adams from William D. Hoard, January 12, Frank Tucker, March 12, Charles I. Brigham, April 17, and Grant Thomas, May 3, 1906, in the Adams Papers.

⁶ *Wisconsin Blue Book*, 1907, p. 1116; Harlan P. Bird to Keyes, November 6, 1906, in the Keyes Papers. See the biographical "Sketch" of Babcock by Harry W. Barney, in the Babcock Papers, in the State Historical Society of Wisconsin.

⁷ *Wisconsin Blue Book*, 1903, p. 1072. See also above, page 22, and Lincoln Steffens, "Wisconsin: A State Where the People Have Restored Representative Government—The Story of Governor La Follette," in *McClure's Magazine*, 23:564–579 (October, 1904).

⁸ Philipp, *Political Reform in Wisconsin*, 53–54; Keyes to E. D. Coe, May 11, 1902, and to Spooner, January 8, 1903, and John C. Gaveney to Keyes, July 2, 1902, in the Keyes Papers.

⁹ Keyes to Fred Dennett, September 22, 1901, in the Keyes Papers; La Follette, *Autobiography*, 276–277.

¹⁰ *Milwaukee Sentinel*, March 22, 1902. The State Historical Society of Wisconsin has a collection of these pamphlets.

¹¹ *Voters Handbook*, a copy of which is in the library of the State Historical Society of Wisconsin; La Follette, *Autobiography*, 279–280.

¹² Philipp, *Political Reform in Wisconsin*, 53–54; Keyes to Spooner, January 8, and to E. D. Coe, May 11, 1902, Dennett to Keyes, June 3, 1902, and John C. Gaveney to Keyes, July 2, 1902, in the Keyes Papers; Arthur G. Douglas to J. C. Harper, May 27, and Edward Kelley to Alfred J. Rogers, June 16, 1902, in the La Follette Papers.

¹³ *Milwaukee Free Press*, July 12, 1902.

¹⁴ *Wisconsin Blue Book*, 1903, pp. 1033–1034.

¹⁵ *Milwaukee Sentinel*, July 15, October 1, December 10, 1902, January 15, 1903; Keyes to Spooner, July 17, 1902, W. H. Stennett to Keyes, August 23, 1902, H. A. Taylor to Keyes, October 20, 1902, and Keyes to Casson, January 17, 1903, in the Keyes Papers.

[16] Bayrd Still, *Milwaukee: The History of a City* (State Historical Society of Wisconsin, 1948), 308 ff.; *Wisconsin Blue Book, 1903*, p. 1043.

[17] *Milwaukee Free Press*, October 1, 1902; *Milwaukee Sentinel*, October 9, November 5, 1902; La Follette, *Autobiography*, 339. See also E. N. Bowers to Davidson, August 1, 1902, in the Davidson Papers, and Marvin B. Rosenberry to La Follette, October 17, 1902, in the La Follette Papers.

[18] *Milwaukee Sentinel*, May 7, 9, 1902; W. G. Bissell (secretary of the Wisconsin Republican League) to Amil Markee, May 23, 1902, in the La Follette Papers.

[19] *Milwaukee Sentinel*, July 18, 19, 1902.

[20] *Milwaukee Free Press*, September 20, 1902; *Wisconsin State Journal*, September 21, 1902.

[21] *Wisconsin Blue Book, 1903*, pp. 447–465. Superintendent-elect Cary lost eleven of the state's seventy-one counties. The schoolbook scandal evidently cost both La Follette and Cary a number of votes.

[22] *Wisconsin Blue Book, 1903*, pp. 1042–1043.

[23] *Ibid.*, 1077–1112; *Wisconsin State Journal*, January 17, 1903.

[24] *Wisconsin Senate Journal*, 1903, pp. 67–81; *Wisconsin State Journal*, January 17, 1903.

[25] "Message to the Legislature," in the *Wisconsin Senate Journal*, 1903, pp. 30–35.

[26] *Congressional Record*, 57 Congress, 1 Session (1901), 85; 57 Congress, 2 Session (1902), 8; La Follette to Cooper, November (n. d.), 1902, in the Cooper Papers.

[27] *Wisconsin Assembly Journal*, 1903, pp. 204–211; Assembly Bills, No. 97A.

[28] *Wisconsin Senate Journal*, 1903, pp. 610–614.

[29] J. V. Quarles to Keyes, March 13, and Keyes to H. A. Taylor, March 27, 1903, in the Keyes Papers; Philipp, *Political Reform in Wisconsin*, 70.

[30] *Milwaukee Sentinel*, April 19, 1903, p. 7; H. A. Taylor to Keyes, March 30, 1903, in the Keyes Papers; *Wisconsin Assembly Journal*, 1903, p. 1375; *Laws of Wisconsin*, 1903, Ch. 451; *Wisconsin State Journal*, June 3, 1903.

[31] *Report of the Wisconsin Tax Commission*, 1903, pp. 150–217, 259.

[32] W. W. Baldwin to George B. Harris, August 18, December 14, 1904, July 25, 1905, in the Chicago, Burlington and Quincy Railroad Papers, in the Newberry Library, Chicago; *Milwaukee Sentinel*, February 11, 1903; *Report of the Wisconsin Tax Commission*, 1903, pp. 216–217.

[33] *Wisconsin Assembly Journal*, 1903, p. 479; *Milwaukee Sentinel*, March 7, 1903, p. 9; *Wisconsin Senate Journal*, 1903, pp. 105, 818; *Wisconsin State Journal*, May 20, 1903; *Laws of Wisconsin*, 1903, Ch. 315.

[34] *Wisconsin Assembly Journal*, 1903, p. 900; *Milwaukee Sentinel*, March 20, 1903. Even in their private and confidential correspondence Baldwin and his railroad associates were consistent in their denunciation of La Follette's quoted rates. They repeatedly charged that he was making unfair comparisons. See Baldwin to George R. Peck, February 1, 1903, and to Thomas Miller, October 19, 1904, in the Chicago, Burlington and Quincy Railroad Papers; Philipp, *Political Reform in Wisconsin*, 217.

[35] *Wisconsin Assembly Journal,* 1903, pp. 1418–1597; La Follette, *Autobiography,* 284–285; *Milwaukee Sentinel,* April 20, 1903, p. 6.

[36] Emanuel Philipp, *The Truth about Wisconsin Freight Rates* (Milwaukee, 1904); Philipp, *Political Reform in Wisconsin,* 221–222; *Wisconsin State Journal,* April 20, 1903.

[37] *Wisconsin Assembly Journal,* 1903, p. 1004; La Follette, *Autobiography,* 287; *Milwaukee Sentinel,* May 16, 1903, p. 8.

[38] C. Edward Merriam, *Primary Elections* (New York, 1908), 70. This statute provided for an "open primary" which allowed Wisconsin voters to participate in either primary election without registering their party allegiance. *Laws of Wisconsin,* 1903, Ch. 451. This feature of the Wisconsin law was not widely copied.

[39] See, for example, W. R. Stubbs to Davidson, February 2, 1907, in the Davidson Papers.

[40] *Wisconsin Blue Book,* 1905, p. 587.

[41] *Ibid.,* 1907, p. 665. The taxes collected by Wisconsin under the ad valorem system were not significantly greater than those levied by her neighbors. For example, in 1911 Minnesota, which retained the gross receipts method, taxed the railroads in the state at the rate of $417.50 per mile as compared with $432.40 levied by Wisconsin. *Report of the Railroad Commission of Wisconsin,* 1912, p. 738; *Report of the Minnesota Tax Commission,* 1912, p. 235.

[42] *United States Statutes at Large,* 37:701 (1913); La Follette, *Autobiography,* 416–417.

5. BUILDING THE PROGRESSIVE MACHINE

[1] "The Menace of the Political Machine," quoted in the *Milwaukee Sentinel* of February 23, 1897; La Follette, *Autobiography,* 37–48, 164.

[2] Granville D. Jones to James A. Stone, July 6, 1900, and Stone to La Follette, July 5, and to George E. Bryant, November 8, 1900, in the Stone Papers.

[3] Interviews with William T. Evjue, editor of the Madison *Capital Times,* June 15, 1948, and John M. Nelson, former congressman from Wisconsin's Third District, June 16, 1948.

[4] See John Chamberlain, *Farewell to Reform* (New York, 1932), 256 ff.; Philipp, *Political Reform in Wisconsin,* 227; and Keyes to Marvin Hughitt, October 2, 1904, in the Keyes Papers.

[5] According to one biographer La Follette kept an elaborate series of lists on the record of every qualified voter in the state. See Albert O. Barton, *La Follette's Winning of Wisconsin* (Madison, 1922), 416; and George B. Carley to John Gamper, April 5, 1915, in the Philipp Papers.

[6] Hall to Haugen, May 7, and La Follette to Haugen, May 11, 1900, in the Haugen Papers.

[7] M. A. Lien to Davidson, August 27, 1900, in the Davidson Papers; La Follette, *Autobiography,* 32; Charles McCarthy, *The Wisconsin Idea* (New York, 1912), 313–317.

8 La Follette, *Autobiography*, 270; *Milwaukee Sentinel*, February 11, 1902, p. 3; March 14, 1902; *Wisconsin Blue Book*, 1901, p. 301; 1903, p. 420; 1905, p. 338.

9 La Follette to Nils P. Haugen, May 7, 11, 12, 25, and F. W. Walker to Haugen, October 16, 1900, in the Haugen Papers; Ira B. Bradford to Keyes, July 22, 1896, in the Keyes Papers; James O. Davidson to T. W. Buell, November 15, 1900, in the Davidson Papers.

10 *Skandinaven* (Chicago), May 10, 1904, p. 4; John C. Gaveney to Keyes, February 11, 1902, in the Keyes Papers. Anderson, who was personally antagonistic to La Follette, claimed that it was because he was sometimes critical of the latter's reform program that *Skandinaven* took the opposite stand and supported La Follette. See *The Life Story of Rasmus B. Anderson, Written By Himself* (Madison, 1917), 616–624.

11 Davidson to P. A. Monason, February 12, 1903, in the Davidson Papers; John C. Gaveney to Keyes, June 20, 1901, in the Keyes Papers.

12 This absence of political solidarity was due perhaps to their lack of a common national background in the "old country" and to the time interval between the migrations of various members of the group. See J. H. A. Lacher, "The German Element in Wisconsin," in Quaife, *Wisconsin: Its History and Its People*, 2:153 ff., and Still, *Milwaukee*, 262–263. See also Keyes to E. D. Coe, May 11, 1902, in the Keyes Papers; J. S. Parkinson to Henry C. Adams, August 10, 1902, in the Adams Papers; Edward L. Kelley to Alfred J. Rogers, June 16, 1902, in the La Follette Papers.

13 Keyes to Spooner, February 6, 1902, in the Keyes Papers. The nucleus of the Democratic organization was to be found in the Irish and Polish Catholic wards of Milwaukee, which usually voted almost solidly for the Democratic candidates. Rose, running on a platform advocating an "open town," was re-elected mayor for five successive terms from 1900 to 1908. Still, *Milwaukee*, 308 ff.

14 *Milwaukee Sentinel*, February 11, 1902, p. 3; March 14, 1902.

15 *Ibid.*, May 19, 1904; *Die Germania*, May 17, 1904; Lacher, "The German Element in Wisconsin," in Quaife, *Wisconsin*, 2:191; Still, *Milwaukee*, 265–266; John J. Kempf to J. C. Harper, June 10, 1902, in the La Follette Papers.

16 Wilbur H. Glover, *Farm and College: The College of Agriculture of the University of Wisconsin* (Madison, 1952), 182; *United States Census, 1910: Abstract of the Census*, 666–667; *United States Census*, 1920, 9:1634–1635; Walter H. Ebling, "A Century of Agriculture in Wisconsin," in the *Wisconsin Blue Book*, 1940, pp. 185–196. For a laudatory account of the relationship of the progressives to the farmers in Wisconsin, see Frederick C. Howe, *Wisconsin: An Experiment in Democracy* (New York, 1912), 174 ff.

17 Stephenson, *Recollections of a Long Life*, 210–213.

18 *Ibid.*, 214–215; Stephenson to Theodore Roosevelt, March 26, 1904, in the La Follette Papers.

19 *Milwaukee Free Press*, June 18, 1901; Stephenson, *Recollections of a Long Life*, 216–219, 237, 239; Stephenson to La Follette, February 21, 1901, January (n.d.), 1902, in the La Follette Papers.

²⁰ Stephenson, *Recollections of a Long Life,* 254; Stephenson to La Follette, about May 26, 1904, in the La Follette Papers.

²¹ John L. Fisher to Davidson, August 9, 1902, and Davidson to H. A. Johnson, August 21, 1905, in the Davidson Papers; La Follette to Arthur Pugh, June 4, 1900, in the Pugh Papers.

²² *Rice Lake Leader* (Barron County), January 16, 1902; *Grant County Witness* (Platteville), March 12, 1902; *Hudson Star-Times,* January 30, 1903.

²³ J. S. Johnson to Keyes, August 18, 1902, and Hiram D. Fisher to Keyes, April 4, 1909, in the Keyes Papers; Warren J. Davis to La Follette, April 27, 1902, in the La Follette Papers.

²⁴ *Milwaukee Sentinel,* January 29, 1902, p. 5.

²⁵ *Biennial Report of the State Treasurer,* 1900, p. 59; 1902, pp. 59, 64; *Wisconsin Blue Book,* 1907, pp. 671–672. The amount listed by the state treasurer for game wardens' salaries in 1900 was obviously for two years, since the amount given for 1899 was only a nominal $125.00. Interview with John M. Nelson, June 16, 1948.

²⁶ Keyes to R. A. Patterson, June 25, 1902, in the Keyes Papers; W. C. Leitsch to H. C. Adams, October 11, 1902, in the Adams Papers; La Follette, *Autobiography,* 343–347; Philipp, *Political Reform in Wisconsin,* 62; G. W. Johnston to La Follette, June 12, 1902, in the La Follette Papers.

²⁷ Up to this time only Lucius Fairchild and Jeremiah M. Rusk had served more than four years as governor.

²⁸ La Follette, *Autobiography,* 321; Philipp, *Political Reform in Wisconsin,* 55; Houser to Esch, April 6, 1904, in the Esch Papers; *Milwaukee Sentinel,* January 20, 1903, p. 7; W. W. Gilman to Keyes, February 12, and Babcock to Keyes, February 23, 1904, in the Keyes Papers.

²⁹ John Hicks to Keyes, November 11, and Edward Scofield to Keyes, December 31, 1903, in the Keyes Papers; *Milwaukee Sentinel,* May 6, 1904.

³⁰ *Wisconsin State Journal,* March 12, 1904; Keyes to Spooner, March 13, 1904, in the Keyes Papers.

³¹ *Milwaukee Sentinel,* May 1, 4, 1904.

³² Keyes to H. A. Taylor, April 21, 1904, in the Keyes Papers; *Milwaukee Sentinel,* May 6, 11, 16, 1904; interview with John M. Nelson, June 16, 1948; *Wisconsin State Journal,* May 14, 1904; *Milwaukee Free Press,* May 15, 1904.

³³ Philip, *Political Reform in Wisconsin,* 75; La Follette, *Autobiography,* 323–326; *Milwaukee Sentinel,* May 19, 1904. The original lists of delegates and contesting delegations are included along with other papers on the "Gymnasium Convention" in a special file in the La Follette Papers.

³⁴ "Memorandum of General George E. Bryant," in the George E. Bryant Papers, in the State Historical Society of Wisconsin.

³⁵ *Milwaukee Sentinel,* May 19, 1904; Keyes to Taylor, May 18, 1904, in the Keyes Papers. Rosenberry was floor leader of the stalwarts and a member of the state central committee. He was given, he later recalled, scant opportunity to present the case of the stalwarts. Interview with Judge Marvin B. Rosenberry, September 4, 1953. At one time Rosenberry had been a supporter of La Follette; see his letter to La Follette, October 17, 1902, in the La Follette Papers.

[36] *Milwaukee Sentinel*, May 20, 1904; *Milwaukee Free Press*, May 20, 1904; Keyes to Taylor, May 19, 1904, in the Keyes Papers.

[37] *Wisconsin State Journal*, May 20, 1904.

[38] *Milwaukee Sentinel*, September 28, 1904. Both Ray and Gaveney were purged in the ensuing election. See Keyes to Marvin Hughitt, October 2, 1904, in the Keyes Papers.

[39] *Milwaukee Free Press* and *Milwaukee Sentinel*, June 18, 1904. Stephenson sought unsuccessfully to persuade Roosevelt to intervene in behalf of La Follette with the Republican National Committee. "The common people are with La Follette," said he; "I am with the people although largely interested in railroads and manufactures." After reminding the president that he had spent more for the Republican Party than any five or ten men in the state, Stephenson concluded, "I presume that you will remember that I was chairman of the Wisconsin delegation in 1900 where twenty-four votes were given you from the start." Copy of a letter from Stephenson to Roosevelt, May 26, 1904, in the La Follette Papers.

[40] H. A. Taylor to Keyes, July 6, August 15, and Keyes to Taylor, September 13, 1904, in the Keyes Papers; H. S. Comstock to John J. Hannan, October 10, 1904, in the La Follette Papers.

[41] Joseph Lincoln Steffens, *The Autobiography of Lincoln Steffens* (New York, 1931), 454–463; *Milwaukee Sentinel*, July 19, 1904, p. 5.

[42] Lincoln Steffens, "Wisconsin: A State Where the People Have Restored Representative Government—the Story of Governor La Follette," in *McClure's Magazine*, October, 1904, pp. 564–579.

[43] *Milwaukee Sentinel*, September 21, 1904, p. 3, September 28, 1904, p. 6, October 3, 1904; *Milwaukee Free Press*, December 2, 1904.

[44] *Wisconsin ex rel. Cook et al. v. Walter L. Houser*, 122 Wis. 534; 100 N. W. 964 (1904).

[45] H. A. Taylor to Keyes, October 8, 1904, in the Keyes Papers; Henry Casson to H. C. Adams, October 22, 1904, in the Adams Papers.

[46] *Wisconsin Blue Book*, 1905, pp. 366–382, 549.

[47] With apologies to Charles McCarthy, who coined the term "soil and seminar" to describe the basis of the "Wisconsin Idea." The progressives combined the farm and labor vote and welded it with college-trained intellectual leadership to produce the "Progressive Machine." For further discussion of the "Wisconsin Idea" see Chapter 9, "The State and the University," especially pages 140–148.

6. COMPLETING THE PATTERN OF REFORM

[1] *Wisconsin Senate Journal*, 1905, pp. 88–90.

[2] Haugen, *Pioneer and Political Reminiscences*, 38.

[3] *Wisconsin Assembly Journal*, Special Session, 1905, p. 29; *Laws of Wisconsin*, 1911, Ch. 200. In the 1914 primary La Follette's worst fears were realized when the second-choice scheme failed to produce a progressive gubernatorial nominee despite the fact that sixty per cent of the voters favored the progressive ticket. Under Emanuel Philipp, the successful conservative candidate, the "Mary Ann" law was repealed in 1915. See page 193.

[4] *Wisconsin Assembly Journal*, 1905, pp. 19–126. The State Board of Forestry is discussed in Chapter 10 in connection with the conservation movement; the Tax Commission is treated in detail in Chapter 7. The other reforms are considered in this chapter.

[5] *Wisconsin Assembly Journal*, 1903, p. 1408; *Laws of Wisconsin*, 1903, Ch. 431. *Report of the Tax Commissioner*, 1906 (Special Report Relating to Back Taxes under Sec. 431, Laws of 1903), 15; *Laws of Wisconsin*, 1905 (Special Session), Ch. 10.

[6] Some of the smaller railroads paid the additional taxes without delay, but the larger roads engaged in seemingly endless appeals that eventually were carried to the Supreme Court of the United States. It was not until 1912 that the attorney general at last reported that the state had recovered some $126,000 in back taxes. *Report of the Attorney General of Wisconsin*, 1912, p. xxii.

[7] Haugen, *Pioneer and Political Reminiscences*, 139–140; Philipp, *Political Reform in Wisconsin*, 231–233; La Follette, *Autobiography*, 341.

[8] *Laws of Wisconsin*, 1905, Ch. 362; *Report of the Railroad Commission*, 1906, p. 38.

[9] *Wisconsin Blue Book*, 1905, p. 957; *Laws of Wisconsin*, 1903, Ch. 315. According to Haugen, there was a difference of only two per cent between the computations of the commission's engineers and those of the Chicago and North Western's own staff. Haugen, *Pioneer and Political Reminiscences*, 134; *Report of the Wisconsin Tax Commission*, 1907, pp. 99–108.

[10] *Laws of Wisconsin*, 1907, Ch. 499, 654. The enactment of a two-cent fare was of course a departure from the principles of scientific valuation by experts and a return to the Granger policy of fixing rates by law. This act, as it applied to interstate commerce, was invalidated in *R. R. Commission of Wis. v. C. B. & Q. R. R.*, 257 U. S. 563 (1922). La Follette, *Autobiography*, 360–363.

[11] *Laws of Wisconsin*, 1907, Ch. 449; 1913, Ch. 756. See also Lewis E. Gettle, "The Work of the Railroad Commission," in Quaife, *Wisconsin*, 2:397 ff.

[12] *Laws of Wisconsin*, 1907, Ch. 578; 1911, Ch. 596. For a thorough, though somewhat overly sympathetic, discussion of the commission's regulation of public utilities, see Fred L. Holmes, *Regulation of Railroads and Public Utilities in Wisconsin* (New York, 1915), 221 ff.

[13] Harley L. Lutz, *The State Tax Commission* (Cambridge, Massachusetts, 1918), 262; Marvin Hughitt to Keyes, July 5, 1905, in the Keyes Papers; *Milwaukee Sentinel*, October 11, 12, 1907.

[14] *United States Statutes at Large*, 32:847; 34:584. For a discussion of federal efforts to curb rebates and enforce regulations during the Roosevelt administration see Carl B. Swisher, *American Constitutional Development* (New York, 1943), Chapter 24.

[15] Cooper had been a member of the House of Representatives since 1892 and except for one brief period continued to serve in that capacity until his death in 1934. Although he was not numbered among the leading administration spokesmen or powerful committee chairmen in the House,

Cooper played a significant role in the drive to enact effective railroad regulatory legislation on the national level. For his part in the battle to put teeth in the Interstate Commerce Commission, see the *Congressional Record,* 58 Congress, 3 Session (1904), 728, and 59 Congress, 1 Session (1906), 1899, 7432. For Cooper's relation to La Follette and the Wisconsin progressives, see La Follette to Cooper, November (n.d.), 1902, January 19, December 23, 1904. See also Ray Stannard Baker to Cooper, November 21, 1905, in the Cooper Papers.

16 Robert M. La Follette, *Railroad Regulation, State and Interstate* (Madison, 1905), 31, 55. In drafting his remarks introducing Roosevelt at Madison in 1903, La Follette praised him as the "progressive leader of a progressive people." The draft is in the La Follette Papers.

17 Ripley, *Railroads: Rates and Regulations,* 629–630.

18 *Milwaukee Sentinel,* February 28, March 1, July 15, 1904; *Milwaukee Journal,* February 27, 28, 1904; Keyes to Spooner, February 28, March 13, 1904, in the Keyes Papers.

19 See the *Wisconsin Blue Book,* 1948, pp. 135–138; *Report of the Capitol Commission,* 1909, 1911; Francis E. McGovern to C. H. Schwerzer, February 29, 1912, in the McGovern Papers, in the State Historical Society of Wisconsin.

20 Laws of Wisconsin, 1905, Ch. 363; John R. Commons, *Myself* (New York, 1934), 102; *Report of the State Civil Service Commission of Wisconsin,* 1906, pp. 12, 61.

21 *Ibid.,* 1906, pp. 20–21; 1910, pp. 17–25; *Wisconsin Blue Book,* 1905, p. 959.

22 Both the intent and the effect of the civil service law were matters of dispute for years, even among well-qualified observers. La Follette pointed to it as evidence of the high-mindedness of his reform efforts. Professor Commons thought that the greatest service La Follette rendered to the people of his state was the Civil Service Act of 1905. It gained for the various commissions, he maintained, the public confidence which was essential to their success. Governor Francis E. McGovern, on the other hand, viewed the civil service law as somewhat less than perfect. He claimed that it was intended to keep La Follette's appointees in office. All of them, he emphasized, had been retained without meeting the competitive requirements imposed on others who sought to enter the service. He thought the law was worth while in that it relieved the heads of departments of much pulling and hauling for political jobs, but he felt that it should be supplemented by an "efficiency bureau" which would seek the most skilled persons for the public service. Even less impressed was stalwart Governor Emanuel Philipp. After three months as chief executive, Philipp commented, "We do not have civil service in state offices to the extent that you might think; but we do have it to a considerable extent where it does not belong." Philipp thought the law was too theoretical and impractical, giving too much weight to academic training. La Follette, *Autobiography,* 365–366; Commons, *Myself,* 105; McGovern to Hiram Johnson, March 26, 1913, in the McGovern Papers; Philipp to Stanley Root, March 22, 1915, in the Philipp Papers.

[23] *Wisconsin State Journal,* January 20, 21, 1905.

[24] *Ibid.,* January 24, 1905; *Wisconsin Assembly Journal,* 1905, pp. 177–178.

[25] *Wisconsin Assembly Journal,* Special Session, 1905, p. 51; *Wisconsin Senate Journal,* Special Session, 1905, p. 116; *Wisconsin State Journal,* December 19, 1905.

[26] During the eleven-month interval between La Follette's election to the Senate and his assumption of office there was much unfavorable comment in the press about his occupation of two public offices. According to the law in effect at that time, Quarles, then a "lame duck," continued to serve until the expiration of the 58th Congress on March 4, 1905. As the new Congress did not convene until December, 1905, La Follette actually lost very little time in taking his seat. He did, however, miss the fourteen-day special session of the Senate, March 4 to 18, 1905, which had been called by President Roosevelt to consider a proposed treaty with Santo Domingo.

[27] Davidson to John L. Erickson, November 2, and to J. D. Stuart, November 13, 1905, in the Davidson Papers.

[28] Haugen, *Pioneer and Political Reminiscences,* 146–149.

[29] Davidson to William Fitzgerald, November 10, December 9, and to Theodore Kronshage, November 10, 1905, and John Anderson to Davidson, March 1, 1907, in the Davidson Papers; letters to Keyes from H. A. Taylor, January 11, Henry Casson, March 9, and M. C. Douglas, July 21, 1906, in the Keyes Papers; *Milwaukee Free Press,* January 6, 1906; *Milwaukee Sentinel,* January 11, 1906; Stephenson, *Recollections of a Long Life,* 229.

[30] *Wisconsin Blue Book,* 1907, pp. 389, 469; Commons, *Myself,* 98–99; La Follette to Davidson, February 7, April 14, 1907; Davidson to La Follette, January 31, 1906, in the Davidson Papers.

7. NILS HAUGEN AND THE TAX COMMISSION

[1] *Wisconsin Senate Journal,* 1873, p. 61; *Laws of Wisconsin,* 1873, Ch. 210. There had been a special Tax Commission report in 1867 which had emphasized the evils of undervaluation and compared assessed valuation of general property with true valuations. See *Report of the Tax Commissioners Appointed by the Governor,* 1867.

[2] Assembly Bills, 1889, No. 383A; 1893, No. 439A; 1895, No. 604A.

[3] *Laws of Wisconsin,* 1897, Ch. 340; *Report of the Wisconsin State Tax Commission,* 1899, pp. 135, 183.

[4] *Laws of Wisconsin,* 1899, Ch. 42, 206.

[5] *Report of the Wisconsin Tax Commission,* 1901, pp. 5–6; Lutz, *The State Tax Commisison,* 240.

[6] *Milwaukee Sentinel,* March 10, 14, 1898; *Laws of Wisconsin,* 1899, Ch. 326, 355.

[7] *Laws of Wisconsin,* 1899, Ch. 111, 112, 113, 114, 326, 355; Philipp, *Political Reform in Wisconsin,* 179.

[8] *Wisconsin Blue Book,* 1901, p. 690; *Wisconsin Senate Journal,* 1901, pp. 27, 56; *Milwaukee Sentinel,* January 11, 1901.

[9] *Report of the Wisconsin Tax Commission,* 1901, pp. 165–171.

[10] *Laws of Wisconsin,* 1901, Ch. 237, 445; *Wisconsin Assembly Journal,* 1901, p. 1309.

[11] Haugen, *Pioneer and Political Reminiscences,* 40–42, 113; La Follette, *Autobiography,* 179–185.

[12] Haugen, *Pioneer and Political Reminiscences,* 131; obituaries in the *Wisconsin State Journal,* April 24, 1931, and the *Milwaukee Journal,* April 27, 1931.

[13] The Tax Commission calculated that in 1902 the railroads would have paid $2,664,950.20 under the ad valorem system as compared with $1,711,900.18 actually assessed by the license fee. *Report of the Wisconsin Tax Commission,* 1903, pp. 216–217.

[14] *Laws of Wisconsin,* 1903, Ch. 378; "Report of Dr. Thomas S. Adams" in the appendix of the *Report of the Wisconsin Tax Commission,* 1907; Assembly Bills, 1907, No. 1035A; *Wisconsin Assembly Journal,* 1907, p. 1302; Haugen, *Pioneer and Political Reminiscences,* 152–153.

[15] *Laws of Wisconsin,* 1903, Ch. 44; *Nunnemacher v. State,* 129 Wis. 190 (1909); *Wisconsin Blue Book,* 1911, p. 375; *Laws of Wisconsin,* 1911, Ch. 450; *Report of the Wisconsin Tax Commission,* 1912, p. 60.

[16] *Laws of Wisconsin,* 1903, Ch. 35, 315; 1905, Ch. 493.

[17] Lutz, *The State Tax Commission,* 238.

[18] *Report of the Wisconsin Tax Commission,* 1907, p. 75; Haugen, *Pioneer and Political Reminiscences,* 143–145, 130–131; *Report of the Wisconsin Tax Commission,* 1903, 1905. One reason for the great reluctance of many public leaders to approve the use of full valuation of all real estate as a basis for taxation was the realization that such a step would throw completely out of balance the legislature's system of fixed mill rates for the support of most of the public institutions.

[19] Lutz, *The State Tax Commission,* 252, 253.

[20] *Wisconsin Blue Book,* 1905, p. 957.

[21] One student of taxation praised the Wisconsin sales method as "undoubtedly the most scientific attempt that has been made in the United States" to equalize local general property assessments. Lutz, *The State Tax Commission,* 248–252.

[22] See "A Personal Letter from Professor T. S. Adams," in Appendix B of Lutz's *The State Tax Commission.* For a detailed discussion of the ad valorem evaluation system and the process of equalizing the general property tax in Wisconsin, see Floyd Franklin Burtchett, "Development of the Fiscal System of Wisconsin, 1900–1925" (unpublished doctoral dissertation, University of Wisconsin, 1927).

[23] *Laws of Wisconsin,* 1905, Ch. 380, 474, 493, 494; Haugen, *Pioneer and Political Reminiscences,* 141.

[24] Holmes, *Regulation of Railroads and Public Utilities in Wisconsin,* 22; *Laws of Wisconsin,* 1907, Ch. 499.

[25] Between 1901 and 1913 railroad taxes increased 233 per cent, total tax receipts 289 per cent. See *Report of the State Treasurer,* 1900, 1901, 1912, 1913. Wisconsin collected under the ad valorem system only slightly more in taxes than did Minnesota under its gross receipts tax.

[26] *Wisconsin Blue Book*, 1911, p. 375; Lutz, *The State Tax Commission*, 267.

[27] *Special Report of the Tax Commission on the Finances of the State Government* (Madison, 1911), 18–20. The failure of La Follette to inaugurate a budget system and an accounting department for the state appropriations had been criticized frequently by the stalwart press. Emanuel Philipp charged that this was "too practical and businesslike" a reform for so "theoretical" and "visionary" a reformer. Philipp, *Political Reform in Wisconsin*, p. 145.

[28] *Special Report of the Joint Committee on Finance* (Madison, 1912), 10–22; *Laws of Wisconsin*, 1911, Ch. 583; 1913, Ch. 728. The legislature of 1911 also tried to broaden the scope of municipal home rule by granting municipal governments the power to tax certain railroad terminal facilities. This law, however, was soon invalidated by the Supreme Court. *Laws of Wisconsin*, 1911, Ch. 540; *Minneapolis, St. Paul and Sault Ste. Marie Railway v. Douglas County*, 159 Wis. 408, 150 N. W. 422 (1915). The desired result was finally accomplished by a somewhat different law passed in 1915. See *Laws of Wisconsin*, 1915, Ch. 407.

[29] *Wisconsin Blue Book*, 1911, p. 629; Haugen, *Pioneer and Political Reminiscences*, 158. Judge Gilson, whose first term expired in 1909, had been reappointed by Governor Davidson but resigned in 1911. Gilson's successor, Dr. Thomas S. Adams, had a distinguished career as a financial expert. In addition to serving as a professor of economics at the University of Wisconsin and as a member of the Tax Commission, Adams was for a number of years financial advisor to the federal treasury department and professor of political economy at Yale. In 1922–23 he was president of the National Tax Association. Obituary in the *Wisconsin State Journal*, February 9, 10, 1933.

[30] Haugen, *Pioneer and Political Reminiscences*, 137, 153–157.

[31] This income tax law was invalidated by the Supreme Court in *Pollock v. The Farmers' Loan and Trust Co.*, 158 U. S. 601 (1895). For the history of federal income tax legislation see Sidney Ratner, *American Taxation* (New York, 1942), 79, 193, 298 ff.

[32] Delos O. Kinsman, "The Income Tax in the Commonwealths of the United States," in *Publications of the American Economic Association*, Vol. 4, No. 4, p. 116 (November, 1913).

[33] *Report of the Wisconsin Tax Commission*, 1912, pp. 24 ff.; *Wisconsin Blue Book*, 1905, pp. 1019, 1028; 1907, pp. 1072–1078; 1909, p. 556.

[34] *Report of the Wisconsin Tax Commission*, 1909, p. 17; *Laws of Wisconsin*, 1911, Ch. 658; Haugen, *Pioneer and Political Reminiscences*, 162–163.

[35] *Laws of Wisconsin*, 1911, Ch. 658; *A State Income Tax*, speech delivered by Francis E. McGovern at the Conference of Governors held in Richmond, Virginia, on December 5, 1912. The provision for a personal property offset was repealed in 1925, and thereafter the state collected both taxes. *Laws of Wisconsin*, 1925, Ch. 57.

[36] *Report of the Wisconsin Tax Commission*, 1914, p. 126; McGovern, *A State Income Tax.*

[37] *Report of the Wisconsin Tax Commission*, 1912, p. 40; 1914, p. 107; 1916, p. 63. Money and credits had been exempted from assessment as personal property, but interest received by the mortgage holder was to be included as taxable income; thus the income tax law shifted the basis of mortgage taxation from the credits to the creditor.

[38] *Wisconsin Blue Book*, 1933, p. 51.

[39] *Ibid.*, 1913, p. 289; David B. Worthington to McGovern, April 12, 1912, in the McGovern Papers; National Industrial Conference Board, *The Tax Problem in Wisconsin* (New York, 1924), 85, 110–111; *Report of the Tax Commission in Response to Resolution of the Assembly Calling for a Statement of Taxes Paid by Wisconsin Corporations in Comparison with Those Paid by Corporations of Other States and for the Effect of the Income Tax Law on Industrial Development*, March 27, 1923. See also the *Wisconsin Blue Book*, 1933, p. 66.

[40] Harold M. Groves, *Possibilities of the Income Tax* (offset reproduction of typescript, unbound [1932]), a copy of which is in the Tax Commission Papers in the Documents Division of the State Historical Society of Wisconsin; George Leland Leffler, *Wisconsin Industry and the Wisconsin Tax System* (Bulletin No. 1 of the Bureau of Business and Economic Research, University of Wisconsin, Madison, 1930).

[41] The aggregate cost of government in Wisconsin—state, municipal, and county—rose from $22,176,239 (including special taxes) to $50,696,150 in 1914. *Wisconsin Blue Book*, 1903, pp. 615–634; 1933, p. 58; *Report of the State Treasurer*, 1900, pp. 6–7; 1912, p. 6.

[42] According to one authority, the general tax system of Wisconsin compared very favorably with that of other states. See Thomas E. Lyons, *Wisconsin Tax System*, reprinted in 1923 from the *Wisconsin Blue Book* for that year.

8. REGULATING THE LIFE INSURANCE COMPANIES

[1] The total insurance in force for American companies increased from $163,703,455 in 1860 to $12,507,937,441 in 1904. Fred L. Hoffman, "Fifty Years of American Life Insurance Progress," in *American Statistical Association Publications*, 12:712, 717 (Boston, 1911).

[2] The "big four" life insurance companies at the turn of the century were the New York Life, the Metropolitan Life, the Mutual Life, and the Equitable Life. Shepard B. Clough, *A Century of American Life Insurance* (New York, 1946), 243; Hoffman, "Fifty Years of American Life Insurance Progress," Table 3, in *American Statistical Association Publications*, 12:715.

[3] Clough, *A Century of American Life Insurance*, 188–200; Marquis James, *The Metropolitan Life* (New York, 1947), 111–130; Louis I. Dublin, *A Family of Thirty Million: The Story of the Metropolitan Life Insurance Company* (New York, 1943), 51–57.

⁴ Hoffman, "Fifty Years of American Life Insurance Progress," in *American Statistical Association Publications*, 12:678–679; Clough, *A Century of American Life Insurance*, 177–178; *Forty-Sixth Annual Report of the Northwestern Mutual Life Insurance Company*, 1903, p. 7.

⁵ *Report of the State Treasurer*, 1900, p. 16; *Report of the Commissioner of Insurance of the State of Wisconsin*, 1907, pp. 66–67. In 1901 the Northwestern Mutual reported an income of $29,471,784.02, assets of $151,944,-756.96, and a total of $574,705,000 insurance in force. *Forty-fourth Annual Report*, 1901, pp. 8–9.

⁶ *Laws of Wisconsin*, 1899, Ch. 326; "Argument of Willard Merrill before the Wisconsin Tax Commission," October 2, 1900, in the Northwestern Mutual Life Insurance Company Papers in the Home Office at Milwaukee.

⁷ The amount of taxes paid by the Northwestern Mutual in 1901 was not significantly reduced by this shift in the tax base, but in the succeeding years the rate of increase was greatly reduced. *Laws of Wisconsin*, 1901, Ch. 21; *Report of the State Treasurer of Wisconsin*, 1898, p. 20; 1900, p. 16; *Milwaukee Sentinel*, February 16, March 1, 1901.

⁸ See "Brief Submitted in Behalf of the Northwestern Mutual Life Insurance Company to the Wisconsin Tax Commission," November 14, 1906, by George H. Noyes, and "Taxation of Life Insurance Companies," by John M. Olin, (1907), in the Northwestern Mutual Papers.

⁹ *Wisconsin State Journal*, July 31, 1903; *Equitable Life Assurance Society of United States v. Host*, 124 Wis. 657 (1905).

¹⁰ *Milwaukee Sentinel*, May 4, June 16, July 27, 1904; *New York Tribune*, May 5, 1904; *Laws of Wisconsin*, 1898, Ch. 1950.

¹¹ *Milwaukee Sentinel*, May 5, 6, 14, 1904; *Report of the Commissioner of Insurance*, 1904, p. 41. This law was eventually amended to make the state responsible for examinations of insurance companies and to require strict accounting of any charges levied against them. *Laws of Wisconsin*, 1911, Ch. 648; excerpt from the Armstrong Committee Testimony, 2:1088–1089, quoted in James, *The Metropolitan Life*, 146.

¹² Hoffman, "Fifty Years of American Life Insurance Progress," in *American Statistical Association Publications*, 12:739.

¹³ Clough, *A Century of American Life Insurance*, 197–216; James, *The Metropolitan Life*, 133–138; *Semi-Centennial History of the Northwestern Mutual Life Insurance Company* (Milwaukee, 1908), 308–310.

¹⁴ *New York Tribune*, February 15, 16, 1905.

¹⁵ *Ibid.*, September 7, 1905; Burton Hendrick, "The Story of Life Insurance," in *McClure's Magazine*, 27:659 (October, 1906).

¹⁶ *Report of the Joint Committee of the Senate and the Assembly of the State of New York, Appointed to Investigate the Affairs of Life Insurance Companies* (*Assembly Documents*, No. 41, Albany, 1906). For a general discussion of the Armstrong investigation see Clough, *A Century of American Life Insurance*, 215–232, and James, *The Metropolitan Life*, 139–165.

¹⁷ Besides Wisconsin the states of Massachusetts, Iowa, Ohio, and New Jersey and the Dominion of Canada appointed committees to investigate life insurance companies soon after the New York exposures.

[18] "Message to the Legislature," in the *Wisconsin Assembly Journal,* Special Session, 1905, p. 44.

[19] *Ibid.,* 44–49.

[20] *Report of the Joint Committee of Senate and Assembly on the Affairs of Life Insurance Companies,* 1906 (Madison, 1907), 3.

[21] Ekern and George E. Beedle, another member of the joint committee, had attended part of the hearings of the Armstrong investigation and had conferred with Prosecutor Hughes concerning the course and aims of the Wisconsin probe. Personal interview with Herman L. Ekern, July 23, 1949; *Report of the Joint Committee on Life Insurance Companies,* 4. For more information on Miles M. Dawson see James, *The Metropolitan Life,* 141, and Clough, *A Century of American Life Insurance,* 220–227.

[22] *Report of the Joint Committee on Life Insurance Companies,* 5. At the same time the report was published and made available to the general public.

[23] *Ibid.,* 6.

[24] *Ibid.,* 11–15, 70.

[25] *Ibid.,* 28–44, 70. For the company's reply and rebuttal to these charges see the pamphlet *To the Policyholders of the Company* (Milwaukee, 1906) by President Henry L. Palmer, in which he explains or refutes each of the charges. A copy of the pamphlet is filed in the Northwestern Mutual Papers.

[26] *Report of the Joint Committee on Life Insurance Companies,* 104.

[27] *Ibid.,* 105–112. See also *The Legislative Life Insurance Committee's Report* (1907) by A. R. Bushnell, counsel for the Wisconsin Life. Bushnell explained that the Wisconsin Life had originally been organized as an assessment company, which accounted for its lack of legal reserves and the frequent reorganizations through which it had recently passed in becoming a legal reserve company. A copy of this pamphlet is filed in the Northwestern Mutual Papers.

[28] *Report of the Joint Committee on Life Insurance Companies,* 17–19, 50–62, 234–235.

[29] *Wisconsin Blue Book,* 1907, pp. 1071, 1079.

[30] Davidson to E. C. Alden, January 31, 1906, and J. W. Estes to Davidson, March 30, 1907, in the Davidson Papers.

[31] *Wisconsin Blue Book,* 1907, pp. 644–645, 1121–1122.

[32] *Report of the Commissioner of Insurance,* 1907, pp. 19–21; George H. Noyes, *The Facts about Wisconsin Insurance Legislation* (Chicago, 1908), 9.

[33] *Laws of Wisconsin,* 1907, Ch. 126, 131, 150, 389, 504, 584, 621, 636, 657, 667, 668. See also *Report of the Commissioner of Insurance,* 1907, pp. 1352–1408.

[34] Assembly Bills, 1907, Nos. 686A, 687A, 688A; *Laws of Wisconsin,* 1907, Ch. 483; Noyes, *The Facts about Wisconsin Insurance Legislation,* 12; "Opinion of Miles M. Dawson on Pending Legislation in Wisconsin to Joint Committee," May, 1907, manuscript in the Northwestern Mutual Papers; *Report of the Commissioner of Insurance,* 1907, pp. 24–25.

[35] "Memorandum to James O. Davidson, July 13, 1907, on Resolutions by Executive Committee of the Northwestern Mutual Life Insurance Company," in the Davidson Papers.

[36] Miles M. Dawson to Davidson, July 5, 10, 1907, telegrams to Governor Davidson, July 10, 11, 12, 1907, and letters to Davidson from H. J. Messenger, July 10, John F. Dryden, July 11, H. B. Stokes, July 12, and Haley Fisk, July 12, 1907, in the Davidson Papers; *Wisconsin State Journal,* July 14, 1907; *Milwaukee Sentinel,* October 9, 1907, p. 7, November 30, December 1, 14, 1907.

[37] *Milwaukee Sentinel,* October 9, November 30, December 1, 14, 24, 26, 1907.

[38] *The Insurance Field* (Louisville), August 22, 1907, p. 16; September 26, 1907, p. 3; December 5, 1907, p. 16; December 19, 1907, p. 4; *Milwaukee Free Press,* November 30, 1907.

[39] "Letters to Policyholders" from many of the withdrawing companies (including the Mutual Benefit, Mutual Life, and Connecticut Mutual) citing reasons for their withdrawal and urging policyholders to keep their policies in force, copies of which are in the Northwestern Mutual Papers. The insurance commissioners listed twenty-one foreign companies that ceased to do business in Wisconsin on December 31, 1907, and two that had retired earlier. Actually there were not twenty-three but twenty-four fewer companies in the state in 1908 than in 1907, according to the Commissioner's *Annual Report* for 1908, pp. 5–6. The leading trade publication referred to the exiles as twenty-three in number. *The Insurance Field,* May 21, 1915, p. 5; June 18, 1915, p. 5.

[40] Quotations in the *Milwaukee Sentinel,* November 27, 28, 1907.

[41] *Milwaukee Sentinel,* December 4, 1907, p. 5. This charge of ambiguity was among the criticisms most frequently made of the new insurance code. See "Letter of Connecticut Mutual Life Insurance Company to the Members Resident in Wisconsin," by John M. Taylor, December 6, 1907, copy in the Northwestern Mutual Papers. Commissioner Beedle had given the opinion that the state would allow the companies to set up the first year's premiums on the basis of term insurance, and each subsequent installment of the total premium on the ordinary life pattern.

[42] Quoted in the *Milwaukee Sentinel,* November 30, December 5, 1907.

[43] *New York Tribune,* December 7, 8, 1907; *Milwaukee Sentinel,* December 7, 1907; *Milwaukee Free Press,* December 8, 1907.

[44] *New York Tribune,* December 20, 1907.

[45] *Milwaukee Free Press,* December 7, 1907; interview with Herman L. Ekern, July 23, 1949.

[46] In a letter addressed to the Wisconsin agents of the Northwestern Mutual on December 17, 1907, H. F. Norris urged them to impress upon every policyholder of the withdrawing companies that his policy was just as sound as it had ever been and that it would be a serious mistake to drop it. Norris warned his agents against "raiding" this field and said the home office would not tolerate such practices. Copy in the Northwestern Mutual Papers.

[47] Among the proposals that were defeated was a bill to require the companies to deposit with the state treasurer securities equal to their liabilities upon all policies in the state. This was similar to the "Robertson Law" of

Texas, which drove most of the foreign companies, including the Northwestern Mutual, from that state.

⁴⁸ Noyes, *The Facts about Wisconsin Insurance Legislation*, 10–12; *The Insurance Field* also called attention periodically to this apparent overtaxation of the Northwestern Mutual; while it did not advocate complete exemption, it favored making the basis for taxation the earnings of the accumulated assets. *The Insurance Field*, June 30, 1911, p. 4; July 28, 1911, p. 8.

⁴⁹ *Report of the Commissioner of Insurance*, 1908, pp. 9–10, 15–16, 18.

⁵⁰ *Laws of Wisconsin*, 1905, Ch. 455; *Report of the Commissioner of Insurance*, 1908, pp. 30–31; Noyes, *The Facts about Wisconsin Insurance Legislation*, 10; also *Address to Northwestern Mutual Agents Association*, July 17, 1907, by John M. Olin, a copy of which is in the Northwestern Mutual Papers.

⁵¹ The rapid growth of industrial insurance in Wisconsin paralleled the increase of interest in legislation providing for workmen's compensation and the general growth of the state's urban communities. By 1914, the insurance commissioner estimated, the 425,184 industrial policies in force in the state represented about one-third of the urban industrial population. *Report of the Commissioner of Insurance*, 1907 to 1912, *passim;* 1915, p. xi.

⁵² *Wisconsin Blue Book*, 1911, p. 375; *Report of the Commissioner of Insurance*, 1912, p. 158; 1915, p. xvi.

⁵³ *Laws of Wisconsin*, 1907, Ch. 447; 1911, Ch. 208, 265, 502, 507; *Report of the Commissioner of Insurance*, 1911, p. 16; 1915, p. xi.

⁵⁴ *Laws of Wisconsin*, 1911, Ch. 484. See above, page 191, for the controversy between Ekern and McGovern over political activity.

⁵⁵ *Laws of Wisconsin*, 1915, Ch. 132; *Report of the Commissioner of Insurance*, 1915, pp. v–viii.

⁵⁶ *Report of the Commissioner of Insurance*, 1916, p. xii; *Laws of Wisconsin*, 1915, Ch. 132, 434.

⁵⁷ *Laws of Wisconsin*, 1915, Ch. 312; interview with Herman L. Ekern, July 23, 1949; *The Insurance Field*, April 30, 1915, p. 5; June 18, 1915, p. 5; July 2, 1915, p. 5; October 8, 1915, p. 11; *Report of the Commissioner of Insurance*, 1916, p. xxi.

⁵⁸ *Milwaukee Sentinel*, March 1, 1904, and subsequent issues; *Report of the Commissioner of Insurance*, 1915, p. xxiii; *Wisconsin Blue Book*, 1927, p. 179.

⁵⁹ *Wisconsin Blue Book*, 1907, p. 1089; *Report of the Joint Committee on Life Insurance*, 1906, Appendix, "Majority Report of Senate Committee on Government and State Insurance," 1. Workmen's compensation is dealt with in a subsequent chapter; see pages 156–158.

⁶⁰ *Laws of Wisconsin*, 1911, Ch. 577; *Report of the Commissioner of Insurance*, 1911, p. 27.

⁶¹ *The Insurance Field*, July 21, 1911, p. 3; November 10, 1911, p. 3; *Outlook*, 103:147 (January 1, 1913), an unsigned editorial entitled "Experiment in State Life Insurance"; 105:565–566 (November 15, 1913).

⁶² *Report of the Commissioner of Insurance*, 1915, p. xxiii.

⁶³ "The State Life Fund," in the *Wisconsin Blue Book*, 1927, p. 179; personal interview with Herman L. Ekern, July 23, 1949.

[64] *The Insurance Field,* in its issue of June 25, 1915, p. 4, noted that Wisconsin led all states in the amount of insurance in force, with $153.88 per capita.

9. THE STATE AND THE UNIVERSITY

[1] Charles Kendall Adams, *The University and the State,* Baccalaureate Address, 1896.

[2] James F. A. Pyre, *Wisconsin* (New York, 1920), 274.

[3] Interview with William T. Evjue, June 15, 1948; La Follette, *Autobiography,* 32, 323; Merle Curti and Vernon Carstensen, *The University of Wisconsin: A History, 1848–1925* (Madison, 1949), 2:10–11.

[4] La Follette, *Autobiography,* 27–28.

[5] *Ibid.,* 30–32; "Message to the Legislature," in the *Wisconsin Assembly Journal,* 1901, pp. 41–43.

[6] Richard T. Ely, *Ground Under Our Feet* (New York, 1938), 228 ff.; Pyre, *Wisconsin,* 291–293. The complete quotation on the plaque at the entrance of Bascom Hall is as follows: "Whatever may be the limitations which trammel inquiry elsewhere we believe the great state University of Wisconsin should ever encourage that continual and fearless sifting and winnowing by which alone the truth can be found."

[7] Charles R. Van Hise, *What the University Can Do for the Business Man,* address given before the Merchants and Manufacturers Association of Milwaukee in 1908 (Milwaukee, 1908); *The Golden Jubilee of the University of Wisconsin* (Madison, 1904), 21–30.

[8] Van Hise, "Inaugural Address," in *The Golden Jubilee of the University of Wisconsin,* 126–128.

[9] *Ibid.,* 125.

[10] *The University* (Bulletin of the University of Wisconsin, Series 666, General Series 478, Madison, 1914); reprint of Van Hise's article on "The Place of the University in a Democracy," in *School and Society,* Vol. 4, No. 81 (July 15, 1916).

[11] La Follette, *Autobiography,* 30.

[12] Frederick Jackson Turner, "Extension Work of the University of Wisconsin," in *Handbook of University Extension,* edited by George F. James (Philadelphia, 1893), 311–313; William H. Lighty, *A Sketch of the Revivification of University Extension at the University of Wisconsin* (Madison, 1938).

[13] The biographer of Charles McCarthy contends, with some reason, that McCarthy was instrumental in persuading Van Hise to reorganize the extension movement. See Edward A. Fitzpatrick, *McCarthy of Wisconsin* (New York, 1944), 249–257, and "Letter to Van Hise," in Appendix I.

[14] Louis Ehrart Reber, "University Extension in State Universities," in the *Proceedings of the First National University Extension Conference,* March 10, 12, 1915 (Madison, 1915), 24.

[15] *Wisconsin Assembly Journal,* 1907, p. 1075; *Report upon the Survey of the University of Wisconsin,* published by the State Board of Public Affairs (Madison, 1914), 80; Mary B. Orvis, "A University That Goes to the People," in the *American Review of Reviews,* 45:457–465 (April, 1912).

¹⁶ Pyre, *Wisconsin,* 277; Turner, "The Extension Work of the University of Wisconsin," in James, ed., *Handbook of University Extension,* 314–316.

¹⁷ *Wisconsin Blue Book,* 1901, p. 506; 1913, p. 355; Frederick W. Mackenzie, "The Farmer at College," in *La Follette's Magazine,* January 16, 1909, p. 7; Charles McCarthy, *The Wisconsin Idea* (New York, 1912) 128–130; Curti and Carstensen, *The University of Wisconsin,* 2:420.

¹⁸ *Laws of Wisconsin,* 1911, Ch. 505, 660; John R. Commons, "Trade Schools and University Extension for Wisconsin," in *La Follette's Magazine,* January 30, 1909, p. 12; Fitzpatrick, *McCarthy of Wisconsin,* 265–271.

¹⁹ Lincoln Steffens, "Sending a State to College," in the *American Magazine,* 67:349–364 (February, 1909); "A State-Wide Forum in Wisconsin," editorial in the *Independent,* 76:245 (November 6, 1913); Edward E. Slosson, *Great American Universities* (New York, 1910), 210.

²⁰ Van Hise, "Inaugural Address," in *The Golden Jubilee of the University of Wisconsin,* 125.

²¹ *Report of the Board of Regents of the University of Wisconsin,* 1904, pp. 42–44; *Wisconsin Assembly Journal,* 1905, Vol. 2, p. 1773; *Wisconsin Senate Journal,* 1905, p. 1235.

²² *Laws of Wisconsin,* 1907, Ch. 428; State Board of Public Affairs, *Survey of the University of Wisconsin* (Madison, 1914), 71.

²³ *Report of the Board of Regents,* 1908–10, pp. 31–53.

²⁴ The amount expended for building before 1903 was $2,399,300. Pyre, *Wisconsin,* Appendix B, 391–394.

²⁵ James O. Davidson, "Message to the Legislature," in the *Wisconsin Senate Journal,* 1909, pp. 29–30, 290, which shows his attitude toward the University; Francis E. McGovern, "Message to the Legislature," in the *Wisconsin Senate Journal,* 1913, pp. 45–47. In 1911 the mill tax was increased to three-eighths of a mill. *Laws of Wisconsin,* 1911, Ch. 574, 631; 1913, Ch. 758; *Wisconsin Assembly Journal,* 1913, pp. 1688–1692. It should be noted that by 1913 McGovern no longer had control of the legislature, and the split that was to wreck the progressive organization was already generally recognized.

²⁶ La Follette, *Autobiography,* 31; Van Hise, "Inaugural Address," in *The Golden Jubilee of the University of Wisconsin,* 120; Van Hise, *Recent Progress of the University and its Future,* Commencement Address, 1908.

²⁷ McCarthy, *The Wisconsin Idea,* 313–317; Lincoln Steffens, "Sending a State to College," in the *American Magazine,* 67:349 ff. (February, 1909); La Follette, *Autobiography,* 26. For a detailed examination of this collaboration see Howard Johnstone Murray, "Some Influences of the University of Wisconsin on the State Government of Wisconsin" (unpublished doctoral dissertation, University of Wisconsin, 1940).

²⁸ For the membership of the important commissions and boards, see the *Wisconsin Blue Book,* 1911, pp. 623–639; 1913, pp. 528–531.

²⁹ In his discussion of "Pioneer Ideals" Turner said: "Nothing in our educational history is more striking than the steady pressure of democracy upon its universities to adapt them to the requirements of all the people. From the State Universities of the Middle West, shaped under pioneer ideals, have come the fuller recognition of scientific studies, and especially those of applied science devoted to the conquest of nature; . . . all under the

ideal of service to democracy rather than of individual advancement alone." Frederick Jackson Turner, *The Frontier in American History* (New York, 1920), 283.

³⁰ *Wisconsin Blue Book*, 1927, p. 395.

³¹ *Laws of Wisconsin*, 1901, Ch. 168; Fitzpatrick, *McCarthy of Wisconsin*, 42–44.

³² Fitzpatrick, *McCarthy of Wisconsin*, 13–31. While a student at Brown University McCarthy was chiefly known as a star fullback on the football team.

³³ McCarthy, *The Wisconsin Idea*, xiv.

³⁴ Circular letter of Charles McCarthy, November 10, 1902, in Fitzpatrick, *McCarthy of Wisconsin*, 44–46; John R. Commons, "One Way to Get Sane Legislation," in the *Review of Reviews*, 32:722 (December, 1905).

³⁵ McCarthy, *The Wisconsin Idea*, 197.

³⁶ Charles McCarthy, "Legislative Reference Library," in the *Proceedings of the National Association of State Libraries*, 1905, p. 20; *Report of the Wisconsin Free Library Commission*, 1908, p. 19; *Laws of Wisconsin*, 1907, Ch. 508.

³⁷ *Laws of Wisconsin*, 1905, Ch. 363; Commons, *Myself*, 101–109.

³⁸ Fitzpatrick, *McCarthy of Wisconsin*, 73.

³⁹ Commons, "One Way to Get Sane Legislation," in the *Review of Reviews*, 32:722 (December, 1905).

⁴⁰ Fitzpatrick, *McCarthy of Wisconsin*, 65–67; James H. Higgins to Davidson, May 8, 1907, in the Davidson Papers; Charles McCarthy to George W. Perkins, December 9, 1912, in the McCarthy Papers, in the State Historical Society of Wisconsin.

⁴¹ Fitzpatrick, *McCarthy of Wisconsin*, 84–89.

⁴² McMurray, "Some Influences of the University of Wisconsin upon the State" (ms.), 34; *Wisconsin Blue Book*, 1901, pp. 721–769; 1913, pp. 629–689.

⁴³ Editorial in the *Survey*, January 13, 1912; William Hard, "A University in Public Life," in the *Outlook*, 86:659–667 (July 27, 1907); Frank Stockbridge, "A University That Runs a State," in *World's Work*, 25:699–708 (April, 1913); Lincoln Steffens, "The Mind of a State," in *La Follette's Magazine*, January 9, 1909.

⁴⁴ Keyes to Henry C. Adams, December 6, 13, 1905, in the Keyes Papers; *Wisconsin State Journal*, December 9, 11, 1905; *Wisconsin Assembly Journal*, Special Session, 1905, pp. 135–137; *Laws of Wisconsin*, Special Session, 1905, Ch. 7; *Wisconsin State Journal*, October 26, 1906; *Report of the Joint Legislative Committee on the Affairs of the University* (Madison, 1906), 14.

⁴⁵ Granville D. Jones to Charles R. Van Hise, November 5, 9, and Van Hise to Jones, November 8, 13, 1909, in the Presidential Papers (Van Hise), in the University Archives, Memorial Library of the University of Wisconsin; *La Follette's Magazine*, July 2, 1910; *Milwaukee Free Press*, February 21, 1912.

⁴⁶ *Laws of Wisconsin*, 1913, Ch. 728.

⁴⁷ State Board of Public Affairs, *Survey of the University of Wisconsin*, 11.

⁴⁸ *Ibid.*, 143, 184–207. The leaders of the faculty group detailed to reply

to the Allen Report were Dean Edward A. Birge and Professor George C. Sellery.

49 The most exhaustive discussion and complete documentation of the fight on the University as well as other phases of Van Hise's presidency are to be found in Curti and Carstensen, *The University of Wisconsin*, Vol. 2, especially pages 276–294. The present study was written independently of this work, but is in general agreement with the findings and conclusions presented there.

50 "Republican State Platform, 1914," in the *Wisconsin Blue Book*, 1915, p. 453; "letter" from Charles P. Cary in the *Survey*, January 13, 1912; George B. Carley to John Gamper, April 5, F. F. Wheeler to Philipp, February 15, and Henry Lake to Philipp, March 6, 1915, in the Philipp Papers.

51 Letters of Philipp to Edward J. James, president of the University of Illinois, April 6, to Nicholas Murray Butler, president of Columbia University, April 6, and to Frank L. McVey, president of the University of North Dakota, April 5, and Chester Lloyd Jones to Philipp, April 9, 1915, in the Philipp Papers.

52 Commons, *Myself*, 110.

10. McGOVERN AND THE SERVICE STATE

1 Charles A. and Mary Beard, *The Rise of American Civilization* (New York, 1930), 2:538.

2 *Lochner v. New York*, 198 U. S. 45 (1905); *Adair v. United States*, 208 U. S. 161 (1908). For a general discussion of the court's attitude toward labor during this period see Swisher, *American Constitutional Development*, 433–435, 520 ff.

3 Excerpts from the *United States Census* of 1910 in the *Wisconsin Blue Book*, 1913, pp. 48–109.

4 *Thirteenth Census of the United States*, 1910, Vol. 5, pp. 486, 548; Vol. 9, p. 1322. During the same period the value of agricultural products increased from 115 million dollars to 200 million.

5 La Follette, *Autobiography*, 425–426; "Speech before the Joint Session of the Legislature on Being Re-elected to the United States Senate," in the *Wisconsin Senate Journal*, 1911, p. 117.

6 "Message to the Legislature," in the *Wisconsin Senate Journal*, 1911, pp. 18–20.

7 "Platform of the Republican Party of the State of Wisconsin," in the *Wisconsin Blue Book*, 1911, pp. 671–675.

8 *Wisconsin Blue Book*, 1913, p. 572; "Message to the Legislature," in the *Wisconsin Senate Journal*, 1911, p. 19.

9 Harry Weiss, "Employers' Liability and Workmen's Compensation," in Don D. Lescohier and Elizabeth Brandeis, *History of Labor in the United States, 1896–1932* (New York, 1935), 3:571–576; *United States Statutes at Large*, 35:65; Second Employers' Liability Cases, 223 U. S. 1 (1912).

10 *Proceedings of the Thirteenth Annual Convention of the Wisconsin*

234 *La Follette and the Rise of the Progressives*

State Federation of Labor, 1905, p. 4; *Seventeenth Annual Convention,* 1909, p. 35; Gertrude Schmidt, "History of Labor Legislation in Wisconsin" (unpublished doctoral dissertation, University of Wisconsin, 1933), 68.

11 *Wisconsin Assembly Bills,* 1907, No. 161A; 1909, No. 18A; *Social-Democratic Herald* (Milwaukee), January 7, 21, February 4, 1911.

12 As has been said, laws setting up compulsory compensation systems had regularly been found unconstitutional by the courts. On the other hand, the laws providing for voluntary systems, such as Massachusetts, for example, had passed, proved ineffective. The compromise written into the Wisconsin act was intended to meet this situation. While the special committee was deliberating the merits of alternate plans the Supreme Court of New York declared invalid the law of that state setting up a system of state industrial insurance. *Ives v. South Buffalo Railway Co.,* 124 N. Y. supp. 920 (1910).

13 *Report of the Committee on Industrial Insurance, Wisconsin Legislature, 1909–10* (Madison, 1911).

14 *Social-Democratic Herald,* January 14, April 29, 1911; *Wisconsin Assembly Journal,* 1911, p. 761; *Laws of Wisconsin,* 1911, Ch. 50. Wisconsin was the first state to put a comprehensive workmen's compensation law into operation, although Kansas and Washington had enacted similar laws earlier in the year. In all, ten states passed workmen's compensation laws during 1911. See Weiss, "Employers' Liability and Workmen's Compensation," in Lescohier and Brandeis, *History of Labor in the United States,* 3:575.

15 *Bulletin of the Industrial Commission of Wisconsin,* Vol. 1, No. 3 (Madison, 1912); Arthur J. Altmeyer, *The Industrial Commission of Wisconsin* (Madison, 1932), 77.

16 *Laws of Wisconsin,* 1913, Ch. 599; Industrial Commission of Wisconsin, *Report on Allied Functions* (Madison, 1914), 39; Altmeyer, *Industrial Commission of Wisconsin,* 32.

17 *Laws of Wisconsin,* 1911, Ch. 548; 1913, Ch. 381. Not until 1924 did the Supreme Court declare this law, as applied to adult women, unconstitutional. See *Folding Furniture Works v. Industrial Commission,* 300 Fed. Rep. 991 (1924). This was indicative of the conservative trend that followed the first World War and reversed such progressive decisions as *Bunting v. Oregon,* 243 U. S. 426 (1917).

18 *Laws of Wisconsin,* 1911, Ch. 485.

19 *Ibid.,* Ch. 485; Altmeyer, *Industrial Commission of Wisconsin,* 106–107.

20 See the editorial on Wisconsin appointive commissions in *La Follette's Magazine,* February 13, 1909; *Wisconsin Blue Book,* 1911, p. 626.

21 Commons, *Myself,* 129.

22 *Laws of Wisconsin,* 1911, Ch. 485; *Borgnis v. Falk Co.,* 147 Wis. 327 (1912). In his autobiography Commons gave Francis H. Bird of the Legislative Reference Library credit for the original idea. Others added to the definition and perfected it. Commons cited this as an example of "collective thinking" and thought it illustrated the best use of the expert by the progressives. Commons, *Myself,* 154–156.

23 John R. Commons, "Constructive Investigation and the Wisconsin Industrial Commission," in the *Survey,* 29:440–448 (January 4, 1913).

[24] Commons, *Myself,* 157–158; Industrial Commission of Wisconsin, *Report on Allied Functions,* 1914, p. 35.

[25] Commons, "Constructive Investigation and the Wisconsin Industrial Commission," in the *Survey,* 29:440–448 (January 4, 1913).

[26] *Ibid.,* 440.

[27] Commons, *Myself,* 141–142. Arthur J. Altmeyer, one-time secretary to the commission, discusses this topic in detail in his book on the commission. He states that "machine" accidents, the class most directly affected by the commission's orders, decreased measurably but that accidents in general increased, perhaps because of speeding up, increase in number of workers in close proximity to one another, and other factors. *Industrial Commission of Wisconsin,* 163–180.

[28] *Laws of Wisconsin,* 1911, Ch. 485, 419; 1913, Ch. 663. Industrial Commission of Wisconsin, *Report on Allied Functions,* 1914, p. 40.

[29] *Laws of Wisconsin,* 1911, Ch. 347; Industrial Commission of Wisconsin, *Report on Allied Functions,* 1914, p. 66.

[30] *Laws of Wisconsin,* 1911, Ch. 347, 499, 616; John R. Commons, *Labor and Administration* (New York, 1913), 363. On the functions of the State Board of Industrial Education see the *Wisconsin Blue Book,* 1915, p. 389.

[31] McGovern to C. A. A. McGee, July 15, 1912, in the McGovern Papers. It should be noted, however, that neither the legislature nor the Industrial Commission seriously attempted to enter the controversial field of mediation of disputes between labor and management.

[32] "Annual Message to Congress," in the *Congressional Record,* 60 Congress, 1 Session, 74–76 (December 3, 1907); Theodore Roosevelt to James O. Davidson, November 11, 1907, in the Davidson Papers; Loomis Havemeyer, ed., *Conservation of Our Natural Resources* (New York, 1930), 5–13.

[33] Wisconsin Assembly Bills, 1897, No. 646A; *Laws of Wisconsin,* 1897, Ch. 367; *Report of the Forestry Commission of the State of Wisconsin,* 1898; Charles R. Van Hise and Edward Griffith, *The Conservation Movement in Wisconsin* (pamphlet, 1912). In 1900 the legislature had cooperated with Minnesota in establishing Interstate Park on the St. Croix River.

[34] *Wisconsin Blue Book,* 1905, p. 796; "Message to the Legislature," in the *Wisconsin Senate Journal,* 1907, p. 56; Davidson to James R. Garfield, June 15, 1908, in the *Report of the State Conservation Commission,* 1909, p. 30; *Report of the State Park Commission* (Madison, 1907).

[35] *Report of the Committee on Water Power, Forestry and Drainage of the Wisconsin Legislature* (Madison, 1911), 25–34; *Report of Senators Paul O. Husting and Henry Krumrey on Water Powers, Forestry and Drainage* (Madison, 1910). This view was the extreme progressive position on the water-power issue. The majority report took a more moderate position.

[36] *Report of the State Conservation Commission,* 1911.

[37] See *Laws of Wisconsin,* 1901, Ch. 354; *Huber v. Merkel,* 117 Wis. 355 (1903); "Minority Report of George A. Whiting and Wm. Irvine," in *Report of the State Conservation Commission,* 1911.

[38] *Laws of Wisconsin,* 1911, Ch. 644; *Wisconsin Blue Book,* 1913, p. 534; Van Hise to McGovern, May 29, 1912, in the McGovern Papers. Prominent

members of the commission were Charles R. Van Hise, chairman, Edward A. Birge, and state forester Edward M. Griffith.

[39] *Laws of Wisconsin,* 1911, Ch. 143, 638, 639. See also the *Report of the State Conservation Commission,* 1912.

[40] Charles R. Van Hise, *The Conservation of Natural Resources in the United States* (New York, 1910).

[41] Editorial, "Stopping Water Power Grabs in Wisconsin," in *La Follette's Magazine,* May 22, 1909, p. 9; February 10, 1912, p. 9; Jones to Van Hise, September 30, November 9, 1909, and Van Hise to Jones, November 8, 13, 1909, in the Presidential Papers (Van Hise). On John Dietz see the *Milwaukee Sentinel* of September 19, 1907, the *New York Times* of October 16, 1910, and the *Wisconsin State Journal* of May 9, 1924.

[42] *Laws of Wisconsin,* 1911, Ch. 652; Leonard D. Smith to McGovern, December 8, 1910, in the McGovern Papers.

[43] *Water Power Cases,* 148 Wis. 124 (1912). See also the *Report of the State Conservation Commission,* 1912, and McGovern to Husting, February 15, 1912, in the McGovern Papers.

[44] *State ex. rel. Owen v. Donald,* 160 Wis. 21 (1915). See also McGovern to Gifford Pinchot, July 29, 1913, in the McGovern Papers.

[45] *Laws of Wisconsin,* 1915, Ch. 380, 406. Under Philipp the Conservation Commission was merged with the Forestry Board into a full-time commission appointed under civil service. See *Report of the State Conservation Commission,* 1915.

[46] *Laws of Wisconsin,* 1911, Ch. 583; *Milwaukee Free Press,* August 25, 1912; Charles McCarthy to McGovern, November 23, 1910, and P. J. Watrous to McGovern, December 24, 1910, in the McGovern Papers; Commons, *Myself,* 153; *Wisconsin Blue Book,* 1911, p. 626.

[47] *General Report of the State Board of Public Affairs,* 1915, p. 17.

[48] *Report of the State Board of Public Affairs of an Investigation of the Efficiency and Cost of State Printing* (Madison, 1915), 5; *General Report of the State Board of Public Affairs,* 22. For the results of the University survey see above, pages 149–152.

[49] *Laws of Wisconsin,* 1911, Ch. 368; State Board of Public Affairs, *Report upon Cooperation and Marketing* (Madison, 1912), 90–91.

[50] "Message to the Legislature," in *Wisconsin Senate Journal,* 1913, pp. 367–376; McGovern to Commons, June 10, 1913, in the McGovern Papers; *Laws of Wisconsin,* 1921, Ch. 571.

[51] *Wisconsin Blue Book,* 1909, p. 588; *Laws of Wisconsin,* 1911, Ch. 377; 1913, Ch. 668.

[52] The legislature of 1911 also passed a corrupt practices act, established the State Life Fund, and made various changes in the state's insurance laws.

[53] *Wisconsin Blue Book,* 1901, pp. 329 ff.; 1913, pp. 275, 528 ff.

11. THE SPLIT IN THE PARTY

[1] Davidson to John J. Esch, November 12, 1906, and La Follette to Davidson, February 7, April 14, 1907, in the Davidson Papers.

[2] *Milwaukee Free Press*, March 4, 1907; Stephenson to O. G. Munson, March 5, 1907, in the Davidson Papers.

[3] La Follette to Cooper, November 27, 1905, Cooper to La Follette, June 26, 1908, and memorandum of Cooper to Samuel Gompers [1905], in the Cooper Papers; O. L. Rosenkrans to Davidson, March 4, and George E. Powell to O. G. Munson, April 13, 1907, in the Davidson Papers.

[4] *Wisconsin Assembly Journal*, 1907, p. 781; Stephenson, *Recollections of a Long Life*, 231–234.

[5] Stephenson, *Recollections of a Long Life*, 235–236.

[6] *Ibid.*, 248.

[7] *Ibid.*, 248–249; *Wisconsin State Journal*, February 16, 1909; *The State* (Madison), August 21, 1908.

[8] *Milwaukee Free Press*, September 2–4, 1908; *Wisconsin Senate Journal*, 1909, pp. 11–13, 74–77, 399–404; *Wisconsin State Journal*, February 12, 1909; Stephenson, *Recollections of a Long Life*, 250–252.

[9] *La Follette's Magazine*, February 6, 1909, p. 3.

[10] *Congressional Record*, 62 Congress, 2 Session, 3865–3896 (March 27, 1912).

[11] Stephenson, *Recollections of a Long Life*, 249–252; *Milwaukee Sentinel*, November 22, 1907; *Charles Pfister v. Milwaukee Free Press*, 139 Wis. 627 (1909); *La Follette's Magazine*, February 20, 1909, p. 3.

[12] *Wisconsin State Journal*, August 31, 1908, January 21 to March 1, 1909; "Platform of the Republican Party of the State of Wisconsin," in the *Wisconsin Blue Book*, 1911, p. 673; *La Follette's Magazine*, February 6, April 6, 1909.

[13] *Laws of Wisconsin*, 1911, Ch. 650; John M. Nelson to F. E. McGovern, May 27, and McGovern to John J. Blaine, March 7, 1912, in the McGovern Papers.

[14] La Follette to Cooper, December 5, 1905, in the Cooper Papers; La Follette, *Autobiography*, 380–383; Steffens, *Autobiography*, 508.

[15] Henry F. Pringle, *Theodore Roosevelt* (New York, 1931), 413–418, 424–428; La Follette, *Autobiography*, 388; Roosevelt to Nicholas Murray Butler, May 21, 1904, and to Lincoln Steffens, June 5, 1908, in *The Letters of Theodore Roosevelt*, edited by Elting E. Morison (Harvard University Press, 1951), 4:802, 1050.

[16] Included among the insurgents in the Senate were William E. Borah of Idaho, Albert J. Beveridge of Indiana, and Jonathan P. Dolliver of Iowa. In the House the most conspicuous insurgent was George Norris of Nebraska. La Follette, *Autobiography*, 427–428. Stephenson's personal ambitions with respect to the enactment of reform measures had been satisfied with the primary and railway laws of La Follette's governorship. As he stated in his autobiography, "There the task ended . . . for me." *Recollections of a Long Life*, 239.

¹⁷ Henry Cooper thought that there was strong sentiment for a Roosevelt–La Follette ticket in the 1908 convention. Cooper presented to the delegates the minority report of the platform committee, which embodied most of La Follette's principles, but it failed to be adopted. Cooper to La Follette, June 20, 1908, in the Cooper Papers; Haugen, *Pioneer and Political Reminiscences,* 150; interview with Charles Skowland, former secretary to Isaac Stephenson, August 31, 1949.

¹⁸ La Follette, *Autobiography,* 495–496; Roosevelt to La Follette, January 3, 24, 1911, in the Roosevelt Papers, in the Library of Congress; Pringle, *Theodore Roosevelt,* 548–549; *Outlook,* January 24, 1911. Senator Jonathan Bourne was elected president of the League, and Frederick C. Howe, municipal reformer of Cleveland, served as secretary.

¹⁹ Walter L. Houser to Duncan McGregor, August 26, 1911, Karl Cochems to McGovern, September 6, 1911, Houser to McGovern, October 23, 1911, and John J. Blaine to McGovern, February 24, 1912, in the McGovern Papers.

²⁰ Pringle, *Theodore Roosevelt,* 553–554; William Allen White to Charles R. Van Hise, May 24, 1912, in *Selected Letters of William Allen White,* edited by Walter Johnson (New York, 1947), 133; William Allen White, *Autobiography* (New York, 1946), 448; Mark Sullivan, *Our Times* (New York, 1932), 4:470.

²¹ Roosevelt to Gifford Pinchot, December 27, 1911, to Walter F. Cushing, January 2, 1912, to William E. Glasscock, January 18, 1912, and to Chase S. Osborn, January 18, 1912, in the Roosevelt Papers.

²² Roosevelt to Frank Knox, January 17, Chase S. Osborn to Roosevelt, January 22, and Roosevelt to William Allen White, January 26, to Richard V. Knott, January 29, to Chase S. Osborn, January 30, to Thomas F. Marshall, February 5, and to Alfred W. Cooley, February 13, 1912, in the Roosevelt Papers.

²³ La Follette, *Autobiography,* 605–607.

²⁴ *Ibid.,* 602–603; Mark Sullivan to Henry A. Cooper, January 23, 1912, in the Cooper Papers.

²⁵ La Follette, *Autobiography,* Appendix A; Sullivan, *Our Times,* 4:474.

²⁶ *La Follette's Magazine,* February 17, 1912, p. 9.

²⁷ Memorandum of Henry A. Cooper with letter from Mark Sullivan to Cooper, January 23, 1912, in the Cooper Papers.

²⁸ Pringle, *Theodore Roosevelt,* 554; George E. Mowry, *Theodore Roosevelt and the Progressive Movement* (Madison, Wisconsin, 1946), 206–207; White, *Autobiography,* 449.

²⁹ *La Follette's Magazine,* February 17, March 8, 16, 1912.

³⁰ Charles Berstrom to McGovern, March 21, and McGovern to A. M. Stondall, May 22, 1912, in the McGovern Papers; *La Follette's Magazine,* April 13, 1912.

³¹ *La Follette's Magazine,* March 2, April 20, 1912.

³² McGovern to Roosevelt, February 26, 1912, in the Roosevelt Papers; telegram from William Barnes Jr. to McGovern, June 1, and from McGovern to Barnes, June 2, 1912, in the McGovern Papers.

[33] Augustus C. Umbreit to McGovern, June 6, and Cassius E. Gillette to Walter L. Houser, June 12, 1912, in the McGovern Papers.

[34] Roosevelt to William R. Stubbs, February 8, 1912, in the Roosevelt Papers.

[35] Roosevelt to Joseph M. Dixon, May 23, 25, to Hadley, May 24, June 4, and to William R. Nelson, May 28, 1912, in the Roosevelt Papers. Roosevelt refers here to Alexander J. Gronna of North Dakota.

[36] McGovern to Drs. P. H. McGovern and J. J. McGovern, June 12, and Alvin P. Kletzsch to McGovern, June 13, 1912, in the McGovern Papers. Doubtless Kletzsch had private assurances that the Roosevelt delegates would also support McGovern. Several students of the period have assumed that McGovern was Roosevelt's candidate for temporary chairman, but it appears more probable that the impetus for McGovern's candidacy came from within the Wisconsin delegation. Henry F. Pringle, *Life and Times of William Howard Taft* (New York, 1939), 804; Mark Sullivan, *Our Times,* 4:515. In the private meeting of the Wisconsin delegation prior to the opening of the convention in Chicago, the delegates had first voted unanimously to support McGovern for temporary chairman; then on the motion of Walter Houser, who was awaiting instructions from La Follette, voted to reconsider; and finally voted to proceed with their endorsement of McGovern despite Houser's opposition. See "Record of Meetings of Wisconsin Delegation to the National Convention of the Republican Party to be held in Chicago, June 18, 1912," in the Stone Papers.

[37] For the details of the inside story of the convention see Victor Rosewater, *Backstage in 1912* (New York, 1932).

[38] *Proceedings of the National Republican Convention,* Chicago, 1912, pp. 42–43.

[39] Herbert Quick, "What Thrilled the Convention," in *La Follette's Magazine,* June 29, 1912, p. 9. The official account of Houser's speech is considerably more subdued. See the *Proceedings of the National Republican Convention,* 1912, p. 54.

[40] Twelve of Wisconsin's delegates voted for McGovern, the other fourteen threw their votes to minor candidates. *Proceedings of the National Republican Convention,* 1912, p. 403; *La Follette's Magazine,* June 29, 1912.

[41] See letters to McGovern, June 19 to June 30, 1912, especially those from Frank T. McNally, M. W. Zeidler, H. H. Henkel, and John Reschlein, June 19, 1912, in the McGovern Papers.

[42] *Milwaukee Free Press,* June 28, 1912; McGovern to M. W. Zeidler, July 6, 1912, in the McGovern Papers.

[43] *La Follette's Magazine,* June 29, 1912, p. 9; July 20, 1912, p. 4; July 27, p. 1; A. J. Provost to McGovern, July 2, and Bob Fanell to McGovern, October 17, 1912, in the McGovern Papers.

[44] Letters to McGovern from George R. Wettengel, September 13, Will M. Cowles, July 29, and Granville D. Jones, July 31, 1912, in the McGovern Papers; *Milwaukee Free Press,* September 27, 1912. See also McGovern to Roosevelt, July 15, 1912, August 2, 1912 (telegram), in the Roosevelt Papers.

[45] *Wisconsin Blue Book,* 1913, p. 166; *La Follette's Magazine,* October 26, 1912. See also the pamphlet *Republican State Platform and Candidates,* a copy of which is in the library of the State Historical Society of Wisconsin.

[46] *La Follette's Magazine,* November 15, 1912; *Milwaukee Free Press,* November 18, 1912; *Wisconsin Blue Book,* 1912, pp. 214, 260.

[47] W. A. Titus to Mr. Wilbur, December 17, 1912, G. R. Wettengel to McGovern, January 10, 1913, and McGovern to Arthur W. Pettit, January 21, 1913, in the McGovern Papers; *Ekern v. McGovern,* 154 Wis. 157 (1913).

[48] For replies to the governor's invitation see the McGovern Papers, March 1–5, 1913. See also McGovern to F. C. Lorenz, April 18, 1913, in the McGovern Papers; *Wisconsin State Journal,* March 6, 1913.

[49] McGovern to James Frawley, April 17, 1913, in the McGovern Papers; Charles McCarthy to La Follette, April 25, 1913, quoted in Fitzpatrick, *McCarthy of Wisconsin,* 114.

[50] *Wisconsin Senate Journal,* 1913, p. 873; John Luschinger to McGovern, June 6, and McGovern to Miss Edythe L. M. Tate, June 13, 1913, in the McGovern Papers.

[51] Three other candidates, Merlin Hull, Henry E. Roethe, and Bruce W. Utman, further divided the vote for governor. The nominees for the lesser state offices were all progressives. *Wisconsin Blue Book,* 1915, pp. 236–245. One friend of La Follette's suggested that he run for governor on an independent ticket and thus recapture the state. Richard Lloyd Jones to La Follette, September 3, 1914, in the Albert O. Barton Papers, in the State Historical Society of Wisconsin.

[52] *Wisconsin State Journal,* September 3, 15, 1914.

[53] *Wisconsin Blue Book,* 1915, p. 228; *Milwaukee Free Press,* November 4, 8, 1914. The rumor was that La Follette vowed to drive McGovern out of political life. If so, he succeeded, for McGovern never held another office. Interview with William T. Evjue, June 15, 1948. See also McGovern to Roosevelt, March 8, 1918, in the Roosevelt Papers, and the *Milwaukee Free Press,* November 4, 1914. Among the amendments that were defeated were proposals to adopt the initiative, referendum, and recall in Wisconsin and to provide home rule for Milwaukee.

[54] In marked contrast to this characteristic were the personal charm and magnanimous gestures by which La Follette would, on occasion, completely captivate his colleagues or bind an erstwhile opponent to him in gratitude. Typical of such a gesture was his approval of the reappointment of old ex-boss Elisha Keyes to the Madison postmastership. In a jocular vein he wrote his old enemy: "You improve with age. That is, I think you are less perniciously and hellishly active in politics than you once were,—or it may be that you play the game with finer hand. . . . Without reference to politics and all jesting aside, the service is good, and I develop a fondness for you as we grow older." La Follette to Keyes, March 1, and Keyes to La Follette, March 13, 1910, in the Keyes Papers.

[55] Haugen, *Pioneer and Political Reminiscences,* 151–152.

12. THE BALANCE SHEET

[1] From the letterheads of the National Progressive Republican League. See letter file for 1911–12 in the Albert O. Barton Papers.

[2] For a discussion of the primary election movement about the middle of the progressive era see George H. Shibley, "Government Reform in the United States for 1909," in *La Follette's Magazine*, June 17, 1909.

[3] See Lescohier and Brandeis, *History of Labor in the United States*, 3:644.

[4] In 1906, for example, Minnesota sent to Madison a delegation headed by political scientist Frank L. McVey (later president of the Universities of North Dakota and Kentucky) to study the Wisconsin Tax Commission and confer with Nils P. Haugen preparatory to establishing a similar commission in his own state.

[5] Letters to Governor James O. Davidson from F. E. Packard (assemblyman, North Dakota), February 12, Walter R. Stubbs (later governor of Kansas), February 14, and Fred W. Warner (governor of Michigan), April 13, 1907, in the Davidson Papers; letters to Governor Francis E. McGovern from Jonathan Bourne Jr., February 2, 1911, Walter L. Houser, August 15, 1911, W. A. Pendergast, February 28, 1913, and Theodore Roosevelt, March 28, 1913, in the McGovern Papers; Martin C. Madsen to Emanuel L. Philipp, February 15, 1915, in the Philipp Papers.

[6] Still, *Milwaukee*, 306–320, 520. The Social Democrats were strongly represented in the Milwaukee trades union movement and presumed to speak for labor in their papers, but they by no means controlled the labor vote.

[7] Francis E. McGovern to P. H. McGovern, March 27, and Judge C. W. Warren to McGovern, May 28, 1913, in the McGovern Papers: *Wisconsin Blue Book*, 1913, p. 271.

[8] Jonathan Bourne Jr. to McGovern, February 11, 1911, in the McGovern Papers; *Milwaukee Free Press*, November 4, 1914.

[9] *La Follette's Magazine*, February 3, June 22, 1912.

[10] Granville D. Jones to McGovern, May 11, 1912, in the McGovern Papers; John Gamper to Governor-elect Philipp, December 28, 1914, and John Saegar to Philipp, March 11, 1915, in the Philipp Papers.

BIBLIOGRAPHY

BIBLIOGRAPHY

★ ★ ★ ★ ★ ★ ★ ★ ★ ★ ★ ★ ★ ★ ★ ★ ★

This list of references does not include all the materials dealing with recent Wisconsin history, but the attempt has been made to include all the significant materials used in the preparation of the study except some minor items cited in the footnotes to document a specific topic. It is intended to be a suggestive rather than an exhaustive list for the reader who wishes to delve further into Wisconsin progressivism.

PRIMARY SOURCES

PERSONAL PAPERS

This book is based in large part on the manuscript collections in the possession of the State Historical Society of Wisconsin, and unless otherwise noted all unpublished materials cited are to be found there. The papers of Robert M. La Follette Sr. became available after the initial draft of this book had been completed and many La Follette letters are cited from other collections. But the papers have been examined and significant additions or modifications incorporated in the narrative.

The more important manuscript collections consulted and the dates covering the part of the collection used are as follows: the Henry C. Adams Papers, 1900–1908, the Joseph W. Babcock Papers, 1899–1906, the Albert O. Barton Papers, 1900–1914, and the George E. Bryant Papers, 1900–1905, in the State Historical Society of Wisconsin; the Chicago, Burlington and Quincy Railroad Papers, 1900–1910, in the Newberry Library, Chicago; the Chicago and North Western Railway Papers, 1900–1920, in the Home Office of the Chicago and North Western Railway Company, Chicago; the Edwin D. Coe Papers, 1894–1902, the Henry Allen Cooper Papers, 1900–1920, the James O. Davidson Papers, 1898–1910, the John Jacob Esch Papers, 1900–1912, the Nils P. Haugen Papers, 1894–1915, the Elisha W. Keyes Papers, 1890–1910, the Theodore Kronshage Papers, 1898–1912, the Robert M. La Follette, Sr. Papers, 1899–1914, the Charles R. McCarthy Papers, 1910–1914, and the Francis E. McGovern Papers, 1910–1914, in the State Historical Society of Wisconsin; the Northwestern Mutual Life Insurance Company Papers, 1900–1920, in the Home Office of the Northwestern Mutual Life Insurance Company, Milwaukee; Papers of the Presidents of the University of Wisconsin: Papers of Charles R. Van Hise, 1903–1918, in the University Archives, in the Memorial Library, University of Wisconsin; the Lewis Patrick Papers, 1900–1912, the Emanuel L. Philipp Papers, 1900–1918, and the Arthur Pugh Papers, 1900–1902, in the State Historical Society of Wisconsin; the Theodore Roosevelt Papers, 1900–1918, in the Library of Congress; the Jeremiah M. Rusk Papers, 1890–1894, in the State Historical Society of Wisconsin; the John Coit Spooner Papers, 1898–1907, in the Library of Congress; the James A. Stone Papers, 1900–1912, and the Ellis B. Usher Papers, 1894–1904, in the State Historical Society of Wisconsin.

INTERVIEWS

Personal interviews were held with the following men who were participants in the events of the progressive era: Herman L. Ekern, former assemblyman and insurance commissioner of Wisconsin, on July 23, 1949; William T. Evjue, editor of the Madison *Capital Times* and long-time progressive, on June 5, 1948, and September 5, 1954; Walter L. Gold, leading Milwaukee attorney who began practice in 1900, on July 20, 1949; John M. Nelson, congressman from Wisconsin during the years 1906–1919 and 1921–1931, on June 16, 1948; Marvin B. Rosenberry, attorney, conservative political leader and one-time associate justice of the State Supreme Court, on September 4, 1953; Charles Skowland, former secretary to Isaac Stephenson, on August 31, 1949; Fred R. Zimmerman, progressive independent and long-time secretary of state of Wisconsin, July 10, 1951.

FEDERAL DOCUMENTS

Congressional Record, 1886–1913.
Federal Reporter, 1909–1924.
United States Statutes at Large, Vols. 24–37 (1885–1913).
United States Census Reports, 12th, 13th, and 14th, 1900, 1910, 1920.
United States Reports, 1876–1923.

Bibliography 247

WISCONSIN STATE DOCUMENTS

ATTORNEY GENERAL. *Report of the Attorney General of Wisconsin,* 1912.

BOARD OF PUBLIC AFFAIRS. *General Report of the State Board of Public Affairs,* 1915.

———— *Report upon Cooperation and Marketing,* 1912.

———— *Report of Investigation of the Efficiency and Cost of State Printing,* 1915.

———— *Report upon the Survey of the University of Wisconsin,* 1914.

CIVIL SERVICE COMMISSION. *Report of the State Civil Service Commission of Wisconsin,* 1906–1914.

CONSERVATION COMMISSION. *Report of the State Conservation Commission,* 1909, 1911, 1912, 1915.

FORESTRY COMMISSION. *Report of the Forestry Commission of the State of Wisconsin,* 1898.

FREE LIBRARY COMMISSION. *Report of the Free Library Commission,* 1908.

INDUSTRIAL COMMISSION. *Bulletin of the Industrial Commission of Wisconsin,* Vol. 1, No. 3. 1912.

———— *Report on Allied Functions.* 1914.

INSURANCE COMMISSIONER. *Report of the Commissioner of Insurance,* 1904–1916.

Insurance Laws of Wisconsin, 1907.

Laws of Wisconsin, 1868, 1873, 1897–1915.

LEGISLATURE OF WISCONSIN. Assembly Bills, 1889–1913. Printed bills arranged by legislative session and number of bill, in the office of the Secretary of State.

———— *Assembly Journal,* 1895–1913.

———— *Report of the Joint Committee on Life Insurance.* "Majority Report of Senate Committee on Government and State Insurance," 1906.

———— *Report of the Joint Committee of Senate and Assembly on the Affairs of Life Insurance Companies,* 1906.

———— *Report of the Joint Legislative Committee on the Affairs of the University,* 1906.

———— *Report of the Special Committee on Industrial Insurance, Wisconsin Legislature, 1909–1910.* 1911.

LEGISLATURE OF WISCONSIN—*continued. Report of the Committee on Water Power, Forestry, and Drainage of the Wisconsin Legislature,* 1911.

———— *Report of Senators Paul Husting and Henry Krumrey on Water Powers, Forestry and Drainage.* 1910.

———— Senate Bills, 1901–1913. Printed bills arranged by legislative session and number of bill, in the office of the Secretary of State.

———— *Senate Journal,* 1901–1913.

———— *Special Report of the Joint Committee on Finance,* 1912.

PARK COMMISSION. *Report of the State Park Commission,* 1907.

RAILROAD COMMISSION. *Report of the Railroad Commission of Wisconsin,* 1906, 1912.

STATE TREASURER. *Report of the State Treasurer of Wisconsin,* 1900, 1902, 1904, 1912, 1913.

TAX COMMISSION. *Report of the Tax Commission in Response to Resolution of the Assembly Calling for a Statement of Taxes Paid by Wisconsin Corporations in Comparison with Those Paid by Corporations of Other States and for the Effect of the Income Tax Law on Industrial Development,* March 27, 1923.

———— *Report of the Tax Commissioner, 1906: Special Report Relating to Back Taxes* under sec. 431, *Laws* of 1903.

———— *Report of the Wisconsin State Tax Commission,* 1899.

———— *Report of the Wisconsin Tax Commission,* 1901, 1903, 1907, 1909, 1911, 1912, 1914.

———— *Special Report of the Tax Commissioner on Finances of the State Government,* 1911.

UNIVERSITY OF WISCONSIN. *Report of the Board of Regents,* 1904, 1908–1910.

Wisconsin Blue Book, 1899–1915, 1927, 1933, 1940. Official publication of the state including population data, election returns, state officeholders, biographical sketches, and other information.

Wisconsin Reports, 1902–1915.

PUBLICATIONS OF NON-GOVERNMENTAL AGENCIES

ADAMS, THOMAS S. *Mortgage Statistics and Taxation in Wisconsin and Neighboring States.* Madison, 1907. A report submitted to the Wisconsin Tax Commission.

Announcing La Follette's Candidacy for Governor, 1900. Pamphlet.

NORTHWESTERN MUTUAL LIFE INSURANCE COMPANY. *Annual Report,* 1901–1919.

REPUBLICAN PARTY. *Proceedings of the National Republican Convention,* Chicago, 1912.

———— *Republican State Platform and Candidates, 1900.* Pamphlet.

STATE FEDERATION OF LABOR. *Proceedings of the Wisconsin State Federation of Labor,* 1905–1913.

PUBLISHED AUTOBIOGRAPHIES, MEMOIRS, AND LETTERS

ANDERSON, RASMUS B. *Life Story of Rasmus B. Anderson, Written by Himself.* Madison, 1917.

COMMONS, JOHN R. *Myself.* New York, 1934.

ELY, RICHARD T. *Ground Under Our Feet.* New York, 1938.

FREAR, JAMES A. *Forty Years of Progressive Public Service.* Washington, 1937.

HAUGEN, NILS P. *Pioneer and Political Reminiscences.* Evansville, Wisconsin, 1930.

LA FOLLETTE, ROBERT M. *La Follette's Autobiography: A Personal Narrative of Political Experiences.* Madison, 1913.

MCCARTHY, CHARLES. *The Wisconsin Idea.* New York, 1912.

ROOSEVELT, THEODORE. *An Autobiography.* New York, 1913.

———— *The Letters of Theodore Roosevelt,* edited by Elting E. Morison. 8 vols., Cambridge, Massachusetts, 1951–1954.

ROSEWATER, VICTOR. *Backstage in 1912.* New York, 1932.

STEFFENS, JOSEPH LINCOLN. *Autobiography of Lincoln Steffens.* New York, 1931.

STEPHENSON, ISAAC. *Recollections of a Long Life.* Privately printed, 1915.

WHITE, WILLIAM ALLEN. *Autobiography.* New York, 1946.

———— *Selected Letters of William Allen White, 1899–1943,* edited by Walter Johnson. New York, 1947.

SPEECHES

ADAMS, CHARLES KENDALL. *The University and the State.* Madison, 1896. Baccalaureate address.

VAN HISE, CHARLES R. *The Idea of Service.* Minneapolis, 1915.

VAN HISE—*continued.* "The Place of a University in a Democracy." *School and Society,* 4:81–86 (July 15, 1916). An address given before the National Education Association.

———— *Recent Progress of the University and Its Future.* Commencement address, 1908. Madison, 1908.

———— *What the University Can Do for the Businessman.* An address given before the Merchants and Manufacturers Association of Milwaukee in 1908.

NEWSPAPERS AND PERIODICALS

The publications listed below are the most useful sources on the politics and personalities of the period. Papers that were used for only a single issue have been omitted.

Die Germania (Milwaukee), 1904. German-language newspaper.

Hudson Star-Times (St. Croix County, Wisconsin), 1900, 1903.

The Insurance Field (Louisville, Kentucky), 1907–1915. General organ of the insurance business.

La Crosse [Wisconsin] *Daily Republican and Leader,* 1900.

La Follette's Magazine (Madison), 1909–1914.

Milwaukee Free Press, 1901–1914.

Milwaukee Journal, 1900–1914.

Milwaukee Leader, 1912.

Milwaukee Sentinel, 1891–1914.

New York Tribune, 1904–1915.

Outlook (New York), 1911–1914.

Skandinaven (Chicago), 1901, 1904. Norwegian-language newspaper.

Social-Democratic Herald (Milwaukee), 1905–1912.

Survey (New York), 1912.

Wisconsin State Journal (Madison), 1900–1915, 1924.

SECONDARY SOURCES

ALTMEYER, ARTHUR J. *The Industrial Commission of Wisconsin.* Madison, 1932.

BARNETT, JAMES D. "The State Administration of Taxation in Wisconsin." *Transactions of the Wisconsin Academy of Sciences, Arts, and Letters,* Vol. 15, Pt. 1, pp. 163–177. Madison, 1905.

BARTON, ALBERT O. *La Follette's Winning of Wisconsin.* Madison, 1922.

BEARD, CHARLES A. and MARY. *The Rise of American Civilization,* Vol. 2. New York, 1930.

BURTCHETT, FLOYD F. Development of the Fiscal System of Wisconsin, 1900–1925. Unpublished doctoral dissertation, University of Wisconsin, 1927.

CHAMBERLAIN, JOHN. *Farewell to Reform.* New York, 1932.

CLOUGH, SHEPARD B. *A Century of American Life Insurance.* New York, 1946. A history of the Mutual Life Insurance Company of New York, 1843–1943.

COMMONS, JOHN R. "Constructive Investigation and the Wisconsin Industrial Commission." *The Survey,* 29:440–448 (January 4, 1913).

————— *Institutional Economics.* New York, 1932.

————— *Labor and Administration.* New York, 1913.

————— *Principles of Labor Legislation.* New York, 1921.

————— "One Way to Get Sane Legislation." *Review of Reviews,* 32:722 (December, 1905).

————— "Trade Schools and University Extension for Wisconsin." *La Follette's Magazine,* January 30, 1909.

CURTI, MERLE, and VERNON CARSTENSEN. *The University of Wisconsin: A History, 1848–1925,* Vol. 2. Madison, 1949.

DEWITT, BENJAMIN PARKE. *The Progressive Movement.* New York, 1915.

DIXON, FRANK H. *State Railroad Control.* New York, 1896.

DUBLIN, LOUIS I. *A Family of Thirty Million: The Story of the Metropolitan Life Insurance Company.* New York, 1943.

FITZPATRICK, EDWARD A. *McCarthy of Wisconsin.* New York, 1944.

GANFIELD [FOWLER], DOROTHY. "The Influence of Wisconsin on Federal Politics, 1880–1907." *Wisconsin Magazine of History,* 16:10 (1932).

GLOVER, WILBUR H. *Farm and College: The College of Agriculture of the University of Wisconsin; A History.* Madison, 1952.

The Golden Jubilee of the University of Wisconsin. Madison, 1904. Addresses given at the inauguration of President Van Hise.

GROVES, HAROLD M. *A Tax Policy for the United States.* New York, 1934. Reprinted from the *New Republic,* 77:297–299, 327–330, 357–359; 78:12–14 (January 24 to February 14, 1934).

————— *Possibilities of the Income Tax.* Offset reproduction of a typescript, unbound, in the Tax Commission Papers in the Documents Division of the State Historical Society of Wisconsin. Madison, 1932.

HALE, ROBERT L. *Valuation and Rate Making: The Conflicting Theories of the Wisconsin Railroad Commission, 1905–1917.* New York, 1918.

HALL, ARNOLD B. "The Direct Primary and Party Responsibility in Wisconsin." *Annals of the American Academy of Political and Social Science,* 106:1–273 (1923).

HARD, WILLIAM. "A University in Public Life." *Outlook,* 86:659–667 (July 27, 1907).

HAVEMEYER, LOOMIS, ED. *Conservation of Our Natural Resources.* New York, 1930.

HENDRICK, BURTON J. "The Story of Life Insurance." *McClure's Magazine,* 27:36–49, 157–170, 237–251, 401–412, 539–550, 659–671; 28:73 (May to October, 1906).

HICKS, JOHN D. *The Populist Revolt.* Minneapolis, 1931.

HOAN, DANIEL. *City Government: The Record of the Milwaukee Experiment.* New York, 1936.

HOFFMAN, FRED L. "Fifty Years of American Life Insurance Progress." *American Statistical Association Publications,* 12:667–760. 1911.

HOLMES, FRED L. *Regulation of Railroads and Public Utilities in Wisconsin.* New York, 1915.

HOWE, FREDERICK C. *Wisconsin: An Experiment in Democracy.* New York, 1912.

JAMES, GEORGE F., ED. *Handbook of University Extension.* Philadelphia, 1893.

JAMES, MARQUIS. *The Metropolitan Life.* New York, 1947.

KINSMAN, DELOS O. *The Income Tax in the Commonwealths of the United States (Publications of the American Economic Association,* 3d Series, Vol. 4, No. 4). 1904.

LA FOLLETTE, ROBERT M. *Railroad Regulation, State and Interstate.* Madison, 1905.

LEFFLER, GEORGE L. *Wisconsin Industry and the Wisconsin Tax System.* Bulletin No. 1, Bureau of Business and Economic Research, University of Wisconsin. Madison, 1930.

LESCOHIER, DON D., and ELIZABETH BRANDEIS. *History of Labor in the United States, 1896–1932,* Vol. 3. New York, 1935.

LIGHTY, WILLIAM H. *A Sketch of the Revivication of University Extension at the University of Wisconsin.* Madison, 1938. Pamphlet.

LOVEJOY, ALLEN F. *La Follette and the Establishment of the Direct Primary in Wisconsin.* New Haven, Connecticut, 1941.

LUTZ, HARLEY L. *The State Tax Commission.* Cambridge, Massachusetts. 1918.

MCCARTHY, CHARLES. "Legislative Reference Library." *Proceedings of the National Association of State Libraries,* 1905.

MACKENZIE, FREDERICK W. "The Farmer at College." *La Follette's Magazine,* January 16, 1909.

MCMURRAY, HOWARD J. Some Influences of the University of Wisconsin on the State Government of Wisconsin. Unpublished doctoral dissertation, University of Wisconsin, 1940.

MERRIAM, C. EDWARD. *Primary Elections.* Chicago, 1908.

MEYER, BALTHASAR H. *Railway Legislation in the United States.* New York, 1903.

MEYER, ERNST C. *Nominating Systems.* Madison, 1902.

NATIONAL INDUSTRIAL CONFERENCE BOARD. *The Tax Problem in Wisconsin.* New York, 1924.

MOWRY, GEORGE E. *Theodore Roosevelt and the Progressive Movement.* Madison, 1946.

The Northwestern Mutual Life Insurance Company: Semi-Centennial History. Milwaukee, 1908.

NOYES, GEORGE H. *The Facts about Wisconsin Insurance Legislation.* Chicago, 1908.

ORVIS, MARY B. "A University That Goes to the People." *American Review of Reviews,* 45:457–465 (April, 1912).

Papers and Addresses on Primary Reform. Publications of the Michigan Political Science Association, Vol. 6, No. 1 (March, 1905).

PHILIPP, EMANUEL L. *Political Reform in Wisconsin.* Milwaukee, 1910.

———— *The Truth about Wisconsin Freight Rates.* Milwaukee, 1904. Pamphlet

PRINGLE, HENRY F. *Life and Times of William Howard Taft,* Vol. 2. New York, 1939.

———— *Theodore Roosevelt.* New York, 1931.

PYRE, JAMES F. A. *Wisconsin.* New York, 1920.

QUAIFE, MILO M. *Wisconsin, Its History and Its People,* Vol. 2. Chicago, 1924.

QUICK, HERBERT. "What Thrilled the Convention." *La Follette's Magazine,* June 28, 1912.

RATNER, SIDNEY. *American Taxation.* New York, 1942.

REBER, LOUIS E. "University Extension in State Universities." *Proceedings of the First National University Extension Conference,* March 10–12, 1915. Madison, 1915.

REGIER, CORNELIUS C. *The Era of the Muckrakers.* Chapel Hill, North Carolina, 1932.

RIPLEY, WILLIAM Z. *Railroads: Rates and Regulation.* New York, 1924.

SCHMIDT, GERTRUDE. History of Labor Legislation in Wisconsin. Unpublished doctoral dissertation, University of Wisconsin, 1933.

SELIGMAN, EDWIN R. A. *Essays in Taxation,* tenth edition. New York, 1925.

———— *The Income Tax.* New York, 1914.

SHIBLEY, GEORGE H. "Government Reforms in the United States for 1909." *La Follette's Magazine,* June 27, 1909.

SLOSSON, EDWARD E. *Great American Universities.* New York, 1910.

SNIDER, GUY E. *The Taxation of the Gross Receipts of Railways in Wisconsin (Publications of the American Economic Association,* 3d Series, Vol. 7, No. 4). 1906.

"A Statewide Forum in Wisconsin." *Independent,* 76:245 (November 6, 1913).

STEFFENS, LINCOLN. "The Mind of a State." *La Follette's Magazine,* January 9, 1909.

———— "Sending a State to College." *American Magazine,* 67:349–364 (February, 1909).

———— *The Struggle for Self Government.* New York, 1906.

———— "Wisconsin: A State Where the People Have Restored Representative Government—The Story of Governor La Follette." *McClure's Magazine,* 23:564 (October, 1904).

STILL, BAYRD. *Milwaukee: The History of a City.* Madison, 1948.

STOCKBRIDGE, FRANK. "A University That Runs a State." *World's Work,* 25:699–708 (April, 1913).

The Story of a Spoilsman. 1902. Pamphlet.

SULLIVAN, MARK. *Our Times: The United States, 1900–1925,* Vol. 4. New York, 1932.

SWISHER, CARL. *American Constitutional Development.* New York, 1943.

TORELLE, ELLEN, ED. *The Political Philosophy of Robert M. La Follette.* Madison, 1920.

TURNER, FREDERICK JACKSON. *The Frontier in American History*. New York, 1920.

The University. Bulletin of the University, Series 666, General Series 478. Madison, 1914.

VAN HISE, CHARLES R. *The Conservation of Natural Resources in the United States*. New York, 1910.

———— and EDWARD M. GRIFFITH. *The Conservation Movement in the United States*. Madison, 1912. Pamphlet.

Voters Handbook. Milwaukee, 1902.

INDEX

INDEX

★ ★ ★ ★ ★ ★ ★ ★ ★ ★ ★ ★ ★ ★ ★ ★ ★

230:n13, 232:n32; and legislative reference library, 141–145, 146; and La Follette, 143, 192

McClure's Magazine, 71, 110

McCormick, Medill, Chicago publisher, 184

McCurdy, Richard A., insurance company president, 106

McGovern, Francis E., and Tax Commission, 98; and Insurance Commission, 123; and the University, 137, 146, 149; as governor, 153–172, 190; and industrial workers, 154–155, 156; and Industrial Commission, 159, 164; and Board of Public Affairs, 169; and Highway Commission, 171; recommends marketing commission, 171; and progressive era, 171; candidate for Senate, 175, 176, 192–193; and La Follette, 180, 184, 188–194; role in convention of 1912, 185, 186, 188, 189, 190, 239: n35, n40; and Civil Service Act, 221:n22; and state income tax,101, 224:n35; and legislature, 231:n25; mentioned, 143, 199, 204

Mack, John G. D., professor of engineering, 139

McKinley, President William, 10, 26

McVey, Frank L., studies central boards, 51, and Tax Commission, 241:n4

Marketing commission, 171

"Mary Ann Law," 75. *See also* Primary elections, second choice

Massachusetts, early tax commission in, 89; regulation of insurance companies in, 106; voluntary compensation board, 234:n12

Merchants and Manufacturers Association of Milwaukee, 157–158

Merrill, Willard, on insurance taxation, 107, 108

Metropolitan Life Insurance Company, 106; investigated, 110; booms sales in Wisconsin, 172

Meyer, Balthasar H., and Railroad Commission, 77, 139, 197

Mill tax, use of, 136, 223:n18

Milwaukee, 20, 23, 27, 61; growth of, 7, 154

Milwaukee Free Press, 44; Stephenson and, 63; supports progressives, 63, 67; and Wisconsin insurance code, 118; announces Stephenson's candidacy, 174; libel suit against, 177; defends McGovern, 188

Milwaukee Sentinel, 14, 20, 34, 64; and La Follette, 17, 19, 21, 23, 24; and primary elections, 30, 33; bought by Pfister, 32; and Stevens Bill, 33; opposes ad valorem tax bill, 38; denounces third-termers, 67; and election of 1904, 67; denounces Steffens, 72; and Railroad Commission, 79; and Prudential investigation, 109; and insurance code, 117

Minnesota, adopts primary system, 54, 212:n7; railroad commission in, 213:n21; tax receipts in, 216: n41, 223:n25; studies Wisconsin Tax Commission, 241:n4

Mitchell, S. Weir, 182

Mortgage taxation, 90, 92–93

Murphy, Jerre, 16, 31

Mutual Life Insurance Company, 106; investigated, 110; returns to Wisconsin, 124

National Conservation Commission, established, 164

National Industrial Conference Board, 102

National Progressive Republican League, 179–180

National republican convention, *see* Republican Party

National Tax Association, 101

Nelson, John M., 42, 65, 140; candidate for Congress, 42; supports La Follette, 60; promotes federal legislative reference service, 145;